ADULTS on the AUTISM SPECTRUM
Leave the Nest

of related interest

Guiding Your Teenager with Special Needs through the Transition from School to Adult Life
Tools for Parents
Mary Korpi
ISBN 978 1 84310 874 0

Providing Practical Support for People with Autism Spectrum Disorder
Supported Living in the Community
Denise Edwards
Foreword by E. Veronica Bliss
ISBN 978 1 84310 577 0

Asperger Syndrome and Employment
Adults Speak Out about Asperger Syndrome
Edited by Genevieve Edmonds and Luke Beardon
ISBN 978 1 84310 648 7
Adults Speak Out about Asperger Syndrome series

Asperger Syndrome and Social Relationships
Adults Speak Out about Asperger Syndrome
Edited by Genevieve Edmonds and Luke Beardon
ISBN 978 1 84310 647 0
Adults Speak Out about Asperger Syndrome series

ADULTS on the AUTISM SPECTRUM
Leave the Nest

Achieving Supported Independence

Nancy Perry

Jessica Kingsley Publishers
London and Philadelphia

First published in 2009
by Jessica Kingsley Publishers
116 Pentonville Road
London N1 9JB, UK
and
400 Market Street, Suite 400
Philadelphia, PA 19106, USA

www.jkp.com

Library of Congress Cataloging in Publication Data
Perry, Nancy, 1946-
  Adults on the autism spectrum leave the nest : achieving supported independence
/ Nancy Perry.
       p. cm.
  Includes bibliographical references.
  ISBN 978-1-84310-904-4 (pb : alk. paper)
  1. Autism. 2. Autism--Patients--Care. 3. Parents of autistic children. 4. Autism--
Patients--Services for. 5. Life skills--Study and teaching. I. Title.
  RC553.A88P47 2008
  616.85'88200835--dc22

                                        2008019089

British Library Cataloguing in Publication Data
A CIP catalogue record for this book is available from the British Library

ISBN 978 1 84310 904 4

Printed and bound in the United States by
Thomson-Shore, 7300 Joy Road, Dexter, MI 48130

Contents

A Message for Parents

There are so many books out now that address the many childhood diagnoses from learning disability to autism. Early intervention is not just a good idea, but a federally funded program of evaluation and treatment available in all states for children under three years of age. Childhood development is scrutinized as never before; treatment modalities have sprung up and information flies around the internet.

This book is for parents who are looking ahead toward the adult lives of their children with disabilities. It is also for those whose children with differences and disabilities have already grown beyond childhood. And, finally, it is for clinicians who treat and consult with these families. All parents hope for complete cure; if that is not possible, they hope for enough treatment and training to allow their children to live independent lives as adults. But some parents wonder, worry, or simply know that their children will not achieve complete independence. This book is for those families.

There are specific brain functions that are impaired in people who cannot learn to manage their lives even though they have normal IQs (intelligence quotients). Some individuals have great vocabularies and have read endlessly on esoteric topics, but they cannot make an adequate meal or protect themselves from unscrupulous people. They make impulsive purchases with money designated to pay the rent. An alarming number end up in jail and prison because they are willing to be seen as guilty of a crime rather than known to be disabled. This book explains, in everyday language, the specific brain functions that underlie these dysfunctional behaviors.

Most books in the field of disability focus on interventions for children. They provide advice and hope, but can be lacking in alternatives if all treatment falls short. This book describes different models of care or support for adults on the autism spectrum of disabilities. The models of care and support differ in the amount of independence the participants can sustain. The last part of the book provides a detailed description of a model program for adults, living in a therapeutic community and receiving daily services tailored to individual needs. A new option that parents might try is included in an appendix. Among the models of care, parents should be able to find one that fits the needs of every adult with disabilities. This is an honest and optimistic book about living a full life with disability.

Acknowledgments

This book represents a culmination and a new beginning. It is the culmination of my feeling full; full of education and training, and then full of experience and esoteric knowledge about the population I am so lucky to have fallen in with. I went to graduate school on purpose, but I fell in love with the brain out of the blue. Then I trained in the field of acquired brain injury, but came upon my first and last job in the field by the lightest connection, a mere conversation between two other people. After many years I felt full of information that could only be valuable when shared. I had to write this book to empty a part of my mind and feel that the information had gone out to others.

The people who inspired me were my teachers and supervisors. Nell Riley, Jeanne Savarese, Helen Fellenbaum, Jim Cole, Claude Munday, Amy Wisniewski, and Lea Bachman are or were stars in the Bay Area neuropsychological community who taught and otherwise influenced me. But my greatest debt is to my teacher for two full years, Michael Shore. Michael talks in fully formed paragraphs, eyes blazing and twinkling. He not only knows his stuff, he also taught and exemplified the way to have an ethical and compassionate career in neuropsychology. I would not have followed this path if not for him.

My debt to clients, families, and co-workers is inestimable. I have not named the clients in the book so I will not name them here, but I owe each of them a world of gratitude for being innocent teachers. They will never know how much our staff loves them. Parents and other family members have become like extra relatives to me.

Our in-house psychiatrist, Dr. John Rostkowski, read the section on medications and advised me, generously, in how to make it better. (Remaining errors are strictly mine.) My co-workers, past and present, with whom I have talked, listened, laughed and cried, must be named to acknowledge the connection and gratitude I feel toward them. Laura Bathel, Albert Bazurto, Angie Beal, Debra Beauregard, Linsley Bock, Jeannine Chang, Paula Chaissang, Nina Ghiselli, Christina Giovannetti, Lori Green, Sandi Inaba, Marquitta Jackson, John Kady, April Kavanagh, Jolanta Kurowski, Steven King, Felton Mackey, Chandra McGunagle, Lindsay Nelson, Lisa Otis, Jane Pinger, Amy Raab, Shana Ring, Jana Scrivens, Shenandoah Sexton, Diana Shapiro, Jeff Smith, Diane Stephens, Doreen Tieman, Randy Thorpe, Conchita Villalba, Patty Wardell, Sonia Marie Wijts, and Lisa Youngblood: thank you all. Don and Nona Bone, you know what you've done.

My deepest gratitude is reserved for Genevieve Stolarz, our founder and Executive Director, the first expert on this population I've encountered. Mentor, teacher, and friend are all labels that fit, but they aren't sufficient to capture an inspiration. Unable to do justice to Genevieve with a label, I'll just say this book was meant to honor what you've created, and let's do another ten years together.

Everyone who writes a book must have had a moment when they turned to a friend, husband, child, sister, brother, mother or father and said, "Do you think I could write a book?" I was with my husband and closest relatives, Kathy and Eric, when I posed that question. I have encountered only support, encouragement, and confidence from my family and friends. Don and Isabel, Susan, David, Jacob, and Zak, Judy and Bill, Brenda and Jerry, Sandy and David, Bree and Bill, Ember, Casi, Eva, Robbie, and Marcia, Ellen and Nick, Pat and Ted, Kelly and Jerry, and John; you were involved or in my heart as I worked. Finally, my coach, Jane Anne Staw, and my other coach, Irene Sardanis, were the best support team anyone could ever want. Susan Weiss came in at the last moment to lend copy-editing expertise, and inexplicably we laughed a lot. Lily Morgan at Jessica Kingsley Publishers offered editing advice that made the book much better and never once hurt my feelings. And my baby, Simone, read the book and offered invaluable suggestions. Kelly, Simone, and Bob are my foundation and my reason for living.

Preface

I found myself working in the field of disability quite unexpectedly. I met Genevieve Stolarz and we had a conversation in which we shared almost no terminology and yet we knew we were speaking the same language. Genevieve came from a nursing background and then learned everything she knows about neurological disability from her son, who was adopted from an orphanage at age six. His disabilities were not recognized until he was home, half way around the world in a family that did not share a language with him. Genevieve soon realized that something was wrong, very wrong, and then she began the process for which I respect her so much. She figuratively rolled up her sleeves and said, "I better figure this out or this kid isn't going to have a good life."

At the time I met Genevieve I would have said my career direction was academic. I had just completed a PhD in Clinical Psychology and training in Neuropsychology. I had trained primarily in the field of traumatic brain injury. Before returning to graduate school I had been a psychotherapist for many years. But none of that would have predicted or accounted for my special connection to Genevieve and the program she founded for adults on the autism spectrum.

My own family was touched by disability. Actually, my family was clobbered by disability. My mother's third daughter was born a normal baby. One day at six months of age this cherished baby developed a fever and convulsions that left her brain ruined. My mother did her best to keep her child home, but after eight years of no successful adaptations, no language skills, and no other signs of normal human behavior, institutional care was found for my sister. She remains there today and is now almost 60 years old. She has no language and no recognition of specific human beings, including her parents and siblings. She spends her time rocking and watching the world go by as she lives from one meal to the next. I consider her completely disabled.

Most outcomes are not as bleak as that of my sister. My mother's fourth daughter was also normal at birth. She lived to three years of age without mishap. Then she fell victim to polio in the last year it was a major disease in the US. She was treated at Warm Springs Hospital in Georgia, a wonderful facility made famous by President Franklin Roosevelt's treatment there. My youngest sister survived, paralyzed from the neck down except for partial use of her left hand. She became an early example of a child with severe disabilities being "mainstreamed" in school. She was mainstreamed because there were not yet terms like special education, resource teachers, aides, exclusion, inclusion, or mainstreaming. She simply was taken to school in her wheelchair, and teachers and students alike helped her as best they could. My mother stopped in about three times a day, every day, to take her to the bathroom. If there was an urgent need, I was brought from my class to help my sister.

On a personal level, it finally felt right to me to end up working with individuals with disabilities. As a child I felt very sad about my sister who was not able to stay within the family. I felt proud of my sister who did stay at home. She was bright and talented and had a great spirit. But at the age of 12 she died of pneumonia. We had been a family of four sisters. My oldest sister went off to college and I was suddenly the only one left. I was the academic type. And the compassionate type. I was an achiever, and I became a therapist. Then I met Genevieve; we talked about brain functioning in our two different ways, and I came home to caring for people with disabilities. We've been working together for over ten years now, refining our theories and trying new strategies, and always doing "whatever works."

My own family history is worth mentioning for two more reasons besides showing my circuitous path toward dealing with disability. The first reason is that it challenges the commonly held belief that professionals don't know what it's really like to live full-time with children with disabilities. In my experience, many professionals choose the areas to which they devote themselves for the most personal reasons. They may know more than you realize about all aspects of disability in the family. In order to maximize your level of trust in the relationship, you may want to seek out professionals who will discuss their own experiences with you. On the other hand, this may not be of much importance to you. You may be the type of person who bases your trust on the practicality and usefulness of the information the professional provides, regardless of his or her personal experiences. However you approach the helping professions, you will ultimately have a better experience if you bypass the lonely notion that no one can possibly understand your plight. Many people can and will.

The second reason I mention my sisters is that my family's experience in some ways represents the whole range of care that is available, from complete isolation to full inclusion in society. The sister who became institutionalized is most safe in that environment. The sister who participated fully in school and clubs and friendships was flourishing in that environment. I am now speaking to parents for whom it is still unknown where their children will end up in the continuum of care, and as well to those for whom the difficult decisions have already been made. I don't believe parents should live out their lives feeling guilty or judged for their choices. I believe that people do the very best they are capable of, given all the factors they have to manage. The full spectrum of care exists because it is needed and it makes sense.

This book will be my attempt to fill a gap I see in the field of disability. Children are the focus of their parents' lives for about 20 years, more or less. Then those "children" may live another 40, 50, or 60 years. Most of those with disabilities are never given the chance to experience independent adulthood. More importantly, they don't have the opportunity to organize their lives in relation to chosen peers, in meaningful relationships, as other adults do. What must be done to provide the richest possible lives and the highest levels of independence for these individuals?

I will discuss the issues I know every parent thinks about; and I will present several models of supportive care for adults with autism spectrum disabilities. I hope I will answer many of the questions that must be answered in order to plan lives of rewarding adulthood for those with disabilities.

My work at the Center for Adaptive Learning (CAL) is a labor of love. And this book is my attempt to put down in plain language what I have learned from Genevieve Stolarz and through my experience with many courageous individuals with disabilities. I truly hope, through this book, to affect the lives of children and adults with disabilities and the lives of their family members. We can all do more to help, but first we need to understand. The following is what I have learned to date; some of it may be wrong and will certainly be clarified through scientific research and through experience. For now, this is what I have learned and what I offer you.

Introduction: Real Lives

Before discussing the brain functioning that underlies the disability I'm writing about, perhaps it would be helpful to be introduced to some real people who live with the disability. Here are four stories of real clients I have known and worked with. Names and other identifying details have been changed to protect their privacy. Each story focuses on a different aspect of the myriad challenges these clients and their families face. One story exemplifies the more old-fashioned practice of dealing with the disability without professional help. Another typifies the newer practice, taking advantage of whatever help is available. The third story describes what can go wrong when the disability is misunderstood. The fourth is a success story.

Howard's story

Howard came to the program where I work at the age of 50. He was the oldest client ever to enter the program, by far. Howard was born the youngest in a family of three children, two boys and one girl. His father was the breadwinner and his mother stayed at home and tended to her home and family. When Howard was discovered to have some kind of poorly understood disability, he was placed in the special education classes at his school. He was among the first generation to have any special ed program, being a Baby Boomer. His mother was a religious and somewhat superstitious woman who believed Howard's condition was a punishment for something she believed she had done wrong in her own childhood.

Howard was considered mentally retarded and therefore unable to learn. But he was a nice boy with a relaxed temperament and friendly demeanor which would serve him well throughout his life. Howard actually was able to learn and remember and he eventually focused his attention on pop music and the history of his town. He knows a great deal about musicians and stars from the 1950s and he knows a lot about his hometown. Howard's school experience was a little better than is usual for these kids; that is, he was teased and ostracized but gradually accepted as an unequal but tolerable member of his class. It was his pleasant temperament that gained him the status of grudging acceptance that many of my clients never achieved in school.

At home, Howard's mother did everything for him in the mistaken belief that it wasn't worth the time and effort to train him to do basic self-care activities. He dressed himself, but that's about it. He never learned to fix any kind of meal for himself; he didn't learn how to do his laundry or any household chores. This was partly due to the social mores of the time; male children often weren't expected to learn any household skills.

One part of Howard's life was managed with great foresight and a little good luck. When he finished high school his father went to a local school and negotiated a job for Howard on the janitorial staff. In those days there wasn't so much concern about liabilities of every kind; an employer was more likely to find a spot for an unusual worker without concern for issues that might crop up, like the omnipresent insurance matters of today. The lucky result was that Howard worked at the same job for 30 years, full-time, and retired with a pension. Revisiting the matter of Howard's lack of housekeeping skills, it's fascinating that his job was in janitorial services, yet he was not considered able to learn the same kinds of tasks at home.

Howard's career was not without problems. He sometimes slacked off in his work and had to be encouraged and lightly warned about the possibility of losing the job. But Howard was so well-liked that when he returns to the school occasionally, staff remember him, smile, and go out of their way to be friendly to him.

At home, Howard's mother developed the habit of criticizing him incessantly for the very things she failed to teach him. His way of eating annoyed her; his appearance became slovenly to her way of thinking. Although all her children were overweight in adulthood, his mother seemed to "see" it only in Howard. His siblings picked up the habit of criticizing what he ate even as they ignored their own weight problems. Even under constant criticism, Howard retained his basic good nature and seemed to get through his daily life without complaint. Who knows what he may have dreamed about the possibility of relationships, friendship, maybe a girlfriend someday. But the years passed with his social network consisting of the relatives that were his parents' social group and, of course, his co-workers.

You may wonder how we came to have Howard as a client in our program. One day his mother took stock and realized that she was over 80 years old. She called her daughter to her side and began talking with her about the future care of Howard. I can only speculate as to what Howard's sister felt when she realized her mother expected her to take on the care of her brother in the same manner that her mother had always done it. Was she surprised or concerned? We don't know her feelings, but she found our program at that time. There was little precedent in those days for Howard's mother to have tried to find a different place for him to live as an adult. And I doubt whether his siblings would have given the matter much thought, as they were focused on their own lives. Clearly, though, neither sister nor brother intended to take Howard into either of their homes and treat him like the dependent child he had become, through no fault of his own. When Howard arrived at our program, his sister provided an extensive list of things she wanted him to learn. After 50 years of being expected to learn virtually nothing, there was hope that Howard would learn everything that had passed him by.

Within a year, Howard was retired from his job and living in an apartment supplied by the program; he took responsibility for his own home for the first time in his life. More significantly, he had friendships among his true peers for the first time. Was it necessary for him to give up his job at that time? The staff decided that it was, because he had so much to learn about self-care, and he was so late in coming to those lessons. In addition, he was obese and in poor health related to his weight. But he absolutely blossomed in expressing his personality and in his ability to make friends and have a social life; he was often invited out to dinner or to the mall or to someone else's home to watch television or movies. And he was able to learn new skills. He never really became a good cook, as a good many of our clients don't, but he gained enough skill to get along as a microwave maven.

Eventually Howard lost a considerable amount of weight, but unfortunately he suffered a series of health problems. He still resides in our program and is still a favorite among all the clients due to his sweet personality. He can no longer learn new skills, as his functioning is limited by the results of a stroke. But he lives in a situation of supported independence; and he feels that he's the master of his own life.

Sharon's story

The story of Sharon takes place about 35 years later than the story of Howard, and that amount of time will make a substantial difference in the course of her life with a disability. Sharon is the only child of parents who are both medical doctors. Parents who choose not to have more children, because of the disability in the first child, function differently than those who have other non-disabled children. It's not a matter of better or worse, just different. For one thing, those who have non-disabled kids have more variety in their parenting experience. They can make comparisons between the developing skills in a typically developing child and in the child with disabilities. Their focus cannot remain exclusively on the child with dis-abilities. And, not least, they can look forward to the blessings of life with a normal adult child who might provide the late-in-life experiences most people look forward to: pride in their children's milestones, grandchildren, and possibly some caretaking in later life. Parents certainly feel pride for the achievements of their adult children with disabilities, especially given the extra efforts and courage required of them, but it isn't what most peo-ple expect when they think of raising a family.

Sharon is a bright, talkative, social young woman of 21 who seems more like 14. As well-educated professionals, her parents knew about the importance of early evaluation and interventions for students with disabili-ties. Sharon is well-educated; she reads and writes well and has a better fund of academic information than most of her peers in the program. For example, she knew how to write a resume and how to search the internet for information when she came to the program. Nevertheless, her social life during the school years had followed the same course as others with disabilities; when she was very young she had a few playmates, but by the time she reached middle school she was isolated and unhappy at school.

Unlike Howard, Sharon was evaluated by a neuropsychologist and had been given a diagnosis that made sense to her parents, Nonverbal Learn-ing Disability. This diagnosis led the family to believe that Sharon's major problems would be in the area of social behavior. Sharon graduated from high school; her parents thought she was capable of doing further academ-ic work, but they realized she did not have the maturity or independence to attend college at any level. I can't say whether Sharon's parents expected her to become "typical," but I believe they still have vague expectations for her to achieve a pretty normal-looking life. I once remarked, probably insensitively, that Sharon would not get married and her mother answered, "Oh, we don't see that door closed yet."

Sharon came to our program three years after finishing high school. In those three years she spent her weekdays knitting while watching daytime TV. She was settling into a pattern of inactivity and had become about 30 pounds overweight by the time we met her. Sharon's mother said Sharon never left the house on her own because they instructed her not to. They sometimes asked her to do chores, but reported that she would appear to have jumped up and begun the first item from the list just as they were coming into the house in the evening. Apparently they never tackled this failure to do chores as an issue of disobedience, I suspect because they thought it too childish to set up rewards and punishments to control a young woman over 18 years of age. Instead, they just hoped their daughter would see the point in helping out, even though there was no evidence leading to that conclusion. Neither did Sharon help with preparing dinner even though both parents worked every day. Her mother told us, a bit sheepishly, that she never seemed to think the right time had come to begin teaching her daughter to cook.

There were other features of Sharon's disability that her parents felt were very important for us to know. They told us Sharon has extremely poor spatial skills and cannot seem to negotiate her way around, not even her own neighborhood. This was the reason for her never leaving the house on her own. They gave an example in which they believed she got lost inside a theatre. She was attending a puppet show with her parents; she went to the restroom on her own, but didn't come back in a reasonable amount of time. Worried, her mother went and found her talking animatedly with a stranger in the restroom. This was interpreted by her parents as Sharon being "lost."

Sharon, like virtually all of our clients, never had friends. However, she has an extended family of relatives and is loved and accepted among her cousins, aunts and uncles. So she doesn't have quite as much the air of suffering and loneliness in her own stories as most of our clients do. She has good self-esteem and a willingness to acknowledge her disability without feeling defined by it. The overall feeling one gets upon meeting Sharon, however, is that she is a child. It was odd when first meeting her to see a young woman with a rather voluptuous body who presented herself as a pre-teen. She giggled and wiggled (and whined!) and said she didn't know in answer to most questions, and deferred to her parents to provide information that she should have known. She was shocked to be called "a woman" by the staff and insisted we start by calling her "an adult" until she got used to that. She referred to the staff as "the grown-ups." For us and for her parents, this led to concerns about Sharon being exposed to adult behavior, including sexual behavior, by her new peers. Were her parents prepared for Sharon to grow up?

As in the story of Howard, the question arises, why did these parents find our program at the particular time that they did? Sharon had been born and raised in a time of much greater awareness of disability, and a greater expectation for interventions to be successful. She was on medications that were working well after a difficult period of trial and error. She had finished high school but was not able to leave the house on her own. Given her level of naivety and her lack of training in adult skills, her parents were undoubtedly correct to continue to protect her, but what, then, could be done to get her life going forward? The program is just right for Sharon and she is just right for the program. She started at a time when she was young enough to be open to new learning and excited about living among her peers with all the opportunities for social contact and growth. After an overly eventful first week in the program, Sharon's life settled into a routine; she has made a number of friends, male and female, and has gotten used to being referred to as a woman. She has lost about 30 pounds and she behaves less like a little girl.

Howard's story rests with his being retired due to his poor health and stroke. But what will be the next chapters in Sharon's story? She has so much to learn about taking care of herself as an adult. She is currently handling friendship on about the level of a seventh grade girl, and that's fine for now. She is helped substantially with meal-planning and cooking because she is in our weight-loss program. But someday it must be determined whether she will be able to maintain healthy eating habits, as well as other kinds of self-care, under her own management. Sharon certainly has sufficient intellectual skills to hold a job. But she would have to manage a habitual tendency to chat about topics of interest only to herself. She would have to be willing to keep to a schedule of work hours even when she may not want to. At this point she is too immature to hold a job in the "real world," but she performs some clerical duties at the program, kind of like an internship. Her vocational goal will be to find a volunteer position of perhaps two hours a day, two to three times a week, as further practice for work readiness. The most important questions the program will need to answer are which of Sharon's talents can be expanded upon and which limitations can be overcome by training and maturity, and which will remain as lasting features of her disability.

Dexter's story

Next I'll introduce you to Dexter. He is a nice-looking young man of boundless energy and an open trusting face with a big grin, most of the time. He has not yet reached his twenty-third birthday, but he eagerly anticipates it. Dexter, like Sharon, grew up in a time that focused much attention on special education and entitlements for kids with learning disabilities and other neurodevelopmental conditions. But, unlike Sharon, Dexter received more attention for his behavior than for his cognitive limitations. Dexter's verbal IQ is squarely in the normal range and his presentation, especially his ability to meet and talk with anyone, appears normal, if exuberant.

Dexter's education proceeded along the lines typical of kids with a disability in his time. That is, he was educated in some special classes and in some mainstream classes. He reads and writes well, with spelling and punctuation as weaknesses that stand out. His behavior attracted more attention than his learning difficulties because he is impaired in his ability to regulate attention and motor behavior. In other words, he is distractible of mind and jittery of body. This aspect of frontal lobe regulatory functioning will be discussed later. What you would see in Dexter would remind you of a restless adolescent, fidgeting and switching his attention from one thing to another, and drawing others into his sphere by his genial good nature and need to talk continuously. Some of you will be saying Attention Deficit Hyperactivity Disorder (ADHD) as you read this. I don't diagnose Dexter with ADHD because his condition is actually more encompassing, more global, than just ADHD. More, later, on that subject as well.

Dexter's family life was, in some respects, not conducive to a good outcome. His parents divorced early in Dexter's childhood and he has no positive memories of a father who now insists upon estrangement from him. He has two brothers who are fairly close to him and a sister who is still frustrated by her years growing up with him. His mother is a kind and intelligent woman who clearly did the very best she could under difficult circumstances, financially and emotionally abandoned as she was. The worst events in Dexter's life unfolded the way they did at least partly because of his mother's need to work during his childhood.

In Dexter's early adolescence, at 12 and 13, he was allowed to spend the time between leaving school in the afternoon, and being picked up by his mother, at a shopping mall. This was disastrous for Dexter. Being impulsive and highly distractible, yet focused, as a young man in puberty, on all things sexual, Dexter began to do things that seemed like deviant or even predatory sexual behavior. I say "seemed like" because the real explanation for Dexter's behavior lies in poor judgment and poor impulse control rather than in planful disregard for the rights of others. Dexter engaged in acts of spying and following women and teenage girls that simply reflected his profound interest in them, but which came across as stalking or worse. Eventually he was arrested. Then, because the nature of his disability was misunderstood, he was placed in residential remedial care for boys with sexual deviancies of all kinds. You can imagine the new information and behaviors he encountered (and learned) in that setting.

Skip ahead a few years to Dexter's release from locked treatment facilities. He had achieved his high school equivalency credential, but he still exhibited the same emotional and behavioral regulation problems. He was placed in a group home. The story takes a turn for the worse at this point. Dexter began to attend a small church where he was befriended by an older man who was a church member and also held a custodial position at the church. Recall that Dexter was lacking any relationship with his own father or an adult father figure. It is understandable that he would be vulnerable to the attentions of an older man who showed an interest in him. Eventually the man sexually molested Dexter. The situation was complicated by Dexter's own history of supposed sexual deviancy, so that when the molestation was revealed his mother was advised not to prosecute because Dexter's own history would undoubtedly be held against him. Finally, the situation was further complicated for Dexter by the fact that he had so trusted and liked the older man that he concluded he must be bisexual. There would be nothing wrong, in other circumstances, with Dexter identifying as bisexual; but in these circumstances it served only to deny his having been exploited and victimized.

This is the point at which I met Dexter. He presented at our program as a wild and wounded young man. He entered into sexual relations with at least two women and two men very quickly. Almost as quickly, he realized he wasn't making friends through his promiscuous behavior, and he wanted friends desperately. He saw that the program could be a safe and fun place for him to live and grow, and he made fairly rapid changes in his social behavior, to the best of his ability. His story, like Sharon's, will unfold based upon the combination of accommodations he will need and his ability to harness and direct his own behavior.

Kevin's story

Kevin is a CAL success story. Kevin's life has reached a plateau that can be called successful stability, which should be of interest to anyone who worries about the adult life of their child. Kevin was adopted by a couple who were both college level teachers. Unable to conceive a child, they made the decision to adopt. This was in the 1960s when the nurture side of the nature/nurture pendulum was in ascendancy. It wasn't fashionable to worry whether an adopted child might have undesirable attributes, so to speak. Everything could be fixed with love and care. But Kevin was unable to learn to read. Dyslexia was just starting to be understood at that time; the many treatments that exist today were unheard of. To complicate matters, Kevin seemed to have other difficulties as well. His judgment and social skills were not the same as his peers. He hated school, of course, being unable to read, but he was clearly not mentally retarded. There didn't seem to be any place for him.

A few years after Kevin's adoption, his parents conceived a child, another son. As luck would have it, he developed as a very bright and studious boy. When Kevin was 11 his parents divorced; both admitted that disappointment and frustration over Kevin contributed to the divorce. Kevin simply remembers that they fought about everything. The younger son remained with his father and Kevin lived with his mother. Eventually Kevin's behavior problems became too much for his mother to manage. He was disobedient about things like eating at the wrong times, and teasing, and he was somewhat hyperactive. He is proud to say he never had contact with the police, so in his own mind his behavior was not so bad. However, his mother found him too hard to manage, and by 15 he was placed in a group home. After about a year his mother found Genevieve, the founder of our program, although the program was yet to be conceived. Genevieve accepted Kevin as a kind of foster child.

By the time Kevin was 16 years old he was able to go to the CCC, the California Conservation Corp. The program provided a closely supervised outdoor work experience for adolescent boys who were not doing well in school. They were not necessarily budding criminals, but boys who hadn't made a good adjustment to sedentary learning experiences. Kevin loved the CCC; he loved working outdoors in activities that did not expose his inability to read. He no longer had a reason to have a chip on his shoulder and so he began to be a very likable young man. He found that he loved hard work.

There was no question of Kevin going back to live with either parent after he finished his time in the CCC. He had tasted independence—at least he thought he had—and he thought himself capable of taking care of himself. By that time, his mother had moved to another state and his father spent limited, structured time with Kevin. Their relationship is best described as distant, which is sad because everyone else who knows Kevin finds him completely charming. Unfortunately, this can be the outcome when a parent is not able to accept whatever comes with an adopted child.

Why is Kevin a success story today? Because any parent would be comforted and proud to have an adult child with disabilities who managed his life as well as Kevin does. Kevin has worked full-time for about 20 years now. With the help of the Center he has been able to get a driver's license and to get jobs that don't depend upon reading and writing ability. He has driven trucks, delivered milk, and moved furniture, and with each job the Center staff has been there to explain his disability and to run interference when he encountered difficulties. Kevin is distractible and he has been known to lock the keys to a truck inside when a whole crew needed the truck to get on with a job. Kevin becomes embarrassed and frustrated when something like that happens, but he has learned to ask for help.

Kevin is fortunate in that he is nice looking and has a pleasant manner with people. He is tall with dark hair, a good build, and a friendly manner. He is the kind of man who is liked by other men and attractive to women. He had taken up line dancing at a western-themed bar for a while; he was very popular with the "regulars" and met many women. Being so likable can be a problem in that Kevin is easily exploited due to his judgment deficits. The Center staff have had to help him protect his bank account on numerous occasions when women he met turned out to have ulterior motives, or to be just as disorganized and disabled as he is. He has also been too generous with his apartment, letting homeless people stay with him until the staff caught on.

Kevin has been successful as a CAL client because he trusts Genevieve more than he wants to follow his own often impulsive decisions. What I mean is that he may think himself in love with a woman, allow her to move into his apartment (often with children), spend money he can't afford to spend, and so on, but when Genevieve points out to him each of those elements of his situation, he trusts her and allows her to help him make the necessary decisions. He is a success because he has dependable and valuable strengths, and because he has learned to seek help and trust staff when his disability gets him into trouble.

Part One

Understanding the Autism Spectrum Disabilities

Chapter 1

What Are Neurodevelopmental Disabilities?

Neurodevelopmental disability is a general term, not a specific diagnosis. It is one of many different terms used to describe a spectrum of symptoms and syndromes characterized by deficits in cognitive and social skills, as well as perceptual, processing, and sensory-motor skills. Broken down, the term means *non-normal brain functioning that is expressed throughout the stages of development.*

Autism is the neurodevelopmental disorder currently holding center stage because it is thought by some researchers, doctors, families, and other professionals to have reached epidemic proportions over the past ten years. Not everyone agrees that the prevalence is a simple matter of dramatically increased numbers of cases. An alternate theory is that awareness, diagnostic acumen, and pressure for services have all contributed to increased numbers of children being diagnosed as autistic. It is not within the scope of this book to take on that debate. A summary statement would be that autism has emerged as a focus among the neurodevelopmental disabilities, and that it has stricken families and subsequently challenged school systems and medical and financial systems that are charged to respond.

Asperger's Syndrome is similar to autism, especially to so-called high-functioning autism. High-functioning autism describes persons with autism who are not mentally retarded and who function so much better, especially in verbal communication, than their fully autistic peers, that it makes sense to give them a separate label. Spectrum theorists tend to see high-functioning autism blending into Asperger's Syndrome. Asperger's kids are both hyperverbal, and impaired in age-appropriate pathways to learning about the environment—crawling, touching, physically exploring the world. Many parents are pleased with the intelligence demonstrated by their verbal little toddlers until preschool experiences show them that their children are, in fact, odd in their grasp of the physical and the social world. As peer relationships fail to develop and interests become eccentric and fixed, parents realize, sadly, that elevated verbal ability isn't everything.

A condition similar to Asperger's Syndrome is currently being labeled Nonverbal Learning Disorder (NLD) or sometimes Nonverbal Learning Disability, though many professionals feel both terms are awkward and misleading. Many laypeople, upon first hearing either term, conclude that the child is *nonverbal*. Just the opposite is the case. These children, like Asperger's children, are very verbal. Yet some of their *nonverbal* skills are impaired, hence the name Nonverbal Learning Disability. And that's not the whole story. In some ways, these children's verbal abilities are also impaired. They are usually impaired in pragmatic language skills, meaning they make many mistakes in the non-literal uses of language when engaging in verbal behavior. Their mistakes have to do with understanding tone of voice, sarcasm and teasing, idioms and sayings, and the give and take of conversation. For that reason—that both nonverbal and verbal skills are impaired—it seems to many professionals that a better term should be found to describe this particular disability.

The confusion over terminology sometimes seems like a turf war, and in fact, can represent a serious struggle for resources. For example, if you attend a conference of people involved with Nonverbal Learning Disorder you will find that some members turn a skeptical eye toward Asperger's Syndrome, thinking it not substantially different from NLD and perhaps not worthy of a separate label. On the other hand, some in the field hold that Nonverbal Learning Disorder is a descriptive profile, not a diagnosis like autism and Asperger's. This assertion is on firm ground based on the authority of the *Diagnostic and Statistical Manual*—4th Edition (DSM-IV), the comprehensive book for diagnoses of mental disorders (American Psychiatric Association 1994). Nonverbal Learning Disorder is not included in the DSM-IV, though it could appear in the forthcoming DSM-V. Its appearance would mean the condition had "graduated" from a profile to a diagnosis. That would be a good thing if the diagnostic criteria that distinguish the condition from all others are clear, meaningful, valid, and reliable. At present they are not.

Pervasive Developmental Disorder—Not Otherwise Specified (PDD-NOS) is the default diagnosis in the DSM-IV for individuals who have neurodevelopmental deficits but don't fit the specific diagnostic criteria for autism or Asperger's. In some ways these are the most interesting individuals to think about in the current climate because they do seem to defy clear categorization. There are children who are given the diagnosis PDD-NOS, but don't really fit into even that catchall category. They are clearly impaired enough to be identified and singled out by their peers at the earliest grades in school. But the criteria for PDD-NOS don't quite fit them, nor do the more specific conditions mentioned above.

When the DSM-IV is used as the authority, we speak of a spectrum of pervasive developmental disorders, or pervasive neurodevelopmental disorders. Thankfully, popular language has taken over, and lately we speak, instead, of autism spectrum disorders. There is no real difference in these terms except for the inclusion of two other very rare disorders in the DSM-IV version: Rhett's Disorder and Childhood Disintegrative Disorder. Because of the recent focus on autism, it makes sense to use a "spectrum" term that clearly indicates we are discussing autism and its closely related conditions. Most of my discussion will be directed toward that subgroup on the autism spectrum who are labeled—perhaps mislabeled—PDD-NOS. I will refer to their deficits as "spectrum" deficits and neurodevelopmental deficits interchangeably. As awkward as the word "neurodevelopmental" is, I like it for its constant reminder that we are dealing with dysfunction in the brain that is expressed through all stages of development. Without that reminder, there is a tendency to think in terms of bad intentions when confronted with the challenging behaviors of these children and adults.

To return to the matter of inclusion on the spectrum, many parents will know that the attention deficit diagnoses (with and without hyperactivity) sometimes function as portal diagnoses into the more serious autism spectrum disorders. This actually makes a great deal of sense, as almost any neurological condition, such as acquired brain trauma from accidents and medical conditions, usually includes disruption of the attention and concentration systems. This is simply a way of saying that if the brain is impaired, the regulation and control of attention will likely be impaired as well.

Finally, many readers will be wondering if learning disabilities and learning disorders should be included in this broad spectrum of neurodevelopmental disabilities we are examining. The criteria for inclusion and the terminology in this field are in flux. For the purposes of this book, I have included anyone who has serious enough impairment to require support in adult life.

A brief look at brain development

The easiest way to understand the autism spectrum disabilities is by reviewing some basic information about brain development. The developing brain can be understood in part by observation of developmental milestones in children. From the first days of life, babies exhibit many interesting behaviors that are the outer manifestations of brain development. Notice babies' eyes as they take in more and more of the world around them. And notice their little hands grasping things, first always using both hands in random, parallel movement and gradually learning to use each hand separately and purposefully. Crawling, standing, walking, and talking are familiar milestones all parents have been asked to report upon during diagnostic interviews, sometimes many years after those accomplishments or failures have become a blur. Delays, irregular timing, or absence of these milestones provide significant evidence that the brain is not developing normally.

Social behavior milestones occur in muddier waters. We don't commonly talk about social development using concrete terms, like walking and talking. Some parents may observe the change from parallel play to interactive play among preschoolers and kindergartners, but many parents are fuzzy as to exactly when these changes take place and why they are important. It is also difficult for parents to interpret social behavior as evidence of brain development when we are more prone to look for signs of failure in ourselves as parents: perhaps little Spike doesn't share with the other children because I spend too much time on the computer in the evenings. Or Judy washes her hands too often because I've made her afraid of germs. If you are noticing things in your child's play, alone and with other children, that set off warning bells, you should follow up on your concerns. Time is lost when parents try to calm themselves by making excuses and hoping for the best. The child's self-esteem also suffers when there are no explanations, and no help, for his or her many failures, in school and in friendship. Due to the tendency to find fault with ourselves (guilt), it is the rare parent who can observe her child as a separate being in order to analyze his behavior productively. But we should aim for exactly that.

Reasoning is one of the milestone skills coming online in adolescent brains. The ability to reason can lead to delight in arguing, where once the child seemed to accept the parental point of view. But again, we confuse our thinking about this developmental stage with guilt and worry about what we've done to raise such "obnoxious" children. The quality of the reasoning is what parents should focus on if there is a concern about development. It can be difficult for a parent to analyze whether her child is more rigid than adolescents typically are; or whether this teenager is less able to tolerate frustration and postpone gratification than his peers. But these are the types of behaviors and traits parents should be thinking about.

The last major stage of brain development produces the executive functions. The development of these functions is gradual, beginning in early adolescence, and closely related to the development of reasoning ability. The endpoint of this development is still unknown. We used to report that it was complete by the early twenties, but estimates are being revised upward in this period of extensive brain research.

If you've been involved with the disability field, you may be very familiar with the term executive functions; otherwise it may be new to you. In any case, hold on to your equilibrium because here again we enter a realm of much confusion. I learned about executive functions while earning my PhD in Clinical Psychology with a focus on Neuropsychology. I believe the concept originated in the work of the great Russian neuropsychologist Alexander Luria (1973), and in the US from the pioneering work of the American neuropsychologist, Muriel Lezak. Her book *Neuropsychological Assessment* (2004) is in its fourth edition; major changes appear from one edition to the next in the area of executive functioning, with a great deal more being known and discussed in each succeeding edition of the book. At the moment, the understanding of executive functions is undergoing a growth spurt, and much remains to be sifted, sorted, studied, and clarified.

What are the executive functions?

The executive functions are often explained through the analogy of the conductor of an orchestra. The individual musicians represent the various intellectual abilities, like reading, thinking, calculating, and perceptions of all kinds. The conductor is needed to keep all the individual skills working together. The conductor controls the members of the orchestra, and without that control there could be a lot of great solo performances that add up to chaos. The conductor's job may look like the easiest job on the stage, but it is the most important for the success of the whole performance. This is the way the executive functions work to organize the other skills, perceptions, and conscious functions of the human brain.

The executive functions are so important that they alone allow us to live as "normal" human beings. They include abstract reasoning and problem-solving ability. They allow us to imagine the future by predicting the consequences of current actions. They allow us to initiate behavior purposefully, and to monitor our behavior while we are simultaneously moving fluidly through a variety of behaviors. They include initiation, judgment, working memory, decision-making, planning, organizing, and sequencing the steps toward a goal. They allow us to use foresight, hindsight, and insight. In the broadest use of the term, the executive functions also encompass regulatory functions, such as the regulation of attention and concentration, and the regulation of emotional states.

It will be easier to understand disability of the executive functions if I paint a picture of an individual with deficits in the long list of skills mentioned above. An individual with executive impairments lives in the moment. This is because he or she can't organize their lives or carry out plans, and can't think about the consequences of their behavior. Not being able to imagine consequences leaves him or her open to doing things on impulse that can have disastrous results, socially, and even legally speaking. Also, they have poor short-term memory so they forget plans and commitments, thus disappointing others unintentionally, and failing to meet all kinds of obligations. They have impaired attentional systems so they may be either highly distractible or, at the other end of the continuum, perseverative, or "sticky," compelled to spend long periods of time doing the same thing, like watching TV or listening to the same music over and over. They usually want close relationships, but they don't know how to treat others and have never had normal childhood friendships.

These individuals are close to their parents because of their failure to make friends, but they assert their right and desire not to be controlled by their parents, even as they make poor decisions over and over again. Money is like water in their hands. They make the same mistakes with money repeatedly, never learning from experience, although they "talk a good game" and can make up very believable excuses for their behavior. Except in truly autistic individuals, all these failures occur alongside virtually normal verbal skills. The conversation, at least the superficial conversation, of these individuals sounds so normal that others expect normal behavior from them. However, they fail over and over again in meeting this expectation.

This is my description of individuals with executive function impairments based upon years of working with them as they go about their daily lives. Researchers tend to prefer a more circumscribed definition of executive functions, emphasizing working memory and organizational abilities. I will make the case for including all these skills and abilities under one label at this stage of our understanding. I take this position because I've seen the way individuals function when they are impaired in all or most of the above-mentioned skills. The skills must be available to be used in a coordinated manner, as a group, and people who are impaired are generally not dysfunctional in just one skill, like working memory, but in the whole array of skills. Also, people with these impairments function similarly to one another, even if the etiologies, that is the organic causes, of their disorders are very different. *Because of their similarities, people with significant executive impairments ought to be members of a diagnostic category of their own.*

Proposing a new diagnosis

Given all the confusion within the spectrum of neurodevelopmental diagnoses, why would I want to propose yet another one? *Because impaired executive functions are so important they should be featured in the criteria of the diagnoses, and yet they are currently not even mentioned!*

The new diagnosis, to be consistent with current DSM-IV terminology, could be called Pervasive Developmental Disorder with Primarily Executive Deficits. The criteria should include executive deficits in the presence of IQ above the mentally retarded range. Individuals with this diagnosis display strengths and weaknesses in their IQ scores as opposed to a generally lowered and flat profile as seen in typical mental retardation (Full Scale IQ below 70). Generally the Full Scale IQ is meaningless in the spectrum population, as these individuals often have a greater than 16 point difference between Verbal IQ and Performance IQ scores. (If you aren't familiar with these terms yet, you probably are not very far along in dealing with disability services. If you have a child who will be tested for learning or attention disabilities, be sure to ask for an explanation of these terms.)

You may wonder why I would exclude individuals with IQ in the mentally retarded range from the proposed new diagnostic group. It is because as the whole intellectual apparatus falls into the retarded range, the executive skills are expected to be similarly impaired. In fact, executive deficits are "normal" in a retarded person. We expect concrete thinking and simple declarative answers to our questions, in conversation with a retarded person. A young woman with Down's Syndrome recently told me about visiting her cousins, and she proudly told me their names. Then she said, "I'm their cousin too." The remark fit the level of her conversation in general, and it was charming.

The individuals I will discuss in this book would not make that kind of simple, naive statement. Both their vocabularies and their reasoning are more complex. But many individuals with Down's Syndrome are more successful in employment than my population because they can learn a task and do it over and over the same way without mistakes, and without becoming bored. It is precisely the discrepancy between intellect and executive functioning that causes most of the trouble for the executively impaired individual.

If there were a diagnosis of Pervasive Developmental Disorder with Primarily Executive Deficits, individuals with many different etiologies would be grouped together according to the way they function rather than according to the way they became impaired. As it is now, an individual who had a birth trauma resulting in lack of oxygen to the brain and an individual who had meningitis in infancy would not necessarily be labeled similarly, even though their skills and deficits would be very similar. Given a diagnosis that clarified their abilities and their limitations, they would likely be served more appropriately.

Reviewing the spectrum

My breakdown of the autism spectrum results in the following categories, which are not discrete, but rather conceptualized as blending from one to another without clear boundaries: full autism, high-functioning autism, Asperger's Disorder, and PDD-NOS.

To qualify for a diagnosis of Autistic Disorder (in the DSM-IV), a child must have significant deficits in three areas: social interaction, communication, and stereotyped interests or behaviors (like self-stimulating motor behaviors, or rituals). An individual with full autism (that used to be considered the typical picture of autism) was mentally retarded, with sensory abnormalities, no language, and low motivation to make contact with other human beings. The newer view of autism, including high-functioning autism, may be a child with intellect in the normal range, some language, some apparent motivation to connect with others, sensory impairments, and poor ability to explain himself and his needs. Clearly, there is more going on than the diagnostic criteria have captured.

We don't know a lot about the sensory experiences of those with autism. Sensory abnormalities, like tactile sensitivity and hyperacute hearing, may constitute the biggest difference between autism and the rest of the spectrum, but we can't confirm that until many autistic individuals can find a way to tell us about their experiences. Perhaps autistic children are preoccupied with processing sensory input that we can't imagine. In that case, it might take a gargantuan effort to pull their focus toward the skills required for communication.

The DSM-IV criteria for Asperger's Disorder include the social interaction deficits and the ritualistic interests as in autism, but a communication disorder is *not* one of the criteria. In fact, surprisingly, to meet the full criteria for Asperger's Disorder there must be *no delay or impairment in development of language, cognitive skills, or self-help skills*. Given such strict criteria, I believe there are many fewer individuals who truly meet the criteria for Asperger's Disorder than are currently being labeled as such. A person with typical Asperger's usually wants friends but is inflexible in his desire to do things his own way. He wants the world to bend to his views and he is definitely able to express himself. If his intellect is in the normal range, he is likely to be capable of analyzing options and making some accommodations to the expectations of others. But he may remain very poor at perceiving a variety of social cues like body language, tone of voice, and idiomatic language in others.

Most importantly for spectrum thinking, executive deficits are present *but not mentioned* in the diagnostic criteria for both Autistic Disorder and Asperger's Disorder. The similar executive deficits seen in high-functioning autism and Asperger's Disorder permit these individuals to be treated alongside—and to live with and socialize with—individuals described above who illustrate executive function deficits. Their similar executive deficits make them alike enough to disregard IQ differences as well as quirky social and communication deficits.

So what is there to say about those with PDD-NOS? Very simply, they have primarily executive function deficits, along with sensory-motor deficits, low muscle tone, and clumsiness. Those who would fit my proposed diagnosis generally do not have communication deficits or social interaction deficits like those seen in autism and Asperger's. They are likely to have intellectual abilities in the normal to borderline range and are not likely to demonstrate the eccentric and rigid interests of the other two diagnoses. Although they will appear, at times, to have similar social deficits to the autism and Asperger's individuals, on closer examination, their social errors result from their executive function deficits.

The social deficit is a fascinating part of the diagnostic and functional puzzle. We theorize that there must be a part of the brain responsible for social behavior. But when the concept of social behavior is broken down, it consists of a number of interconnected perceptual and cognitive inter-related skills. Our PDD-NOS clients have trouble doing the socially correct thing when their focus is pulled elsewhere. Unlike a person with Asperger's or autism, these individuals are very context-dependent; unlike the others on the spectrum, when questioned about social behavior, they can correctly answer what is expected, as long as their focus is not pulled to some other need or interest. Knowing the right answers does not guarantee the correct behavior when the situation arises, however.

Those with Asperger's respond very differently to the same social questions. Although they don't know the correct answers, they tend to be overly confident about their interpretations, even self-righteous. And they don't accept others' interpretations even when they would obviously ben-efit by doing so. On the other hand, intelligent individuals with autism or Asperger's can sometimes train themselves in social behavior to an extent that they can get by, although awkwardly, in the world of "normals." They like to follow rules, and can train themselves in the mastery of social rules, and find comfort in using them. Temple Grandin is the most famous ex-ample of a person with autism who taught herself to do as others do even though social skills did not develop normally for her (see Sacks 1995, pp. 244–296; Grandin 1995).

An unambiguous social situation will illustrate the differences between these groups. At the program where I work, we have members of all three diagnostic groups as clients, given that those with autism are high func-tioning. When prospective clients and their families visit, we like to ask a veteran client to show his or her apartment to the visitors. This is an unam-biguous social situation in that there is a specific point to the interaction; it is meant to be friendly, informative, and brief. Our executively impaired clients have no difficulty accomplishing this task and passing for normal, if the contact remains brief enough and superficial enough. They have sufficiently good social behavior to greet strangers with eye contact and a hand shake, to make small talk while walking to the apartment, and to point out obvious features of the environment (this is my bedroom and this is my roommate's bedroom). The clients who have autism or Asperger's are not able to accomplish this simple behavior without revealing their social disability.

Quirky social behavior that looks similar but is actually different in cause, severity, and capacity to be modified can be seen across the autism spectrum of diagnoses. And it should be noted that individuals with autism and Asperger's are likely to be more anxious than the others on the spectrum.

What about ADD and ADHD?

The autism spectrum is often called upon to include those with attention disorders as their primary diagnosis. As most readers will already know, the attention disorders have received a great deal of focus over at least the past 20 years. In my opinion, these diagnoses remained difficult to understand until Russell Barkley began writing accessible books that explained the interconnection between control of attention and the executive functions (see Barkley 1995, 1997).

The H in ADHD stands for hyperactivity. So the attention disorders are differentiated by whether or not there is hyperactivity present along with a dysregulation in attention and concentration. The main focus of these disorders is the dysregulation of attention, but when hyperactivity is present, it tends to take center stage. Hyperactivity can be understood as too high a level of arousal too much of the time, with too little personal control. The typical picture is of a boy who can't be still. He's fidgeting constantly or running around, bothering other students in his class with random remarks and outbursts. He can't focus on his own work or even his own personal space.

Attention Deficits without hyperactivity are actually very interesting, but they aren't as dramatic-looking and well-known as those accompanied by hyperactivity. Individuals with attention deficits without hyperactivity are not overly aroused, visibly. They may have very aroused minds, however. Their focus can be very wide in the normal range, just enough to be difficult to control. Or it may be completely unbounded and experienced as multiple channels of sensory input bombarding the mind all at the same time. Imagine very loud music with a video playing a different story and all the while a teacher trying to get through with difficult, technical material. Along with all this, the person is tuned in to a few channels of thoughts that might be considered "their own" thoughts. But there is no excess movement to call attention to the sufferer.

There are many books that address the attention deficits exhaustively. For those who suspect attention deficits without executive deficits, those books should be consulted. My focus is that executive function disorders always have an element of dysregulation of attention and concentration. Most clinicians working with attention deficits are working with children, and are focused on school work and behavior. My point, in my discussion of initiation and the organizational abilities and social skills, is that control of one's attention is a subskill without which the higher executive skills cannot be achieved.

Chapter 2

Families Living with Disability

When a diagnosis is sought, the search begins with the question: what's wrong with my child? Your first red flag may be "floppiness" in your infant, or prolonged crying and inability to be soothed; or you may not become worried until developmental milestones show a delay. You may get through the stages of walking and talking, but notice social problems in preschool or kindergarten. The question "What's wrong?" leads to numerous visits to pediatricians, child psychologists, and perhaps a neuropsychologist. Diagnoses are considered, and reconsidered. Parents are encouraged to see their children not as having something "wrong" with them, but as having challenges or differences. We don't want to stigmatize children and we certainly should not view the whole child as the disorder or disability. Nevertheless, a parent's first impulse is to say, "There's something wrong," and we must respect the depth of despair behind that statement. For it grasps the truth: that this particular child is different and the differences are not normal, and they may represent lifelong challenges for the whole family.

Once they have voiced the question, "What's wrong?" parents have a multitude of difficult tasks ahead of them. Rarely do they have time, or realize they must take time, to comprehend their own feelings and learn to have a different kind of optimism about their child with disabilities. They may not feel they can devote time to their own feelings because they are dealing with the child and with the disability every day. Their own feelings may be the last thing to occupy their busy and worried minds.

When parents first face the evidence that their child will have disabilities, there is inevitably shock and disappointment. Then concern and worry for the child set in. There may also be concern for other children in the family, or even for whether to have more children. Those are universal emotional reactions that should be experienced with self-acceptance. Emotional reactions and coping patterns can vary widely depending upon the personalities and talents of parents. There is no reason to feel guilty for any of the many feelings parents are likely to experience.

Regardless of the extent and depth of feelings, the most important step in the care of the child is acceptance, and parents achieve it in various ways. The model of parental acceptance has been provided for me by three sets of parents, all of whom happened to be adoptive parents. They have told me they were able to look at the child as an individual for whom they felt responsibility without guilt. This point is so important that I cannot emphasize it too much. These adoptive parents felt responsibility to love and care for the child, but they did not feel responsible for having caused the disability. Many biological parents of kids with disabilities spend inordinate amounts of time and energy worrying about what they might have done wrong during the pregnancy, during the birth, during early childhood, or even in their choice of a mate! I wish I could tell every parent what a waste of energy this is. In the end they are left with exactly the same option as the adoptive parents: to look at the child as an individual they love and are responsible to care for. Acceptance includes making peace with an outcome that is different from what they had expected and hoped for when they had a child. But acceptance does not have to mean devotion to the care of the child, in the home, for the rest of their lives. Both the child and parents have a right to look forward to a natural separation at the time of adulthood, just like family members without disability.

After some measure of acceptance has been achieved—this stage may require years and may not happen in a linear way, but in a series of steps forward and backward—the next adjustment is just as important. This is the stage in which parents have to balance the search for treatments and interventions with the knowledge that the child cannot be "fixed." (I'm speaking, of course, of children who have an autism spectrum disability that cannot be cured within the present state of medical knowledge.)

Obviously parents need help in the form of information, guidance, and treatment for their children as soon as a diagnosis is made. Naturally, they want solutions that can be started immediately. Early intervention is the term we hear throughout the disability community these days. But early intervention may be misunderstood if certain questions are not answered. What promises are suggested by early intervention? Do professionals make informed predictions about the level of success they expect to achieve with their young clients? Do parents bring their own expectations to the table and forget or fear to ask the difficult questions? The most difficult question to ask, surely, is what the future holds for this particular child. It is important not to fear thoughts about how limiting the disabilities might be. What are the child's strengths and weaknesses? Which behaviors lead to what kinds of consequences? What training programs can be used to foster adaptive skills in place of deficits? And perhaps the most important question: will this child be able to live as an independent adult?

Parents should proceed with the search for appropriate treatment, but at the same time they must accept the child as a worthy and lovable person just the way he or she came into the world. I cannot stress enough how important this acceptance is. I've heard parents say things like, "I know in my heart my child doesn't have to be like this." They don't realize that the child hears, and feels, that his parents don't want him to be the way he is. He then internalizes the disappointment and doesn't want to be the way he is either, which is rejection of the self. In the presence of rejection of his very nature by his parent, it becomes difficult for a child to have self-esteem.

A valuable strategy at this point is to focus on what is charming about your child. If he has a beautiful smile or curly hair that strangers always notice, cultivate those positive attributes. We all learn to highlight our best features, and children with disabilities benefit even more than the rest of us by having likable traits or behaviors. In the future, you and your adult child will need to rely on strangers for some of her care. Having a nice personality and manners will go a long way toward the positive response you want your child to elicit from others.

Another invaluable tool will be a support network. Most parents, especially mothers, draw strength from knowing they are not alone in their situation. In a support group, parents can share the feelings they may believe no one else will understand. They may also use the group to brainstorm and develop new coping strategies. A social group for the kids will naturally emerge from among several families facing similar disabilities. And who knows what latent talents various members of a support group may possess? You may be good at leading a group of kids in games, while your new friend has a talent for studying legislation, and someone else may be adept at organizing advocacy efforts on behalf of the whole group.

A balancing act begins. Parents must express their natural love for the child with disabilities as easily as they do for their other children. In addition, they should express their disappointment and sadness with each other, or with a counselor, or in the support group. And while they seek treatment and intervention, they must not hold the child at arm's length, emotionally speaking, waiting for the treatment "to work."

More important than any other strategy, parents must make themselves the experts on their child. Watch your child as she plays or tries to do new things. Don't be too quick to help or correct or make judgments about the way things "should" be done. Your child can do amazing things the "wrong" way. When you talk with teachers, pediatricians, neurologists, and psychologists, you will be leading the evaluation process as you tell those experts how your child does things. How does she learn new things? Does she watch other kids and try to copy them? Does she have to touch and feel everything in order to accomplish new skills? Does she listen very carefully to your use of words when you explain things? Do you explain today but not see the result until a week from Tuesday?

Too many parents have an exaggerated respect for experts these days. They seem to believe they shouldn't contribute to the expert's evaluation by voicing their layperson's observations. Nothing could be more wrong. Professionals generally test your child to find out how far off the norm he or she is in various skills. That's important, but in the long run it is not more important than knowing how your child does things adaptively, in his or her own idiosyncratic way. *All treatments work best if they are designed to take advantage of your child's strengths.*

You, the parent, should be the person who can explain your child's strengths. This may require that in addition to observing your child, you read the existing literature on the disability you suspect you are dealing with. You might find it difficult to understand jargon you encounter in books, but if you start with the diagnosis your child seems to have, and read all you can about that disorder or syndrome, you will find yourself gradually putting together the experts' terminology and your own. It is a process like anything else you might want to learn. Think about when you learned to ski or to sail or to grow a garden; anything that requires special knowledge has its own jargon. Learning about your child's disorder will be similar, but much more important in the long run.

Parents first have to come to terms with the disappointment of having a child with a disability. They also need to seek treatment, support, and education, all the while learning to balance the pursuit of help with the acceptance of the child as a lovable and capable person, just as he is. Finally, they must begin to think about how this particular child should be raised. Should they treat her just the same as the other kids in the family? Should they let the child pursue his own interests and not direct him in any particular way? Should they leave those decisions to teachers and other experts?

Growing up with disabilities

In my work with families, I have been amazed and impressed by the variety of ways different families face the issues of disability. In my family, disability first appeared in the late 1940s, when my baby sister developed a fever that led to seizures and the almost complete destruction of her brain. She became what was termed gravely mentally retarded, with no language and no recognition or connection to other people. She remains institutionalized to this day. In 1953, my last baby sister contracted polio just before the polio vaccine was invented. She became paralyzed from the neck down, with partial use of one hand. She was not mentally impaired and enjoyed school and friendships throughout the early school years. In those days, there were few services; and families felt shame in a way I'm glad to say does not occur as much today. Mental retardation brought with it a greater feeling of shame than did polio, which inspired fear. In those days, conditions that might have been inherited seemed to be the most shameful, I suppose because your child was regarded as an advertisement for your "bad genes" or "bad bloodline." When mental retardation was the obvious, visible disability, one felt the desire to tell people that the baby was normal at birth and then something happened. Now, it seems sad that that mattered so much.

Behavior is the aspect of disability that matters so much because others witness it. My profoundly retarded sister engaged in no normal behaviors except walking and eating. Therefore she could not connect with other people. Being able to connect with other human beings is one of the hallmarks of human identity. In that way, my sister was similar to the most affected autistic children seen today. On the other hand, my sister with polio was emotionally and intellectually normal. Paralyzed and using a wheelchair, she couldn't do many things that other kids could do, but she could engage with others verbally and socially in a normal manner, once the others got used to seeing beyond the wheelchair and braces. She was very popular in grade school and was someone the other kids wanted to help and to play with. Junior high school brought about the expected age-appropriate self-consciousness in her, and in her peers, and her social position began to change. The ways in which we family members negotiated that developmental stage would have mattered a great deal to my sister's future in terms of confidence and self-esteem, but tragically for me, she died before we could experience that outcome.

Today, I don't see families experiencing shame when their child's disability is visible and understandable. But some of the neurodevelopmental disabilities have only subtle markers, or none at all, to alert the onlooker that there is a reason for the behavior on display. When a child has a deficit in social skills, behavior in public can be eccentric, intrusive, and even frightening to others. This is difficult for parents—and at times for the children themselves—because they feel that others expect them to maintain or regain control when they cannot. One teenager on the spectrum, aware of her disability but unable to control herself, explained her wish to be understood by saying, "I wish I had a bandage."

In embarrassing situations, some parents develop a down-to-earth response and are able to say, in effect, "Excuse us, there's a reason for this behavior and we didn't mean to disturb you." The ideal that parents should aim for is an internalized acceptance of disability in the child, and at the same time, an internalized expectation for the best possible behavior in public. When parents are successful in getting their child to internalize both acceptance of the disability *and* a requirement for good behavior, it goes a long way toward developing self-esteem and pride in appropriate behavior in the child.

Many parents who are not comfortable with their child's disability will go to extremes to control the *appearance* of normalcy. I know parents who, in effect, went to school all over again with their child with a disability. They seemed to believe that if they could get the child through school, something would be different by the time she graduated; the child would have a high-school diploma to fall back on, just like her peers. It is easy to imagine a parent feeling sorry for her child, knowing she is not able to perform in the classroom, or is being teased and bullied at school. She wants to help, so she does whatever she can think of, or what she has been advised to do by teachers and other professionals who may have incomplete knowledge of the disability.

As the years go by, the child is passed from grade to grade, falling farther behind each year. Time that could be better spent developing adaptations for the child is instead spent trying to help him "pass for normal."

By the time he is old enough to leave high school, with or without a diploma, the parents are exhausted and feel they've done so much that they deserve to see results. The now-adult child is ill-equipped to enter the adult world because too much was done in the service of getting the education to which the child was "entitled" and too little attention was paid to acquiring meaningful skills for the kind of life he will actually have. (Much more will be said later about the kinds of skills I think should be pursued during the educational years of a child with a spectrum disability.)

Whether parents and teachers have been realistic or not, eventually the adult child ends up in the proving ground of adult life in one way or another. If academic skills are pretty good, as with some Asperger's kids, young adults may try college, perhaps community college. The experience is particularly difficult if they leave home. They may experience continued academic success, but be dismayed by social challenges that had been mediated by the parents during childhood. They may ignore hygiene and even adequate eating because they don't have the parental cues and direction to keep them aware of those needs. Usually money is a pitfall for the young adult with disabilities. Failure is often accompanied by depression and anxiety, then more failure and decline in functioning. At this point, young adults with disabilities may be vulnerable to be drawn farther off course through inappropriate relationships, including dangerous sexual behavior, alcohol and drug use, or exploitation by unscrupulous people.

Frequently, as a result of the scenarios described above, young adults with misunderstood disabilities end up back at home. Parents' responses are varied at this point. For some the hope is that another year at home or an undemanding part-time job will be the answer. They find the job for the young person, only to discover that they are taking more responsibility for the job than their child does. Self-care and hygiene may still be a problem, as well as unwillingness to contribute to household chores. The cry, "I'm 18, you can't tell me what to do," is commonly heard. The young person is lonely and unable to find appropriate friends. Frustration increases for all concerned.

Some parents realize at this point that the disability has not been "cured," and that adaptations are not in place. Then the search for adult services begins.

An example of a successful approach

Wendell's story illustrates a successful approach to disability. Wendell is a young man who was adopted from an impoverished country. He had lived in an orphanage since birth and although he was six years old at the time of his adoption, he was about the size of a two- or three-year-old. He had received inadequate food all his young life and his brain impairment was likely due to poor nutrition. No other etiology was ever determined.

Wendell's adoptive mother felt no remorse about his condition. On the contrary, she observed a tremendous will to survive in the little boy, and she so admired that character trait that she bonded with him immediately. She knew other adoptive parents who returned children to the orphanage upon discovering their serious disabilities. She did not judge those parents, but felt they knew themselves well enough that they must be making the right choice for their nature or circumstances.

Wendell's mother had a gift for seeing the big picture. She believed that Wendell was an admirable and valuable human being just as he was, even if his limitations couldn't be corrected. She wanted a child and she had gotten one; now she saw that she had a different kind of child than she had imagined. So she made a mental and emotional adjustment. That doesn't mean she didn't try to find every kind of help for her son. Over time, he received virtually all the diagnoses mentioned in the first chapter, and then some. His mother read all she could about each condition. But she also became the expert on her son. She taught him how to do things and she watched the way he learned. She emphasized his skills and figured out how to get around his limitations. She saw early on that he would not benefit from a typical education. She wanted him to have useful skills. She taught him manners, good habits, and values from the very beginning of his life with her.

In school Wendell had the same general experience as most of the clients I've seen and will be describing. That is, he was known to the other kids as different, not normal, not like them. But his parents fostered self-esteem in Wendell. They were successful in that effort because they understood that self-esteem is based upon the love and acceptance of the parents *and* increasing accumulation of real skills by the child. Wendell made friends from among others who were like himself. He had the good fortune to have one wonderful teacher, a woman who collaborated with his mother, and was flexible in her approach to teaching Wendell. When he was placed in too many time-wasting activities, she was helpful in getting him transferred to a class where he could learn a useful skill. He learned keyboard skills when computers were first being used in schools; later on, he worked in data entry for ten years.

The final piece to the good outcome for Wendell was that his mother recognized early on that he would not be able to function as a fully independent adult. She knew he would need help with self-care decisions, with money, and with motivation to develop useful routines and habits. She spent no time trying to picture Wendell living on his own. Nor did she think for one minute that she would keep him at home with her as an adult. Why? Because she knew Wendell would never feel like an adult if he continued to live in his parents' home. Therefore, there had to be another option. When she didn't see a good one, she became instrumental in developing such an option, for Wendell and for others like him.

The elements that worked for Wendell and his family were, first of all, the temperament and values of his mother. Not everyone can find acceptance in the face of disappointment and challenge, as fully and quickly as she did. But if you are going to raise the child you have, it is essential to work toward that acceptance and to find help and support wherever you can. Second, it helps to be able to attack the problem with your intellect. Observe and analyze your child in addition to having feelings for her. You may uncover talents you never dreamed of in yourself. Perhaps you will become a special ed teacher or a political organizer; perhaps you have the ability to inspire others. In the process of finding your own talents, you may bond with your special child differently than you would have with a normal child. The third element for success is to be able to picture your child leaving home. If you can't picture it, it probably won't happen. And if it doesn't happen your adult child will be left, at least partially, with the life of a child. He will be denied the experience of living among his peers, having his own place to be in charge of, and feeling like an adult.

Looking toward adulthood

Parents and other relatives of adults with disabilities generally expect to remain involved with them over the whole course of their lives. It is still the case that most adults with disabilities live with their parents throughout their lives. This arrangement, which many people experience as their only choice, has always been difficult for families. There is a high incidence of divorce in families with a disabled child; in many the divorce does not occur until the disabled child's adulthood. Frequently, parents disagree about why the now-adult child still requires so much help. It is a generalization, but I think a valid one, that when parents disagree, the mother usually knows more than the father about the child's needs. The mother, generally, has coped with the myriad problems that crop up in daily life with the child. Tasks have been taught and cued over and over, and still the growing child cannot do them automatically. The father, who works away from home and may see the child for only a couple of hours at night, may conclude the child is lazy, spoiled, manipulative, or "playing dumb." Often the mother is accused of coddling the child, or recently the term "enabling" might be used. Sometimes disagreement between the parents leads to an ultimatum for the adult child: get a job or go to school, or move out. After the inevitable failure there is guilt and remorse enough for everyone.

If there are brothers and sisters in the family, they often report they felt the disabled child took more attention from the parents, to their detriment. Sometimes they say, poignantly, that they know the parents had to do what they did, but they still felt they received less than they would have liked of their parents' attention. Some siblings are openly critical of the way the parents raised the special child, feeling they made the disability worse. Siblings often say they know the parents expect them to take over the care of their sibling when the parents are gone, but they won't do it the same way the parents have done. Everyone in the family is generally troubled by the gravity of these decisions.

The typical living situation, adults with disabilities living in the parental home, is not only difficult for family members but is not the best arrangement for the adult with disabilities either. It is important to state why this would be true, in case parents might feel that a false argument is being made in order to excuse them from the duty of continuing to care for the adult child.

The most important reason for adults to live away from their parents is to ensure that they experience true adulthood, including relationships with their peers. One could suggest that having a job is just as important, or learning all the independent skills one needs to keep a life going. Those are important, but in my opinion there is nothing that makes adults with disabilities feel as much like their non-disabled peers as having true peer relations: acquaintances, friends, and romantic relationships that include the possibility of sexual relations. It is impossible for a parent to provide those relationships for an adult child who lives at home. And it is categorically impossible for a parent to direct the life of his or her child without all parties being aware that their relationship is still parent to child and child to parent.

The second most important reason for adults to live away from their parents is to prepare them for the likelihood that they will outlive their parents. It is much too difficult and too sad to have to learn to live without parents beginning on the day they die. Most parents do have concerns about dying before their children who need them so much, but they don't know what to do to prepare for this outcome. If there are siblings, the parents often persuade themselves that the siblings are taking careful notice of how much they will have to take on when the parents die. As mentioned above, siblings often have decided long before the time comes that they will not provide the kind of care the parents have provided, whether because they misunderstand the need or because they are not prepared to make the same kinds of sacrifices.

The idea of sacrifice reminds me, again, of the feeling that is present in every discussion of this population and these issues: guilt. Parents feel guilty for having kids with disabilities; then they feel guilty for wishing their kids were different, even though they are really wishing for a better life for the child. Then they feel guilty for not doing enough, or for doing things the wrong way, or for getting tired of all that they have to do. I would feel that this book has achieved its purpose if it causes parents of adults with disabilities to feel guiltier for keeping their kids home with them than for finding other options.

Part Two

Understanding Executive Functions

The second part of the book consists of a detailed description of the executive functions and the abilities, deficits, and behaviors associated with each function. For the sake of clarity, they will be described separately, but it is important to remember that these functions are actually inseparable. Behaviors are very complex and, when unimpaired, there is constant fluidity of movement between various brain functions. Picture a person swimming. You may see the arm and leg movements as the most important element of swimming; but then you may realize that breathing correctly is just as important, along with being aware of the position of one's body in the water. Taking off in a direction and holding that line is another component. It would be awkward to try to master each element separately when they all must be learned in coordination. This is the way to think of the executive functions.

Chapter 3

Initiation, or Getting Started

Initiation may be one of the most difficult executive functions to comprehend. Even the word "initiation" seems vague. It is related to the concept of taking initiative, but it is more basic. It really means having the ability to *start* anything at all without assistance from outside oneself.

Initiation deficits can be seen and understood more easily in persons who have suffered traumatic brain injury as adults than in the population we are considering in this book. In those individuals who have had productive, active lives and who then suffer brain trauma, the change in their initiation can be dramatic. They may do many things when asked to, yet never start anything without being directed. Similarly, they may not see the time to move from one step to the next in a complex behavior, yet as soon as someone else suggests moving to the next step, they are able to do so.

Picture a person who once enjoyed putting together jigsaw puzzles. After a brain injury, he may express an interest in doing a puzzle, but when you hand him the box, he seems not to know what to do. When you remind him that he used to dump out the pieces and turn them all face up, he will do that, then you will find him sitting at the table staring at the pieces of the puzzle. You suddenly realize that he will not be able to engage in the trial and error of comparing pieces by shape and color, and fitting them into place. He will need a prompt to pick up each piece of the puzzle. It finally dawns on you that the activity won't be fun for the brain-injured person or the helper.

In living with traumatic brain injury patients, failures of initiation are inevitably confusing and frustrating to loved ones. They can't see why the person doesn't think to start any activity. They seek explanations. Is he depressed? Has there been a personality change resulting in defiance? Could he be teasing, or is it a memory problem? But these brain-injured people haven't forgotten how to engage in activities, they just can't get started on their own.

In our population of adults on the autism spectrum, this deficit looks a bit different. Because they have lived with the same brain from childhood to adulthood and there hasn't been a sudden trauma, the deficit may not be as severe as it is when resulting from brain trauma. And our population typically have learned to use the behaviors of others as cues. So when mom says "good morning," they know not only to say good morning back, but to do other things that are triggered by saying good morning. Perhaps they are expected to set the table for breakfast, or take the cereal boxes down from the cupboard. These steps can be learned, even out of awareness, like a habit. However, the person with a neurodevelopmental disability is not able to initiate the ritual. Once started, she knows exactly what to do, yet day after day, she fails to begin the process on her own. And she cannot adapt the process to unexpected changes. Suppose there is no milk and you mention that you'll be making eggs and toast for breakfast. Undoubtedly, you will see the cereal boxes on the table anyway.

A person with poor ability to initiate will appear to be unmotivated, apathetic, or dull. You can just see the word *lazy* coming next. However, as you think more deeply about "lazy" behavior, you can almost always find a richer and more accurate explanation. For example, the person with poor initiation, who appears dull and unmotivated, will at other times show as much commitment and determination and perseverance as anyone else. It's just that he's gotten past the beginning point of the activity. Once started, he has the energy and the motivation to continue. For the jigsaw puzzle aficionado, you might have success by suggesting that each piece be tried in a given spot. This is mind-bogglingly inefficient to a normal puzzle-maker, but it just might work to overcome an initiation deficit. And chances are the impaired puzzle-maker would not experience the repetitiveness with the same sense of boredom as one would with a normal brain. Clearly, someone who would spend hours devoted to filling each space in a puzzle could not be described as lazy.

The elements of initiation

To further understand the initiation deficit, let's see how initiation works for normal people. My way of making sense of initiation is to analyze it step by step. When I wake up in the morning, the first thing I become aware of is whether it's a weekday or a weekend day, based upon whether or not I have set my alarm clock the night before. Knowing what day it is tells me whether I'm going to work or not. Knowing whether I'm going to work or not triggers two different routines, thus telling me what I need to know to get started. If I'm going to work, I get right to my morning routine of showering, dressing, breakfast, collecting briefcase, cell phone, appointment book, purse, keys, lunch.

If it's not a work day, then I may have more choice. But my first job is to be sure of that fact. It could be a Saturday, but one that is fully committed to errands or chores at home or social plans. Do I have any flexibility? May I change my plans based upon the weather, or a phone call from a friend? Do I feel well? How many people live with me, and do I need to know their plans as well as my own? All of these factors affect the way I initiate my day.

You probably have some feelings as you read my description. Perhaps you are the kind of person who loves to be organized and scheduled. You don't have to make new decisions each day because you live by cherished routines that assert themselves in your mind when you wake, and you have no desire to change them. What could be simpler? Or perhaps you feel the burden of responsibility as you read my description. You pull for it to be Saturday and for the day to be open to all possibilities. You welcome the chance to decide, on the spot, what you will do based only upon what you feel like doing (although if you are reading this book because you have a child with a disability, you probably can't remember when you felt that carefree).

Now suppose you don't feel anything like the description above. Suppose you wake up and you just are you... You are just there... You wait for the next thing to happen. I think that is how an initiation deficit feels. Generally the first thing that will assert itself will be the need to go to the bathroom. Then perhaps hunger. Or the need to smoke. These are called internal cues; your own body is cueing your mind to tell you what it wants. External cues would be things like the alarm clock or the conversation of the people you live with. People with normal initiation can respond automatically to both internal and external cues, and we automatically prioritize them. We can head for the bathroom while also thinking about the day ahead. Thinking in a self-aware way (like the thinking in my example above) is an internal type of cueing. One thought leads logically to the next thought, and, eventually to a decision. This is typical of the organization provided by normal executive functioning, and to various degrees it is impaired in persons with executive deficits.

Imagine if that little monologue you live with disappeared from your mind. As we will see later, that monologue is the equipment for self-monitoring, and is something most of us can't imagine turning off. (We don't know whether persons with executive deficits have the internal monologue, since it is difficult to get reliable answers from them about this phenomenon.) There is no functional way of getting started and directing one's life without the internal voice of initiation. Responding to primitive cues, like the need to go to the bathroom, is an inadequate means of directing a complex human life.

So we've seen the beginnings of normal initiation in the simple fact of being awake and alert, and able to think. The second step is the awareness of options that lead toward decisions. To be aware of options by thinking rather than seeing them or responding to internal cues is an abstract act. We can choose to turn some of our attention to abstract thoughts while still seeing and hearing what is all around us. The brain automatically prioritizes the abstract thoughts and the ongoing cues of the environment. We then combine our automatic responses (need to go to the bathroom) with our thoughts (it's a Saturday) and that takes the process away from being automatic and toward being purposeful.

The last step is difficult to understand as part of disability: the need to compare and evaluate choices against one another. With normal brains, we do this kind of weighing and choosing so automatically by the time we are adults that it's very hard to imagine being without this skill. Even when we make a poor choice, say calling in sick to work because we want a free day, we are aware we are on thin ice. We may rationalize (I hardly ever do this), justify (my co-workers do this more often than I do), or be rebellious (I don't care if they fire me). But we are aware we are making a choice that might not be a good one. We know there may be consequences that will be stressful the next day when we go back to work. We even know in advance how we will handle those consequences. We may have a plan that includes lying to boss and co-workers, so we already know we are going to feel guilty. We even know approximately how long it will take to stop feeling guilty! None of this high-level thinking is going on for the person with an initiation deficit. Later, we'll see this comparing of options, and imagining thoughts in the future, as part of self-monitoring, arguably the most complex and valuable of all the executive functions.

Summary of the elements of initiation

- Alertness.
- Awareness of options.
- Response to internal and external cues.
- Evaluation of choices for appropriateness.
- Action.

How initiation works with the other executive functions

Remember, the executive functions are inseparable. As we move in discussion from one function to the next, it is important to keep in mind that they must work together in coordination. When they are impaired, the deficits affect each other in various ways. How does an initiation deficit interact with the others? Well, imagine trying to make a plan for your day, or something more ambitious like a weekend trip. If you can't even recognize that you have options for the next five minutes, how could you organize your immediate future? You are likely to become overly dependent on the cues of others in your environment. Being overly dependent, you will appear cooperative and agreeable. This is one reason why individuals with executive deficits are so easily exploited by unscrupulous people. Keep in mind the initiation deficit as we move on to the next executive function.

Chapter 4

Concrete Thinking and Response to Novelty

A concrete thought is a thought about tangible objects, people, or events that can be pictured easily. The normally developing person is learning to think abstractly by adolescence. Abstract thinking makes use of concepts and ideas with symbolic meaning, ideas that are not circumscribed by pictures of familiar objects. Abstract thinking also involves the application of known principles to new situations, or generalizing. When we say "modes of transportation" instead of listing "cars, trains, and planes" we are moving into abstract thinking. Similarly, when we hear a list of concrete examples, we can supply an abstract phrase that encompasses the particulars.

When talking with a preteen child we don't expect much abstraction to be included in the conversation. But we begin to modify our own language with the increasing age of a child because we unconsciously know that complexity is developing. We might say, "What will you be doing for fun today?" to a ten-year-old, whereas we might say, "What toy do you want to play with?" to a five-year-old. If an adult fails to grasp or use abstract language we know immediately, if only on an unconscious level, that something is wrong. We modify and adapt our own language until we feel that a common ground for understanding has been reached. Let's look at how this is related to executive functioning.

"Bill and Joe got into a fight" is a more concrete statement than "I felt tension building between Bill and Joe." This example illustrates that people who think concretely appear to miss a lot of the complexity of life. They don't seem to register or report abstractions, in this case tension building between two people. They only have words for the action they observed, not the critical thinking that could have been done before the action. The question is whether this is a way of thinking—or not thinking—or a social deficit. If this example were analyzed as primarily a social deficit, the important feature would be the failure to perceive or understand tension between two other people. As an executive function deficit, the important feature is the inability to think about one's own perceptions and to articulate these perceptions. Perhaps tension was felt, but the observer has no cognitive structure to detect and talk about a non-concrete perception. With so much focus on impaired social functioning in those on the autism spectrum, it is important to find ways to differentiate social deficits from deficits in complex thinking and in perceptual information processing. When we analyze examples taken from social settings, interesting questions are raised about whether social skills are a discrete skill set, or are a domain in which concrete thinking pervades other skills.

One way to investigate is to ask simple step-wise questions of the observer, in other words, to supply the analytical skills of an intact brain from outside the thinker. We might ask how the two boys sounded when they encountered one another. We might ask how their faces looked and whether they moved toward one another. We might ask what they said to one another, and if it was a surprise when one hit the other. If all of those questions were answered in a way that showed the observer did notice *and understand* many cues leading to a fight, then we could move in the direction of poor ability to think abstractly and to self-monitor as the cause of the concrete reporting of the event.

On the other hand, a man with Asperger's demonstrates a circumscribed social deficit by beginning a conversation with me every single time he sees me, without regard for the context. If I'm moving quickly down the hall in a way that indicates I don't want to stop, he talks to me anyway. If I'm already in conversation with others, he talks to me without apparent awareness of the ongoing conversation. Each time I say something that should be understood as calling attention to his social error, he accepts what I say as the condition of the moment, such as, "I'm talking with Joe right now." But he does not use that information to guide his social behavior in the future. This is an important point: perhaps this young man does not change his behavior because his social deficit is not modifiable. In other words, he may never be able to scan quickly for the cues the rest of us use to make immediate, unconscious, social decisions. Or, he does not change because he fails to think the following: "Nancy told me she couldn't talk to me right now because she's talking to Dan. I should have noticed that she was talking with someone else and I would be interrupting." We find that clients can train themselves to use cues to make better social decisions, but it is never quite the same as having intact social abilities. The difference is inexpressible, but noticeable and significant. The difference in the purity of the social deficit can be seen by comparison to another type of client who might interrupt others in conversation because of poor impulse control, but who fully understands what it means to interrupt.

Consider the normal progression from concrete to abstract thinking. It is an evolving process that occurs throughout adolescence and continues into adulthood. A hallmark of adolescence is the stage of individuation between child and parents, or that time when the young person realizes he or she is separate. Brain development makes individuation possible. Younger children who identify with their parents accept, without conscious thought, that their parents' values are their values. They say "we" like Fords or Macs or hiking in the mountains. Individuation can begin when brain development allows for thoughts like, "I'm not the same as my parents because I can like things and think things that my parents don't like and don't think."

Individuation (and obnoxious arguments) assert themselves into the family at this point. Parents will often use the phrase "having a mind of his own" to describe a teenager at this stage, and that is actually a very apt expression. It is developmentally accurate to regard the teenager's mind as becoming a separate, autonomous mind. When a younger child is described that way, it is generally considered a precocious trait, as in, "he had a mind of his own from day one!" Again, the observation represents developmental accuracy: the younger child is not expected to have the thoughts of a distinctly autonomous being.

The executive functions spring forward in development as a result of what one neuroscientist calls "the expensive cells" being activated at the appropriate time (Sapolsky 2000). If that neuronal system is damaged, these higher-level thinking skills don't develop. Or, more typically, they develop in spotty or incomplete fashion. So an adult with impaired ability to think abstractly will seem childish in his thinking, or will appear to be joking. The use of money provides many good examples of concrete thinking where abstract thinking is expected. Money is being used concretely when we buy things with cash. But money also has abstract elements that my clients can't comprehend. They believe, for example, that checks may be written with confidence as long as the checkbook still contains checks. When *we* make that well-worn joke—I must have money if I still have checks—we know why it's a joke! Understanding credit cards similarly requires the ability to think abstractly. The card stands for an amount of money that can change out of our awareness, such as when new charges hit the account or when payments are applied.

Examples of concrete thinking supplied by my clients often have a charm that stems from their naivety. A young man with the deficit of concrete thinking drives a car and works full-time in a government office. When fueling his car, he goes to the same gas station and even uses the same pump every time. Once he was given a prepaid gas card as a gift. But it was from a different gas station than the one he uses. He remarked, in complete seriousness, "It's too bad I don't go to that gas station."

It is tempting to regard concrete thinking as simply an example of low intellect, but that would be misleading in many cases. The man in this example has an IQ in the normal range. But IQ tests do a poor job of calculating the effect of reduced executive skills on functional intellect. This man happens to be an extremely concrete thinker in real-life situations, although he reads the newspaper and comprehends the complexities of news stories. It is likely that he fails most completely when abstract thinking meets with novelty.

What is novelty?

"Novelty" is the academic word given to the experience of sudden unexpected events requiring some kind of response. What is considered novelty by any given individual depends in part upon the extent of abstract thinking he is comfortable with. If you go through life with beliefs like "the only constant is change," then you are likely to be more comfortable with a great amount of novelty in daily life. You regard many occurrences not as novelties, but simply as life unfolding before you. You expect a lot of randomness and therefore are not so surprised by it. In order to live that way, you must have an expectation of flexibility: flexibility in thinking, in changing course, in modifying ideas and opinions. People who live this way appear to others as spontaneous and open-minded.

In contrast, think of individuals who know they don't like a lot of change, and are able to think and plan in order to reduce novelty in their lives. Although they may not enjoy the unexpected, they can respond when they have to. Think about being stuck in a traffic jam on the way to work.

The person who hates to be caught off guard would probably have left early enough to take an alternate route and still arrive on time. Or, these days, the efficient person would set up phone, fax, or laptop right in the car and get some work done. On the other hand, the person who isn't as bothered by chance occurrences might think of the delay as more time to listen to her book-on-CD in the car. Thus both styles can be functional.

The problem for people with executive deficits is that they have neither an alternate plan nor an alternate attitude when faced with a novel obstacle. Every novel occurrence feels the same. They feel surprised and sometimes paralyzed with the inability to respond. They don't have an automatic "mind search" function that says *how is this situation similar to something I've done before?* Being poor at abstract thinking, they are also poor at imagining what might happen if they act, especially when a quick response is necessary. An intact individual will know, for example, that a novel event while driving probably requires slowing down, but also checking the rearview mirror before slowing down too abruptly. For a more mundane example, imagine your waiter returns to the table to tell you the order you placed is no longer available. You have to order something else even if you had your heart set on a particular meal. Or you could leave the restaurant, but you should consider the needs of others in your party before deciding to leave. Failing to be guided by a quick mind search, the impaired individual generally acts on impulse or in response to the most compelling cue in the environment. There are many examples of truly dangerous responses of these types: running from a policeman, yelling back at someone who yelled first, saying yes to an offer of a ride or a suspicious substance. Individuals with executive deficits do all of these things, and they do them over and over again, regardless of the consequences.

Problem-solving is a skill closely related to response to novelty. Problem-solving, however, like decision-making, might be thought of as the situation in which you have plenty of time to respond to novelty. In other words, the problem you want to solve doesn't spring up in front of you like a ladder in your lane on the freeway. It presents itself without urgency. You may deliberate and analyze, taking all the time you need. These would be problems like what food to serve at a party, or what kind of new car to buy. Even eliminating the time pressure, some individuals with executive deficits cannot problem-solve because of the inability to think abstractly, to generalize, to do the mind search for similarities and differences, and to ponder the consequences of various options.

Meet Joe

Joe is actually the young man you just met in the example above. He is an interesting client because his problem-solving deficit is so complete, and stunningly incongruous when compared with his other intellectual abilities. As mentioned above, he reads a newspaper daily and follows the stock market in his own way. He works in a government office and is valued as an employee, for his affable nature. He's always ready with a quip or a pun. He drives and has not been defeated as yet by the novelties that occur to all drivers, though he has had his license suspended for a time, following an accident.

Joe once found that a new roommate had moved some items into the kitchen they were to share. In the process, the roommate had moved Joe's toaster oven a foot or so and had unplugged it. Another appliance had been plugged into the wall socket and was placed in such a way that it covered the set of outlets in the wall. Both appliances could be plugged in at the same time by simply moving the one that hid the outlets. Joe spent four days not using his toaster oven because it wasn't plugged in, *and he couldn't solve the problem of getting the oven plugged in again.*

Now, if you really like to analyze puzzles like this, you might speculate that Joe didn't want to reverse the appliances thus doing to the other man what had been done to him. Or you might guess that he was frightened to speak to the other man about the situation. You might wonder why he didn't seek help from staff, who are available for situations like this. The problem went on until staff happened to ask Joe why he wasn't eating the meals he always cooked in his toaster oven. He said, "My oven is unplugged and the outlet is covered up." The problem for Joe was not an interpersonal dilemma about manners, or a power struggle for control of the kitchen. He just could not think of moving the two appliances around so that both could be plugged in at the same time.

Another of Joe's dilemmas is interesting in that it could appear to be a social deficit, but analysis will show that it isn't. Joe is very social and has a friendly manner and a delightful wit when talking with staff and others in his comfort zone. But on one occasion he requested help from staff to ask a woman for a date. The staff person assumed Joe just needed to get started in conversation with the woman, and then he would be able to invite her out. So he suggested an opening remark like, "Do you like to go to the movies?" Joe walked across the room to the woman and asked if she liked to go to the movies. When she answered that she did, Joe turned on his heel, went back to the staff and reported her answer, then waited for his next line to be supplied by the staff. Joe had no idea that this would be seen by the woman as odd behavior, because he was being concrete about getting help with conversation. Once he was in that mode, his own very charming conversational skills were set aside completely. Joe could not mesh the two behaviors—getting help and making conversation—at the same time. And he could not think about his nervousness and eagerness to ask for a date, and also monitor the social expectations of the woman.

I can't resist telling one more story of Joe's problem-solving disability, because it is also my favorite illustration of concrete thinking in an otherwise intelligent person. Joe had a minor accident with his car and had to stop driving for a while. He learned to commute to work by public transportation, including taking a bus as part of the commute. After a few months he was able to drive again, but staff wondered if it wouldn't be less stressful for him to continue using public transportation. We posed the question to him: would you rather go back to driving your own car or continue using public transportation? Joe answered, "Well, I have to use the bus for a while longer." Oh, why is that? we asked. Joe answered, "I still have some bus quarters left."

Concrete thinking and moral reasoning

Besides leading to problem-solving difficulties, concrete thinking creates some other serious deficits in our clients. It can cause behaviors that are perceived as moral failures, when they should be understood as organic deficits. Moral development is interwoven with the more complex abstract thinking skills. Our executively impaired clients are definitely able to think about right and wrong in the same way that a young child does. This means they will act to avoid getting caught and punished for something everyone agrees is wrong. But whether they achieve an abstract conception of moral behavior *when not observed by others* varies considerably in our population.

Higher moral development is most likely to be seen in our population when other factors are put in place to override poor brain development. Young people with disabilities can learn, by rote, what is acceptable and what is not, at least in broad strokes. And some can carry into adult life a habit of behaving according to those rules. But they face compelling organic obstacles that can prevent the achievement of higher levels of moral behavior. One of these obstacles is the poor ability to imagine abstract outcomes in the future, which is the subject of this chapter. In the next chapters that examine other executive functions we'll encounter further obstacles to moral behavior in the form of impulsivity and lack of empathy. All these obstacles to moral behavior stem from executive dysfunction.

The more abstract and subtle aspects of good behavior are likely to be poorly understood, and poorly carried out, by people with impaired executive functions. The following examples can be explained as errors caused by concrete thinking, poor problem-solving and decision-making, poor appreciation of consequences, and failure of empathy. And all fall under the general heading of immoral or "bad" behavior that would not be expected from a normal adult.

Real examples of bad behavior

- A man writes checks against an account that hasn't enough money and, when confronted, denies having done it.

- A young man breaks into his roommate's bedroom while he is away in order to use his computer, telephone, and video games.

- A woman convinces the teller in her bank to allow her to write a counter check for cash and spends all her rent and grocery money.

- Friends tease one another even though they report that being teased was the most painful part of childhood.

- A young woman discovers chat sites on the internet and invites a stranger into her parents' house and has unprotected sex with him.

Most of the behaviors mentioned above sound childish (albeit dangerous in some cases), because they exemplify self-centered behavior unchecked by moral self-monitoring or even self-preservation. Unfortunately, my executive function impaired clients have the intellectual ability to conceive of and carry out such self-serving schemes, along with the inability to solve the problems they create. Given this tendency, it is evident that these clients can be dangerous to themselves and can end up committing crimes unwittingly. Methods to combat these unfortunate behaviors will be taken up in a later section.

Chapter 5

Planning, Sequencing, and Organizing

Planning and being organized in brain terms are similar but also different from what those words mean in everyday life. There is a wide range among normal people in the way they can be organized or disorganized. But having a brain deficit in this area goes beyond normal everyday disorganization. Again, to understand this concept, it is helpful to think of children and their development.

Most parents would not make the mistake of asking a five-year-old to clean his room. They know the child doesn't have the organizational skills to plan and put in order the steps to complete the whole job. However, the clever parent could definitely begin coaching the child toward orderliness by giving him a basket or box and asking him to put all the cowboys in the box. After he has completed that task, if he still seems involved, he could be asked to put all the blocks into another basket. As the child grows older, and based upon earlier training—and never forget temperament—he may become a pretty good room-cleaner by adding steps in an age-appropriate way.

School homework is also assigned according to the principle of incremental planning skills. By the last years of high school, a student should be capable of planning and completing complex projects. This involves knowing the different tasks necessary to complete the whole project, understanding how to put the steps into a logical sequence, and estimating the amount of time each step will take. Parents are often frustrated by the child's apparent poor judgment shown in not allowing enough time for each step and ending up overwhelmed the night before the project is due.

The wise parent of a teenager might employ a combination of helpful guidance and freedom to learn through failure, depending again upon the temperaments of all involved. In other words, if the parents are very "hands-on" they may divide and sequence the steps for the child and require that the steps be completed by certain times, as they would have done with the child's homework in the lower grades. Their hope would be that the young person would be so relieved at avoiding the last-minute pressure to complete the project that they would learn the lesson of sequencing the steps and working steadily over time. On the other hand, many teenagers insist upon their autonomy and refuse all help by this stage in school, and end up learning about time management "the hard way." Again, both paths are functional and much depends upon temperament and family style.

For the person with an impaired brain, issues of organization and planning go much deeper. It's not that the person doesn't organize his world, it's that the person's brain isn't organized. Steps toward a goal are not apparent and logical. The passage of time isn't perceived accurately, which leads to the inability to estimate how much time is needed to complete various activities. Short-term memory is not reliable. Sustained attention toward a problem cannot be maintained.

Nora and I were discussing her messy bedroom. She said she would like it to be cleaner and neater. I asked her to picture her room and tell me what it would take to be the way she wanted it. She ticked off on her fingers, "I'd have to make the bed, and pick up all the clothes off the floor, and clear off the top of the desk, and vacuum, and throw away the newspapers and junk mail." I remarked that she knew what to do to clean the room, but she answered that she wouldn't know where to begin. So I asked her to tell me again the things that had to be done. Again she ticked them off on her fingers, in the same order. I said, "So now you know what to do." Her list amounted to a very competent analysis of the necessary steps to clean the room. But she looked at me with a completely blank stare and said, again, that she had no idea how to clean the room. For Nora, a description of her room that she could picture in her mind bore no relation to knowing how to go about cleaning the room.

The example above illustrates the way in which the executive functions cannot be separated. Part of Nora's problem was an initiation issue: she couldn't begin the project. But she couldn't begin because she couldn't organize the project in her mind. She couldn't think of sequential steps even though she created a list when asked. She didn't even realize that a list is a sequence. Most importantly for understanding this deficit, she could answer questions about cleaning her room, but she couldn't ask herself the same questions as a way of getting started and analyzing the problem. The brain deficit is largely in not realizing there is an analysis to be done. We do these analyses all day long, automatically, and at various levels of awareness. If we know we need to go to the cleaners and the post office and the bank and the grocery store, we don't drive back and forth across town; planning an efficient route is so automatic that we may not even realize we've done it. And we never buy the ice cream first!

How dysfunctional is a deficit in planning, organizing, and sequencing? It is important to remember that the executive functions are impaired together, albeit to different degrees. People with a deficit in planning are not just messy and disorganized "normals." In employment, this deficit can be the source of failure after failure. Obviously, employees with this challenge would not do well with multi-step tasks. They function more like the five-year-old who has to be told what to do one step at a time. And they will most likely need to be reminded of the steps to complete a task long after the supervisor would expect a sequence to have been learned. Furthermore, once a sequence is learned, the employer cannot expect generalization of the learned sequence to different tasks. Where the employer sees the similarity of two sets of tasks, the impaired person sees only the differences.

This organizational deficit also takes place on a larger scale than the examples discussed so far. Planning over the lifespan can be just as problematic as organizing the tasks of a day. Individuals with this disability try to master what they consider to be adult behavior; but they do this largely by copying the most eye-catching or trendy aspects of culture at the time of their late adolescence. There is no regard for a style being a good fit or having specific meaning to the individual. A young woman may dye her hair green at 16 and then stick with that "look" into middle age. Individuals with an organizational deficit, along with poor abstract thinking, and other executive deficits will tend to stay stuck in these patterns indefinitely. Due to the inability to plan for developmental change on a large scale, these individuals can come to seem ageless. They tend to dress in the style of young adults far too long; they remain committed to the music and other fads of their early adolescent years. They don't seem to register the passage of time or changes in social conventions. And they continue to talk of things they will do "in the future" long after the time has passed for those events to be pursued or given up.

Some of my clients talk about leaving our therapeutic program for people with disabilities. They have dreams of life "in the real world." Ironically, they usually imagine only that the apartment they would live in would be in a different complex than the program's apartments. They might still want a roommate, or not, and other than the re-location they don't have a clear picture of how they would occupy themselves. Many say they would have a pet. The most unrealistic feature of their fantasies is that they would have unlimited supplies of whatever they want most. Money is the first commodity that they imagine would be more plentiful if they were to be released from supervision. Or they would meet their ideal romantic partner, get married, and have children. Or they would have a more exciting and better paying job. For the majority of our clients, these ideas are stupendously unrealistic fantasies.

Asking the clients, in a logical manner, what it would take to have the things they want stimulates good, reasonable answers. This is because they are generally not impaired in intellectual ability. But because they aren't organized in their analytical and thinking skills, they fail to ask the same questions of themselves. And, amazingly, after such a conversation, they return to the wishful thinking and failure to analyze their circumstances, as if the conversation had never happened.

What life skills are affected by an organization deficit?
Almost any aspect of daily living can be affected by an organization deficit. And since the executive functions are inseparable, this deficit does not exist by itself. The organizational deficit looks different depending upon the extent of initiation deficit, and different based upon the extent of regulation deficits (which we haven't discussed yet).

Aspects of daily living that are affected by this deficit include following routines and schedules, and completing multi-step tasks like making a meal, cleaning, and shopping. In addition, responding to mail appropriately, knowing when and how to get medical care, and keeping track of social engagements may be problematic. And managing money is almost always a problem for people with this deficit. Imagine how it would feel if the arrival of your benefit check was a surprise each month. Or if someone told you how important it was to pay the rent on time, but you just didn't quite understand what "on time" meant. Imagine if you couldn't figure out when a bit of money would be yours to spend without supervision—you might just spend whatever ended up in your hands whenever that happened. It is so difficult to comprehend the effects of this deficit in our clients because their verbal ability sounds so normal and competent. Simply put: it's hard to believe someone who sounds so normal could make such ridiculous mistakes.

With a greater initiation deficit, the individual may not appear to have any plans at all. Each day may require extensive cueing of the day's tasks and activities. A cue can be as simple as another client saying "Aren't you going to morning meeting? You aren't dressed." The remark serves as a cue to get dressed and head over to the program building where morning meeting takes place. Following morning meeting, there are cues in the environment in the form of conversation about what else takes place throughout the day. Staff are quick to ask if a client knows what's next on her schedule. This is really a cue to look at one's schedule and go to the next class or appointment.

If initiation is not so much in deficit, then the organizational deficit shows itself differently. The person who has lots of ideas and impulses may be inclined to set off in many directions at once. Anything in the environment that attracts her may start a "new plan." But with poor ability to analyze the steps toward a plan, she will likely make many false starts. This is when clients fail to attend classes, miss appointments, spend their money on the wrong things, or hurt others' feelings by ignoring plans they may have made together. This version of the organization deficit often provokes criticism of the person's character because it looks like they are making selfish decisions based upon disregard for others. On the contrary, it is a deficit in brain functioning and much pain can be avoided by understanding it as such.

Decision-making is a specific skill that is impaired when organizational abilities are impaired. To make decisions in any way other than by "gut" reaction, some evaluation of options is required. A choice is not always a decision. A choice made purposefully is called a decision because it is based upon prioritizing options in a variety of ways and choosing one over all others for reasons that have been compared and considered. Granted, many of us make our decisions based on prior experience or hunches or going along with others far more often than we might realize, but the intact brain is capable of judicious decision-making and the disorganized brain is not.

Sequencing is a part of this executive function that deserves an extra bit of explanation. We touched on sequencing in the failure of Nora to understand that her list of tasks was an organizing tool. A sequence that is written down like a list doesn't adequately emphasize the fact that sequencing involves time. It means one thing happens before or after another, and time has passed. When my clients make plans for later in the same day, they are poor at factoring in the amount of time it will take for various things to happen. On Friday afternoons when they receive their discretionary spending money, most rush to the bank or grocery store to cash their checks. They often go out to dinner in groups on Friday evenings. A newcomer to the community was most eager to be included in the dinner plans. But he left the bank with his cash and then wandered home by way of several of his favorite stores. He knew the time he was supposed to meet the others for dinner, but he didn't know how to perceive or calculate the amount of time it would consume to stop in at each store on his route. When he arrived 40 minutes past the meeting time, he was confused, hurt, and angry to see that he had been left behind. When the interaction of sequencing and time is analyzed this way, it becomes clear that memory is affected by a deficit in sequencing ability, and vice versa.

My clients have very poor memories for when something happened and poor judgment for the feeling of how much time has passed since a specific event occurred. The same is true for events coming up in the future. The date of an upcoming concert may be memorized, but the feeling of how imminent it is, is not accurate. The inevitable caveat is that some of the clients memorize things by date as their idiosyncratic special interest. But they may still have the deficit in estimating how long ago something happened even if they can provide the date. They don't feel the passage of time the way we normally do.

Again, if the conversational ability of an individual sounds normal, people will not expect to encounter the sequencing/memory problem. Consider this type of conversation that occurs frequently with doctors. In this scenario, the client will be on medication that was prescribed by a different doctor, perhaps some time ago. The current doctor will want to record in her records how long the client has been on the medication. So she asks the client, who has no idea how long, but wants to appear normal. The client will answer vaguely, "Oh, I've been on that med a long time." The doctor might ask, do you mean more than a year? The client will answer, "Oh yes, more than a year, maybe five years." At this point, if the doctor writes down one year or five years or between one and five years, her information will be completely unreliable. The client doesn't mean to lie, but he cares a great deal about passing as normal, so he won't simply say he doesn't know how long he's been on the medication. Interestingly, if the doctor asks in a different way, if she says, "Do you know the date you started this medication?" the client will generally answer, "No, but my mom does."

Chapter 6

Attention and Concentration

I mentioned that the terminology surrounding the executive functions is not set in stone. There is still disagreement as to which skills should be included as executive functions. Not all theoretical models of brain functioning include *regulatory functions* as executive functions.

It makes sense to me to include regulatory functions with the executive functions because they oversee and control some *other* behavior the brain is performing. Much of the discussion so far has included examples of the executive functions monitoring and controlling, or regulating, other brain activities. The specific regulatory functions I'll include and discuss here are control of attention and concentration, and, in the next chapter, control of emotions.

Regardless of how the terminology gets sorted out over time, the salient fact is this: there are behavioral functions that require constant regulation. Some of the same parts of the brain that perform the other executive functions, primarily the prefrontal lobes, are also involved in these regulatory functions. In traumatic brain injury, regulatory functions tend to be affected as part of an executive dysfunction syndrome, which is another indicator that they should be grouped together for practical understanding.

When we consider attention, we must think of a continuum. If a skill, or function, exists on a continuum, something has to control where on the continuum the attribute is at any given moment. Think of the power used in a golf swing. The drive off the tee requires the most power the golfer can produce, whereas the putt is a stroke that requires a softer touch. The way the golfer controls the power in his swing is an example of regulation of an output on a continuum.

Attention is a fascinating skill that we often take for granted. We are in command of an amazing range and fluidity where attention is concerned, and we don't even realize it most of our waking hours. Consider how our attention fluctuates throughout a normal day. We wake up each morning and we begin to consider, both automatically and with effort, where we are—indeed, who we are. I awake and immediately sort out where to direct my attention, based upon whether or not I awoke to an alarm clock. Once we know what kind of day it is to be, we direct our attention toward certain tasks. In addition, we direct ourselves as to whether there is urgency or not. My waking to an alarm clock may signal urgency to me, but compare it to a fireman awaking to the fire bell!

Throughout the day we make thousands of little adjustments in our attention. When we choose a certain level of directed attention, we call that concentration. We may stay in a state of focused concentration for an hour or more, and then we usually take a break of some kind. A break in terms of attention can simply be turning the eyes toward a different view. Or listening to ambient noise instead of a lecture. Yet most of us have some activities to which we can devote ourselves at an intense level of concentration for as long as we want to. How are we able to make that choice? And what would it feel like not to be able to do so?

A two-part model of attention

Attention is a two-part function. It has what can be viewed, metaphorically, as a vertical component and a horizontal component. The vertical component of attention is level of arousal and the horizontal component is breadth of focus. Picture the vertical aspect of attention as a pole standing upright in a large empty room, like the pole firemen use to get "downstairs" quickly. The pole represents the arousal part of attention. The lowest level of arousal, in a living person, would be a coma. So place coma at the bottom of the vertical pole. Moving up the pole, imagine the state of being asleep, first deeply asleep, then higher up the pole, lighter sleep. Then continue upward through a range of normal states of wakeful arousal. This should take up most of the pole from the low middle up almost to the top. This middle range represents all the various levels of arousal we pass through normally. The continuum consists of states like lethargy after a meal, boredom at a bad movie, involvement with a lecture, excitement upon seeing someone we love, enthusiasm for an activity we know requires stamina and focus, and all the other routine and arousing aspects of a normal life.

Toward the top of the pole would be the heightened arousal required for states of concentration that are called upon for athletic competition, the arts, sophisticated intellectual achievements, and endeavors like operating dangerous machinery or performing complicated surgery. We've all heard of feats performed by people who were in states of unusual arousal. They sometimes report that they felt calm and not stressed by the difficulty of the feat. Many of us don't enter the higher states of arousal often, if ever. On the other hand, some people find the state of highest arousal so invigorating that they seek ways to achieve it, like engaging in daredevil activities.

What, then, would be at the extreme top of the pole, representing the extreme of heightened arousal? We might assume that position is reserved for sexual arousal. Unfortunately, even more arousing than sexual feelings are the feelings of fear, terror, and rage. Also at or near the top would be the abnormal state of arousal that exists in bipolar disorder and other psychotic states of arousal. (There is a misconception that manic states are fun and invigorating. In fact, a manic episode may start out that way, but it becomes an engine that can't be turned off, and is very disturbing and disabling.)

In Attention Deficit Disorder with Hyperactivity, like a manic episode, there appears to be an engine perpetually revving inside the individual. Movement is compelled from within and the individual cannot explain why. They try to do things that will make the need to move seem logical and purposeful, but this ploy doesn't work because the need to move doesn't allow them to stick with any one activity long enough to accomplish it. If the attention deficit is restricted to activities of the mind, bodily movement won't be seen, but the mind can be as chaotically active and out of control as the body of a hyperactive child. This is not a psychotic state because loss of contact with reality doesn't occur, but it is a very disabling, exhausting, and distressing condition nevertheless.

As we have seen, the very top of the vertical pole representing arousal is a dysfunctional state, as is the bottom, the coma. Many normal levels of arousal occur in the midrange of the continuum, in the same way that so many other natural phenomena have normal conditions in the midrange, with the two extremes being rare or dysfunctional (think of height and weight). Arousal naturally seems best represented by a vertical image, contrasted with the other aspect of attention, which is best pictured as a horizontal field.

The horizontal aspect of attention refers to the breadth of possible things one can pay attention to at one time. Picture a ring hovering around the vertical pole, like a hula hoop. The ring can move up and down to be located at different levels of arousal, but more importantly the ring can change size, from small and close to the pole, representing concentration on one item or activity, to larger, suggesting a wide field of attention.

In the normal course of a day we regulate our attention constantly without conscious awareness of the process. Picture a state of arousal somewhere in the middle of the vertical pole, with a ring around it wide enough to encompass the variety of things you are able to attend to at the same time. You may be driving a familiar route to do errands that are not unusual. You are able to drive, plan the route to complete the errands, and, at the same time, think about a friend who's having a baby any day now, along with an unfinished project at work, and the child who has a birthday coming up. It is only when you miss a turn that you realize something captured your attention to such an extent that you lost track of your main focus, driving to a particular place.

In fact, driving offers a perfect example of how we regulate our attention. Experienced drivers drive automatically in familiar situations. Even people in blackout states of drunkenness can get home without conscious attention to their driving. But what is the first thing we do when something unexpected happens while we're driving? Most people turn down the radio and tell the children to be quiet. What we mean to say is: "I have to pay attention to my driving now." The ring that represents the breadth of our attention immediately shrinks so that all the things we were attending to leave our minds while we focus on driving in the new conditions.

Focus is a small tight ring; daydreaming is a big widespread ring. Focus on brain surgery, or on "fourth down and goal to go" in the Superbowl, is a small tight ring up toward the top of the vertical (arousal) pole. Daydreaming is a widespread ring down low on the arousal pole, maybe just above a light sleep. Watching an involving movie with no other distracting thoughts might be a moderately small ring around the middle of the pole; the ring is not at its smallest, though, because you still notice your foot touching something sticky on the floor, or someone talking in the next row. Attempting to focus on a movie not to your taste when you feel you really need to be somewhere else makes the circle of focus expand, as you realize you are unable to concentrate on just the movie, but are thinking about many other things.

This is the flexible and fragile nature of attention: we control it but it also controls us. This is undoubtedly a survival mechanism. If we were able to tune out everything but what we choose at any given moment, we would be vulnerable to all manner of dangers around us. We might miss the moment when the casual drive changed to an emergency situation; we might not hear a crying baby, or smell the smoke of an imminent fire. And socially we would seem less than normally involved with others, as those on the autism spectrum exemplify.

How attention and concentration shape social behavior

Attention and concentration are interwoven with the other executive functions. Consider, again, an example stemming from brain injury. A young woman suffers a stroke somewhere in the frontal lobes of the brain. She may recover many abilities, especially the basics of walking and talking and memory for the routine activities of her life. But her friends find her different, and they describe the difference as a personality change. Why would the woman's personality change following a stroke?

The answer lies in the fact that what we call personality includes many little traits that are actually separate brain functions, or skills. This is a profound concept that may require a pause for contemplation: what we consider personality is actually made up of many skills that can be impaired either together or one-by-one, allowing us to see in bits and pieces what goes into the making of a "personality."

Perhaps the woman with the stroke and her best friend take walks together. During the walks they confide in each other about their families and other concerns. Now, however, the woman doesn't seem to care about her friend's troubles. She may appear to be listening as she would have in the past, but suddenly she'll point out a flower that has caught her eye, and the interruption of her friend's conversation is startling.

The woman has suffered diminished control of her attention. Her mind is more apt to wander (the circle containing her focus is widespread); she is likely to say whatever comes to mind, and she is unaware of the effect this has on her friendship. Her poor awareness of the change in social behavior is actually a greater problem, and that's another executive skill, self-monitoring, that we'll examine in a later chapter. At this point, consider what a small thing it may *seem* to be, to comment spontaneously on whatever pulls your focus. But in a social context, where a friend believes you are listening intently to her every word, it can be devastating.

Another way poor control of attention can intermingle with social behavior is that people with this impairment will fail to keep appointments and fulfill commitments. It's not that they don't remember, but rather that they continue responding to all stimuli more or less equally, and thus they miss the time when they would have had to take control to attend an appointment, or take the necessary steps to meet a commitment. People find them inconsiderate and selfish—again, personality traits—but the behavior stems from their impaired ability to control their attention and to direct their behavior purposefully.

As with so many of the executive functions, the two extremes on the continuum are the areas of dysfunction. So, attention and concentration can be impaired by being either too focused or too loose; that is, the horizontal circle can be too small or too large. Both are examples of dysregulation. The ability to regulate or control one's attention is impaired, leaving the individual with too much or too little ability to focus. In either condition, such a person is literally out of control.

The individual with too little ability to focus is highly distractible and impulsive. Every stimulus in the environment exerts an equal pull on their attention. It would be rare to have this impairment and not to have, accompanying it, poor social judgment. In order to have social judgment, one must notice the subtle reactions of others. When every stimulus attracts you forcefully, you cannot choose to focus on the subtleties of the facial expression of another. So these individuals tend to say whatever comes to mind and feel it's not their fault if someone gets hurt. They didn't intend to cause pain.

On the other end of the continuum are people who are too focused, who perseverate on one narrow topic and don't notice that others are bored with their monologue, or feel they can't make a connection. They also fail to notice the subtleties of another's facial expression, but in this case it is because their focus is entirely devoted to their one thing. Persons with Asperger's are particularly apt to ignore the social component of any interchange, as they are overly reliant on and interested in their own verbal abilities. Generally, they are oblivious to the boredom or irritation that may be quite obvious on the faces of their captive audience. Many clinicians are working with young children to develop the habit of paying attention to facial expressions of others. It remains to be seen if this is a skill that can be developed in some way other than the natural developmental way of the normal brain.

Wayne is a middle-aged man with Asperger's Syndrome whose favorite subject is birthdays. He has memorized the birthdays of many famous people, and within the first minutes of meeting he asks to know the birthday of everyone he meets. This is an especially odd topic for conversation because there's so little to converse about. When Wayne is lucky enough to encounter someone willing to throw out names of famous people so he can supply the birth dates, an even stranger thing happens. Wayne doesn't enjoy the surprise and acknowledgment others inevitably express about his odd accomplishment. Instead of graciously accepting the compliments, he impatiently prods them to keep supplying names. This makes him seem even more socially inappropriate, as he rejects the only interpersonally connecting part of the conversation, the compliment.

Because these traits fall on a continuum, there are individuals whose verbosity and poor social awareness are noticeable to those around them, but are not considered to be worthy of a clinical diagnosis. In other words, these people wouldn't be diagnosed with a brain disorder or with Asperger's, but everyone recognizes them as slightly inappropriate in aspects of their interpersonal behavior. We have all encountered the co-worker or neighbor or church acquaintance who talks relentlessly about subjects of interest only to herself and who fails to notice cues that we want to end the conversation. Similarly, there are those at the other end of the continuum who jump from subject to subject, and appear to be just on the verge of loss of control. In both cases, greater dysfunction would be required for clinical diagnosis, and we can appreciate that these individuals remind us of the wide range of human behavior that is considered normal.

Chapter 7

Regulation of Emotions

The regulation of emotions is another subject of controversy in terms of inclusion with the executive functions. I include it because it is often affected in conjunction with the other executive functions when brain injuries are sustained. As with attention and concentration, regulation means that control and management are exerted by the brain. A person experiencing emotions is using a brain that, ideally, can interpret, control, regulate, and express those emotions. As with all brain functions, this one can also be impaired.

To understand the role of regulation of emotions, first we must acknowledge that a very wide range of emotional behavior can be considered normal. Individuals have characteristic ways of expressing themselves emotionally. Some are low-key and mild in all emotional states; others are impressively vivid in their range and expression of emotions. Still others are mild in some emotional states and intense in others. Some people, particularly those who are especially concerned with being nice, are more comfortable with the friendly and warm emotions and more inhibited in expressing the supposedly negative emotions. All of this can be called normal.

After acknowledging individual differences in emotional expression, second, we must recognize that acceptable expression of emotions is dependent upon the situation or context. In hospitals, public expressions of anxiety or sorrow are not surprising, and are treated with respect. A football game provides a context for loud and exuberant behavior. A wedding is a setting for all kinds of intense emotions. The examples go on and on. Once we've taken context into account, it's interesting to realize that we recognize non-normal expressions of emotion *when we see them*, and within cultures we are remarkably consistent in making these judgments.

To return to the first point, we all know people who are more expressive, or more sensitive, or more explosive, that is, more demonstrably emotional than ourselves, and probably people who are less so as well. Or we may feel that we are at the extreme in one kind of emotion, but not in all kinds. To use myself as an example (again!), I am overly sentimental. I cannot give toasts at weddings or tell stories about kindness or the innocent charm of children without feeling my eyes tear up and my voice crack. On the other hand, I do not cry when I'm angry as many women do. I enjoy telling jokes and funny stories, and I can speak before a large audience. For me, the emotional tender spot is kindness, or public expression of sentiment or love.

For others, anger is the difficult emotion. We all know people who barely contain themselves while driving. They criticize other drivers and take things personally that are probably random occurrences. Or, in social situations, they turn every conversation into a debate and then an argument. Sometimes people who appear angry to others will say that they feel stimulated or invigorated or involved, but not angry. They characterize people who don't like to argue as boring or bland.

Individuals differ in the amount of emotion they express, whether it is anger or sentiment or enthusiasm or joy. Some people tend to have very personal, very loud, conversations in public and on cell phones. They seem not to care that strangers overhear their business, even the most intimate details. Others are more reserved, and choose the time and place and person with whom to have personal conversations. Again, the variability that is considered normal is extensive. And we assume people are more or less in control of their behavior. That is, we assume that people behave the way they do because they are in a personal comfort zone.

Another consideration in the regulation of emotions is context. There are times and places where any one individual's emotions will not be scrutinized, such as at home, or walking through a park with a friend. On the other hand, there are settings that dictate a particular emotional tone, as mentioned above: ballparks, weddings, or hospitals, and the list goes on. Human beings seem quite able, in general, to adjust our level of emotional expression to the occasion or setting. This point is exploited to great advantage in movies: when the moviemaker wants to create tension or humor, she may place distraught characters in a restaurant. The quieter and more upscale the restaurant, the more potential there is for misbehavior on the part of the characters because quiet, restrained behavior is the norm in such restaurants. How many times have we seen a movie character accidentally spill food on an innocent bystander, or have an emotional outburst to the embarrassment of another character at his table? As drama, it works because we are troubled or amused by seeing the characters break the rules. For the most part, we follow social/emotional rules.

These days we are all more and more aware of cultural diversity. As a general rule, emotional behavior varies by culture. If we become dogmatic in our beliefs about culturally determined emotional behavior, we risk stereotyping others. But there are generalizations that are considered valid, and we all have opinions about them. For example, some cultures are considered *warmer* than others. Some are regarded as more comfortable with expression of conflict, or public expressions of affection, or self-disclosure to strangers. Sometimes we might tend to be critical of a certain behavior, but if we perceive the individual to be significantly different from us, we withhold a negative judgment based upon tolerance of diversity. The more we perceive the other person to be similar to ourselves, the more we feel secure in our judgment of what to expect from him or her. These are feelings and judgments that often occur completely unconsciously, or out of our own awareness.

The third consideration of emotional behavior mentioned above is that we all know "not normal" when we see it. Even though tolerance differs from one person to another, most of us are quite clear when a line has been crossed. Consider this: no matter how many acts of violence we've all seen in movies and TV, real violence, in person, is shocking. We don't want to see people fight in real life; we generally don't like to witness aggression, or threatening behavior, or even verbally abusive behavior. Also, too much intimacy can be disturbing to witness. Most of us believe that certain things are private and we know what crosses that line, even in this permissive and demonstrative twenty-first century American society.

In addition to shocking violence and immodest intimacy, there are other emotional states we all recognize as not normal. Anyone who has seen the distress of a person with schizophrenia responding to inner voices knows they are seeing something abnormal. Other abnormal displays of unregulated emotion might be seen in drunkenness, delirium, or tantrums in non-age-appropriate children. All of these events, when witnessed, can arouse curiosity, pity, or even revulsion. We may also feel relief that the problem is not our own.

Regulation of emotions in disability

Dysregulation of emotions is the term sometimes given to impaired functioning in this area. Individuals with traumatic brain injury again help us understand the disability in the neurodevelopmental population. Traumatic brain injuries are generally sudden and often catastrophic. And yet brain-injured persons' disabilities are likely to be labeled as alterations in personality, as we saw with deficits in control of attention. It is easy to see why this happens. If a person was formerly mild-mannered and now he curses and loses his temper at the drop of a hat, it seems reasonable to call that a change in personality. Perhaps a better way to analyze this problem is to ask: what is personality anyway? Perhaps the way we display emotions is inseparable from the way others will describe our personality. But if the emotional display is not done willfully, purposefully, then is it fair or accurate to interpret it as an expression of the individual's personality? Ultimately, personality cannot be separated from brain function, but many people are not ready to accept this. There is a feeling with every new discovery in brain functioning that uniqueness and other mysteries of human nature are under attack. I personally don't find this to be a problem. To me, the universal questions and mysteries remain awe-inspiring even when explained, and why shouldn't human nature be the same?

In any case, adults with neurodevelopmental disabilities are often judged to be displaying unpleasant, out of control personalities, when they are actually suffering from emotional dysregulation. They may have outbursts of anger they cannot control, or they may weep at the least provocation, or be consumed by anxiety they can't modulate. Impaired ability to control one's emotional expression is a brain dysfunction. The resulting behavior may not be a major feature of personality, though it appears to be.

Margy is a woman in her mid-twenties who has simple likes and dislikes. She listens to the records of one female singer and she has one hobby to which she devotes a great deal of time. She is generally pleasant to her peers, and is equally comfortable with other people or in her own company. However, if anyone criticizes Margy's hobby, her anger is immediate and stunning to behold. Margy is quite tall and thin, and she draws herself up to full height and holds her breath and her eyes seem to grow larger. She hasn't much to say at these moments; she is just a picture of pure anger.

These displays don't last very long if Margy can get away by herself. She knows her anger is not reasonable, and she is usually able to control her physical behavior, but she feels anger at 100 percent and nothing less. Interestingly, if Margy is warned that someone might say something critical of her hobby, and advised not to get mad, she is usually able to short-circuit her angry response.

Adults with Asperger's often have great difficulty with anxiety. They may be engaged in a conversation with a peer, and something begins to go wrong socially. Since they are overly dependent upon their verbal ability, they might try to salvage the situation by talking more or louder or faster, always about the same subject. This strategy doesn't save the situation. An observer can see the individual's struggle with anxiety, but he or she generally is not able to recognize the feelings as anxiety. These are individuals who cannot soothe themselves easily. They usually have one calming strategy and no flexibility about its use. Generally, they must immerse themselves in their one activity of choice—which Asperger's individuals invariably have—such as a collection of something no one else would be interested in. Obviously this is a poor strategy, since the soothing activity may not be portable!

If an individual has poor judgment about the setting in which she is expressing herself, even expressions of happiness can be a problem. Barbara, a middle-aged woman with emotional dysregulation, demonstrates the inseparability of this problem from that of poor judgment. Barbara is a kind person with a sunny disposition. Her facial expression usually displays a smile. She particularly likes one of the teachers at the community college she attends. Barbara has an IQ in the normal range, a sophisticated vocabulary, and a profound dysregulation of attention. I conceptualize her emotional dysregulation as a by-product of her attention deficit. When she sees the teacher she likes, she is apt to say, "I love you, Sally," no matter what the circumstances. She has poor judgment because her attention span is such that she cannot stop and think about what to do next. Her "love" for this person is expressed immediately because she feels it immediately and, again, she cannot stop and think. Under most circumstances, Barbara is perceived as a non-disabled person, at least briefly. Imagine, then, witnessing this inappropriate, childish-sounding, emotional expression. She actually endangers herself by saying whatever crosses her mind in any situation. She literally doesn't have time for judgment.

Inflexibility, or rigidity, is another expression of emotional dysregulation that can be perceived as a negative personality attribute. Inflexibility is a feature of childhood that most parents remember from the time their kids were two years old. It lasts long enough in some kids to begin to be viewed as a personality trait—stubbornness. But generally, in an intact young person, the feedback from parents and peers guides them toward becoming more flexible. Kids will refuse to play with someone who always dictates what game will be played, or otherwise insists on being in charge. (Very different are those rare individuals who display the charisma of leadership from an early age: they acquire followers who are pleased to be led by them.) Imagine, then, a young adult who has retained the inflexibility of a two-year-old. When this behavior is far outside the normal range, it is a form of emotional dysregulation.

Harry has the problem of inflexibility. He wants to do something and his mind is made up. Harry's choices are often not unreasonable, so his inflexibility isn't challenged all the time. When his plans are reasonable, he appears to be a leader. But sometimes he recruits others into his plans with no regard for their wishes. Once Harry planned a New Year's Eve party. He chose the guests, which is reasonable, but then he pointedly did not allow others who were popular with some of the chosen guests to come to the party. When he was pressured to invite the others, he felt his "authority" was being questioned; this exacerbated his need to control the situation. In response, Harry assigned specific costumes to be worn by each guest.

Harry cajoles, manipulates, and eventually threatens social consequences if his wishes are not accommodated. When Harry's inflexibility becomes too intense, he has to be managed by someone else, because he cannot control himself. The strategy that works best is just what one would do with a child past the stage when a parent could use simple physical control. Harry must be told that something concrete will happen if he persists, and it has to be a consequence logically related to the plans, and something he doesn't want to have to do or endure. The best choice is a consequence that can easily be imagined, something real and definite like, "no one will come to your party if you don't let them wear the costumes they've already chosen. You'll be all alone and embarrassed." Harry's dread of being all alone at his party has to be strong enough to wrench his mind away from his inflexible stance. Most people would not require such a concrete intervention because intact judgment would guide them to be more fluid in emotional regulation. In other words, they could persuade themselves to accept something different from their preference without having a tantrum.

Summary

The examples of emotional dysregulation seen most often in the autism spectrum population are anxiety with no cause or out of proportion to its cause, anger that goes from 0 to 100 percent with no modulation, and the spontaneous display of any emotion without the mediating influence of judgment. Dysregulation of emotions also means that the emotional behavior on display is often *not* what the individual wants to feel or convey. It feels "out of control," and it is. In addition, inflexibility, or rigidity, is frequently seen in persons with neurodevelopmental disabilities. Normal brains can solve the problem of regulation of emotions by overriding feelings with judgment. "Normals" may "talk themselves down" or seek privacy until they can regain control. Most people are able to get through daily life without drawing critical attention towards their emotional behavior. Individuals with executive deficits often cannot do so.

Chapter 8

A Glance at Memory

Memory is a very complex and extensively researched part of brain functioning. However, I know of no studies of memory function conducted on my population, those with Pervasive Developmental Disorders, or the autism spectrum. Most people like my clients have taken memory tests as part of psychological or neuropsychological evaluations. Their scores tend to correlate with their IQ scores, and they may have a particular strength or weakness in visual or verbal memory that stands out. But the usefulness of these findings is surprisingly very limited. For example, we have a young man who tested with zero ability to remember anything he reads. In our experience having gotten to know him, we believe this result was due to anxiety. He becomes so anxious in a test situation that he cannot concentrate and do his best. In daily life, when reading for his own reasons, he is quite capable of remembering at least some of what he reads. Other test results have a similar frustrating failure to correlate with experience. Some of our clients score well in the normal range on tests of memory, yet in daily life they "forget" important things like promises to their friends.

Many researchers include working memory as part of executive functioning. By working memory they mean the skill of holding something in mind for use within a few moments. The typical example is the quick memorization of a phone number just long enough to dial it. Short-term memories, in research terms, are bits of information intended to be dumped after use. Long-term memory, in researchers' terms, can mean what we might think of as the kind of memory required to get along in daily life. Long-term memory, in research, can be demonstrated by learning a list of words and repeating the words 15 minutes later, then repeating them again seven days later. Thus, long-term memory is not the same thing as remote memory, which is the storage of events from as far back as we can remember in childhood. Remote memory is known to be very robust, even in the elderly. We can all think of examples of an elderly person telling a personal story from her childhood that is filled with names and addresses, even days of the week when something occurred. Yet the same elderly person may not be able to recall the events of yesterday, or to say the names of familiar faces seen on television. We're so familiar with this phenomenon that we chalk it up to aging, which is usually accurate. In the neurodevelopmental population, however, remote memory may or may not be vivid, full of details, or reliable. As with so many other factors, our clients tend to be at one extreme or the other.

There are so many complex aspects of memory, and so many terms used to categorize them, that I will not attempt to discuss memory in a scientific way here. I will instead attempt to describe what appear to be memory deficits in my population. Some features of my clients' memory failures certainly represent deficits in the frontal lobe's role in memory, as it is the frontal lobe that is primarily implicated in executive function deficits as well. I do not know if the other major memory system structures—the hippocampus, thalamus, and others—are impaired in my clients, but my hunch is that they are not significantly impaired. As mentioned above, test results of my clients don't generally suggest focal memory deficits. And most significantly, their memory problems, when closely analyzed, seem best explained by their disorganized approach to all functioning, perception as well as output. Disorganization of the mind cannot be overestimated as a cause for my clients' failures in memory functioning.

Memory and executive functions

Consider how you would navigate the following situation. In thinking about each step, try to decide whether memory is the most essential element, or one or another of the executive functions we've been reviewing. Here's the situation: you are in an unfamiliar town, let's say visiting a friend who is ill and needs your help. You see that your friend needs a few things from the supermarket. You decide to buy milk, bananas, and paper napkins. First, you have to get directions to the store, and you are going to drive your friend's car. As your friend tells you how to get to the store, you would be estimating how complicated or simple the directions seem to be, in order to decide whether to write them down or memorize them.

You might base this decision on what you already know about yourself and your spatial abilities. Maybe you noticed on the way from the airport that the town is laid out in a very geometrical pattern—that it seems an easy place to get around. How do you remember that you noticed this a day or so ago? Well, you might be the kind of person who always notices the lay of the land; or you might have been anxious about doing errands for your friend in a place that's strange to you. You started noticing pieces of information you might need because you have the ability to organize your experience in useful ways. And you know certain things about your-self, so you call on them in making decisions that relate to memory. How purposeful are you in deciding to remember these things? Depending upon how consciously you decide to remember, how easy or difficult is it?

Continuing with the story, next on your list of brain-related organi-zational tasks is everything related to driving a strange car. You've rented cars before and you know that it's a good idea to find the turn signals, the lights, the air conditioner and heater, the radio, the wipers, the emergency brake, before you set off. How do you remember this? You've organized your experience into efficient memories that can be called upon when you need them. If you've ever had a mishap related to not being familiar with a car, your memory will be more vivid and more dependable for this step.

So now you're in the car, ready to go with simple directions that you didn't feel the need to write down. Did you write down the items you plan to buy? If you're over 40 you probably made a joke about remembering three items; and if you're over 50 you probably did write them down, "just in case."

Once in the store, another whole set of organizational abilities is acti-vated in the normal brain. The items you want to buy can be categorized automatically as produce, dairy (kept cold), and non-food item. You realize, without thinking about it consciously, that these items will all be in specific parts of the store that can be found logically by category, and they will not be near each other. (Is this based upon a memory of other stores, or is it analytical reasoning?) My guess is that most people would go for the bananas first because the produce area can usually be seen easily in large stores. You might go for the milk next because it's likely to be between the produce and the non-food items. Why would I make that assumption? Is it an aspect of memory? I picture non-food items grouped together in aisles that are near one edge of the whole set of aisles. I picture cold items along a wall because refrigeration is easier to set up in a wall than in an aisle in the middle of the store. But I could certainly be wrong about any given supermarket. What would I do then?

The more time-consuming way to shop for a few items is to walk the aisles, covering the whole store. Some people do that because they enjoy seeing what a new store has to offer that might be different. But it is a choice, not an inability to approach the problem logically. If you are in a hurry to get back to your friend you will probably forgo that little pleasure to save time. Now you take your three items, you pay and leave the store. What did that unfamiliar car look like? Did your friend mention the make of the car so you could look for it that way? Are you a person who notices the color of a car and not much else? Perhaps the keys in your hand contain a clue, like the brand name emblem stamped on the key. Or perhaps you've been through this before and you always note where you are parked, using some landmark of the parking lot. Are you so visual that you can just close your eyes and picture the way the lot looked as you drove in? Can you remember a landmark if you didn't verbally rehearse it to yourself? In other words, did you say to yourself, "I'm parked way over here by the dumpsters. Remember, green car by the yellow dumpsters."

You've found your friend's car, you know how to play the radio, and off you go to find your way back by reversing the directions that you memorized rather than writing down. But, wait, are you leaving by the same way you entered the parking lot? There's a big intersection, but where's the gas station that was on the left? Well, at least you know your friend's address. If you get tired of driving around lost, you can always ask for directions to the specific address. Oh, your friend moved recently and you don't actually have the new address memorized? You gave it to the taxi driver at the airport and then stuck the scrap of paper in your big heavy appointment book that you didn't bring on this errand. Well, maybe you'll remember (remember, or reason, or guess?) that your friend's registration is in the glove box; I hope she's had her change of address registered.

I'm having fun with this scenario—for once I'm not really out there going through it! Of course most of the problems would be alleviated these days by use of the ubiquitous cell phone. But that's not the point.

In analyzing this story, the interaction of memory with planning, sequencing, reasoning, and organizing abilities is complex and difficult to tease apart. Taking the same scenario and describing what my clients would likely do, it's difficult, again, to distinguish which of their mistakes would be due to poor memory and which to disorganization of their minds. They would fail to take most of the shortcuts and safeguards one would think of based on prior experience; they would be faulty in estimating their own ability to remember something like directions; they would be poor at categorizing and searching their memories for prior knowledge of similar situations; they would be unlikely to recognize when to use rehearsal to enhance memory; and novelty of any kind, including distracting or enticing items in the store, would derail them even further.

In terms of memory specifically, my most successful clients would be those who approached this task with a visual learning predisposition. Several of the male clients who drive are very reliable in finding their way to and from new places, and remembering forever how to go there again. The men I'm thinking of are not highly verbal, so are less likely to verbally mediate—that is, talk their way through a new experience—than to rely on their visual and spatial abilities. They could tell you years later that there is a particular tree or building at a particular spot on the route to their best friend's parents' home. Inside the store, the same skills would be used by visual learners. They probably would not categorize the three items the way we did above, but once they found them they would remember where those same items were on another day. But, interestingly, they would probably not be able to find apples and aluminum foil by noticing that they are of the same categories as two of the other items they could already locate. This is just a hunch, but I believe if someone said, "Don't you remember where the fruit is?" these men would realize pretty quickly that bananas and apples are found together; but asking the same question about paper napkins would not produce the same quick realization that aluminum foil belongs to a known category. "Non-food items" just isn't as compelling a category as fruit.

Other than the visual learners, most of my clients would have been less efficient in encoding bits of information for memory storage; and they would then have problems with retrieval of information because it wasn't efficiently stored. Their strategy for finding things would be the same as on the first visit because they wouldn't realize that they now know more about the store than they did last time. Their recognition memories, that is, recognizing something even though you couldn't recall it from scratch, so to speak, would be least impaired. But even recognition would be limited by the failure to have scanned the environment efficiently in the first place. So, when a visual client says the soda is near the bottled water, that direction is useless if you never saw the bottled water in the first place.

Let's turn our attention to how normals would follow up this task with another trip to the same grocery store within a week. I think it's safe to say most of us would write the directions down if we weren't sure of them. Once in the store, there is probably a lot of variability as to how much of the store layout would be remembered. Visual learners would be best at remembering the layout; but others would be comfortable and efficient at reading the aisle labels instead of wandering through the aisles randomly. Most normals would appreciate the distinction of categories and where they are usually found, and, in addition, would remember some features of this particular store from the first visit. In short, the grocery store is a pretty reasonable place to navigate with intact executive functions and memory.

This is by no means an exhaustive look at memory and memory problems. It is meant to be an introduction to a way of thinking about memory. Memory failures in the absence of damage to the specific memory systems in the brain can be due to frontal lobe damage and to executive function deficits. That is the point of this trip through the supermarket.

Chapter 9

Judgment,
Self-Awareness,
and Self-Monitoring

Working on my dissertation in the late 1980s, I was able to read every reference that included the term "executive functions" in a reasonable amount of time. That could no longer be done easily. There has been a huge amount of research and general interest directed toward the executive functions. And yet the notion persists that they are best understood as the cause of messy school notebooks. On the contrary, the brain itself is disorganized, inefficient, and out of control. As I've tried to show in earlier chapters, the impaired brain fails to perceive accurately; to organize and store material logically; to sequence the steps toward a plan; and attention can be haphazardly directed to all stimuli without the ability to prioritize. This is what I mean by inefficient brain functioning.

Executive function deficits are disastrous to the management of a normal life. In my early reading, I encountered researchers who called self-awareness "the pinnacle of mental functioning" (see Stuss and Benson 1986, p.248). The more I thought about and worked with the issues of executive functioning, the more I came to understand what they meant.

Self-awareness and judgment are the sine qua non of an independent adult life. Without judgment, which includes common sense, we cannot negotiate the thousands of little adjustments in thought and behavior we make throughout every day. Beyond judgment, self-awareness is the added dimension of knowing that we are making judgments when we are. Self-awareness means knowing what we are thinking and feeling while we think and feel and perceive, and while our thoughts and feelings and perceptions change right before our eyes. Self-awareness means acting upon those thoughts, feelings, and perceptions, both automatically and by deliberation, and moving between the automatic and the deliberate with recognition of that movement. And, amazingly, we use the brain to think about the functioning of that very same brain. This is, indeed, the pinnacle of being human.

A walk in the park will illustrate these functions. Suppose you are walking in your own neighborhood park, a place where you've walked a hundred times. You have chosen to do it because you know you enjoy being outdoors, walking and letting your mind wander. You believe your park is a safe place. Then, from the corner of your eye, you notice a child in the playground area who appears to be unsupervised. You become alert to the possibility of having to act to protect the child. But first you scan the environment efficiently and quickly. In fact, there's a woman approaching the child now. Subtle perceptions tell you she is probably the mother, but she could be a kidnapper. You watch and see that the child smiles and raises her arms to be picked up by the woman. The possibility of a crisis is over and you continue your walk.

There are so many issues of judgment in that story it would be tedious to list them all. Some occur out of awareness while others require a state of heightened awareness. Deciding whether you have time for this walk might happen out of awareness—it's Saturday and you have been aware all day that you have no commitments; the weather or the proximity to a meal time might also be "noted" out of awareness. On the other hand, on a different kind of day, those factors might have to be carefully considered. Once in the park, the event concerning the child prompts some spontaneous and some considered reactions: is the child in imminent danger? This question pulls your attention no matter how immersed you were in your thoughts. Am I a man, who could be perceived to be threatening the child if I rush toward her? Have I noticed everything I need to notice to come to a decision? Individuals with judgment deficits would react very differently than would those with normal brains in this type of situation. They might remain completely unaware of danger to a child even if the situation was as serious as the child running into the street. Or, in the case of my clients who have been impaired all their lives, unlike those with acquired brain damage, they are likely to defer to "real" adults to take charge of a dangerous situation.

How does self-awareness go wrong?

To understand how this complex brain function goes wrong, first consider the perceptual part. Perceptions are the information we receive from the outside world through our sense organs and into our brains. Seeing and hearing are easy senses to think about. We know whether we can see or hear. We know what we are seeing and hearing—or do we? You can probably remember a time when you thought you saw something, but someone else saw the same thing very differently. When you talked about this with the other person, your interpretive judgment came into the picture. If you weren't frightened or anxious or embarrassed or competitive, you were probably able to calmly compare what you thought you saw with the other person's interpretation. Maybe you were able to find reasons for the distortion of one view or the other. Maybe it was funny or interesting, or the discussion became heated, or maybe one of you learned that you need glasses.

It can be even more problematic when the disputed perception is a heard perception. How many times do we think we heard something in conversation and the other person denied saying it, or insisted they didn't say it with the tone we perceived? Or how many times have we heard a sound from outdoors that several people identified entirely differently? One heard a car backfiring, while the other heard a door slamming, and another heard a gunshot. Sounds are generally gone and cannot be revisited, leaving us to analyze without the data.

The point is that we need more than the sense organs to sort out our perceptions. We also need judgment about our own sensory perceptions. There are parts of the brain, called the association cortex, whose function is to interpret perceptions. First your brain performs this interpretation automatically, but then you can engage the process actively by turning your conscious judgment toward the problem. You can think about your own perceptions. Imagine you hear a dog barking. Your brain decides instantly that it heard *your* dog barking. And upon conscious reflection you add that it's your dog's fearful bark; this makes a substantial difference in the interpretation.

But what if you couldn't do the added judgment about perceptions? What if your attention span was so impaired that you were always on to the next perception before you could think about the first one? Or if an extreme emotional reaction to perceptions always threatened to turn you into a bundle of nerves or caused you to act out in anger? Then you would find yourself attending to that emotional state or behavioral problem instead of the original perceptual problem. Unfortunately, this is too often the world of the person with autism spectrum disabilities.

Barbara, whom we met earlier, often misinterprets others. She fires back an angry answer to a perceived attack or intrusion, making her misbehavior more important than the original remark. If someone asks Barbara what she plans to have for lunch, she might interpret that as a demand to make lunch for both of them immediately. Barbara's attention deficit is such that she is dealing with mental chaos, rarely having the peace of mind to hear things the way others intend them. She might answer angrily that she has no intention to make lunch for the other person, who was not asking for that at all. The hearing part of her brain did not make a mistake, but the interpretive judgment part did. Another client, who is perpetually anxious, had to give up a job because he couldn't override his anxiety when addressed by his supervisor, no matter how innocuous the remark might be. He was counseled to listen and think about what the supervisor was saying before assuming it would be a criticism. But he could not use judgment to overrule his habitually anxious reaction.

We've discussed judgment applied to perceptions. Judgment is also needed in more abstract situations. Most of us apply judgment automatically to a variety of situations that are not precipitated by a sensory perception from the outside world, but stem from our own thoughts. Most of us have an internal thinking monologue going on virtually all the time. In fact, we are so unable to turn off this monologue that we have a special regard for the rare times when it slips away from our consciousness. During sexual climax, and other activities that demand intense concentration, like performing surgery, or dance, and certain moments in sports, we may lose the monologue, and afterward we may feel that's what makes the activity so special. We return to such activities with delight because we experience a kind of pure doing, or pure feeling, without analyzing.

What must the inner monologue of the person with neurodevelopmental disabilities sound like? I imagine it is more firmly lodged in the present, in the moment, than is the case in normal functioning. And it is probably more self-referencing and less complex. I even wonder if it exists at all for some individuals. I've known several clients who cannot be alone. I wonder if it is because they have to do their monologues aloud, speaking to another person. When such an individual is alone and not speaking, perhaps she cannot feel (or hear?) her "self." I imagine that another client, who is afflicted with dysregulation of attention in the form of extreme distractibility, must have a chaotic monologue. How could it be otherwise? I imagine her inner voice, if she has one, saying something like: "look at that, look at that, listen to that, oops I spilled that, he's looking at me funny," and on and on in that manner. A normal inner monologue, by contrast, is more linear and logical, able to go off on tangents, but able to come back to a thread that wends its way through the inner life of the mind, making a record of the day's thoughts and feelings, and sometimes being turned with more purpose toward reviewing past events, solving an upcoming problem, or fantasizing about the future.

Another kind of impaired internal monologue could be one that only "talks about" feelings, but doesn't analyze or reach conclusions. "I'm cold, I'm hungry, I'm mad at so-and-so, I'm late for class, I hate it when the staff get mad at me, I'm feeling rushed." In that example, you can see a thread of analysis beginning in the remarks about staff being critical and client feeling rushed, but then the thread is not pursued in an organized and self-aware manner. But this is only speculation because, as I said, I haven't found a way to help my clients tell me, reliably, about their inner monologues. Each individual's self-awareness is a mystery.

The importance of judgment in daily life

Most of my clinical examples—the humorous, the poignant, and the truly frightening stories—center on failures of judgment by my clients. Failures of judgment occur in all aspects of daily life, but those that have the most impact on the clients' capacity for independence are those that concern safety, money, and interpersonal behavior. Social behavior is so interconnected with judgment that it blurs the diagnostic implications of labeling social behavior as a separate and discrete domain of brain skills, as in autism. In my experience, failure of judgment, self-awareness, and self-monitoring, the "pinnacle" executive functions, encompass and explain most failures of social behavior in those clients who are not diagnosed with full-blown autism or Asperger's.

Many of our young men come to the program in their early twenties. They are usually sexually inexperienced and very much look forward to finding romance and a sexual partner. A particular young man, diagnosed with Asperger's, did succeed in forming a relationship that included sex, but he also wanted different kinds of sexual experiences. So far, he's not unusual. The trouble began when he got an idea. Unbeknownst to the staff, he discovered a website on which he could post a message about the various kinds of sexual acts he wanted to try. He requested that his readers think about joining him *and his girlfriend* in any sexual behavior they wanted. He supplied his full name and phone number and requested that interested parties contact him. He thanked them very politely. If our young man inadvertently contacted minors, he could have been arrested, convicted as a sexual predator, and required to register as a sexual offender for the rest of his life. Other clients with spectrum disabilities have ended up in that status through similar misguided schemes. In this instance, staff learned about the internet posting and managed to stop him. He still does not understand how the incident exemplifies poor judgment.

It is worth asking whether this incident exemplified poor judgment, or failure to use judgment at all. Any parent of a teenager will recognize that the phrase, "what were you thinking?" is likely to fly out of your mouth when you believe your kid didn't actually think at all. Teenagers, like my clients, will often be so caught up in a plan, so excited by the expected outcome, that they fail to think about the consequences. That's why teenagers continue to need supervision until they demonstrate adequate ability to think before acting. This is the development of judgment. But the question remains whether the choice they make when they do stop and think will be a good one. In the case of our young man on the internet, his Asperger qualities left him unable to make good judgments even when he was questioned in the logical manner we typically use. When we asked what would happen if a college girl showed your message to her boyfriend, our young man answered, "They might want to call me." When we asked what would happen if a high-school girl showed it to her father, he answered, "He'd probably tell her not to call me." There was no awareness that the outcomes could be more dramatic, even dangerous to him. This is not the case with our clients who have executive function impairments, but not Asperger's Syndrome. They may initiate the same scheme with the same failure to use judgment, but when asked logical questions about the outcome, their answers would show better awareness of the likely motives and actions of others. This is an important element of diagnosis, and would be a feature of the diagnosis I've suggested for those currently labeled PDD-NOS.

Many of the judgment errors of daily life in which we must intervene with the spectrum population have to do with money. Our clients are, almost without exception, unable to grasp the abstract aspects of managing money. They certainly can shop, in fact it tends to be a favored activity. But they usually do not understand what banks do, what a checking account is, how a check translates into money, where the money comes from for an ATM, and the relationship between income and expenses. Nevertheless, like all adults, they want to feel independent in the use of their money. The most frequent, typical mistake they make is the impulsive spending of designated money (for rent) on something else (an engagement ring, a stuffed animal, a car). Also typically, without a shopping list and supervision, many would buy such poor choices of food that they would soon have health-related consequences. I imagine many readers thinking poor food choices are pretty typical for "normals" too. Most of us eat poorly from time to time, and indulge whims more often than we should. For my clients, it goes to a matter of extremes. I'm talking about purchasing only soda, chips, ice cream, and candy every time they go to a store. Whether this is poor judgment or failure to use judgment is, again, a good question. It highlights the concept that the executive abilities are inseparable, with impulsivity and disorganized thinking contributing to what ends up looking like poor judgment.

I happened to be in a grocery store one day when several of my clients entered with their shopping list. I watched, unnoticed, as they took a cart and set off, presumably to find the items on their list. It was fascinating to see them completely waylaid by a large display of sodas, a pyramid designed to instigate impulse purchasing. They loaded their cart with sodas, without thought for the items they would then be unable to buy due to their limited budget. Analysis shows that the ability to be drawn off task (distractibility) affected them first and then impulsivity overruled decision-making. In addition, they failed to imagine consequences in the immediate future, that is, not having the food to make planned meals with staff, and they certainly showed no regard for consequences in the more remote future, such as becoming obese and unhealthy. All these elements of executive functioning together caused the failure to carry out a plan or to use judgment in the moment.

The clients in my program come to know one another very well. They attend classes and groups together, they are paired as roommates at staff discretion, and they socialize together. Although they cherish these friendships, relationships that have eluded them all their lives, most of them do not hesitate to say terribly mean things to and about one another. They will tell one another that they smell bad, that they are fat, or ugly, or don't like the right music. But if a staff member intervenes and asks whether that was the right thing to do, most of our clients know, on reflection, that the comments were rude or insensitive or mean. They just aren't able to *monitor* themselves continuously, which would be required to prevent the hurtful and rude behaviors. Only our clients who are autistic or have Asperger's

Syndrome are genuinely puzzled by our questions about the appropriateness of interpersonal behaviors. That group of clients defend their behavior on the grounds that the remark was "true," therefore always the acceptable thing to say.

Another example will show how social skills interact with executive deficits. I know a young man who lives alone in an apartment purchased for him by his parents. He is considered high functioning and able to live independently with minimal supports. But he is lonely because he lives away from his true peers. He would prefer to make friends within the non-disabled population, so he goes out looking for new friendships. Recently we found out that he had been exploited by a group of new "friends." And, sadly, he accepted the offer of one of the new friends to help extricate him from the situation, and instead the man took further financial advantage of him. It was only after the second incident that the young man admitted he was in over his head and sought help from his family.

To analyze this situation, one would think that the client has a social skills deficit in being unable to recognize lack of sincerity or an exploitive nature in another person. But another way to analyze the situation throws more weight onto his deficient judgment skills. How many of us would bring someone home, or expect a new acquaintance to want to come to our homes, after a chance meeting in a public place? In other words, we wouldn't do what the client did whether we detected insincerity or not. We would enter into friendship more cautiously as a general matter of good judgment. In some circumstances we develop friendships with less caution, such as in college dormitories, in clubs based on a common interest, and in situations where we meet through known acquaintances. But adults in their thirties, who meet someone in a bar or a store or at a bus stop, tend to take more time to feel friendly enough to invite that person home, *even when they do not detect unpleasant traits in the new acquaintance.* In this view, the client was harmed because he didn't have a rule of thumb about getting to know people, regardless of his ability or inability to read sinister intentions. A "rule of thumb" is a way of saying a judgment made in advance that is called upon as an applicable situation develops.

This is probably too fine a point to belabor, however. We do know that individuals with the spectrum disabilities have judgment and self-monitoring deficits that affect all aspects of social life. They may be lax in their hygiene, or dress eccentrically; their conversation is self-focused, or they make their desires known without regard for the social cues of the other. Or they can't engage in small talk, yet they expect non-disabled individuals to overlook that and find them desirable. And while all of this is going on, they are baffled by it.

Self-monitoring and the mundane

Self-monitoring is judgment about ourselves from moment to moment. For an unimpaired brain, self-monitoring is a constant part of whatever else we happen to be doing. For most of us, it occurs in the internal monologue we discussed earlier in this chapter. Self-monitoring is intensified whenever we do something new. We talk ourselves through the new experience in a way that is characteristic of our own style. A timid person may focus on doing the new activity correctly and not calling attention to herself, while a bold person might focus on her ability to attract attention.

Childhood is a time for mastery of so many new skills, and self-monitoring can begin to develop along with the myriad other skills. Picture a five-year-old boy playing with cars and trucks. His play may seem entirely haphazard until you join him and do something "wrong." The blue truck never faces backward, you are told emphatically. There is a reason for the child's decision, even if the reason is just to experience making choices, or being in charge. Making choices involves some level of reflection, and that reflecting and prioritizing is what grows and develops over time and with experience.

Parents unwittingly teach self-monitoring every time they call out a reminder to a child to "watch what you're doing." Picture a small child walking from the kitchen to the dinner table with a glass of milk. If he hasn't yet learned to keep the glass upright without watching it constantly, he is at risk to trip because he can't also watch his feet. If he looks down at the floor, the glass is likely to tip in the direction of his head. To "watch what you're doing" in this example is actually a pretty complicated maneuver, yet children master this and hundreds of other physical accomplishments every day. And along with the individual accomplishments, they are learning to monitor themselves without experiencing it as a separate skill.

When I was ten years old I loved to iron. There was a sense of accomplishment in taking wrinkly clothing and my father's cloth handkerchiefs, and making them warm and smooth all over. Ironing is a good task for increasing a child's sense of mastery because the goal is so clear, and success is obvious immediately. Self-monitoring is being developed each time you look at a part of the cloth and see (analyze) that if you point the iron in at a different angle, you accomplish the task just a bit better. The habit of "watching what we are doing" and storing away the skills never stops in the unimpaired brain.

Self-monitoring in social behavior

Empathy is an important feature of normal interpersonal behavior. It is a part of the executive function sometimes called theory of mind. Theory of mind means one person recognizes that others have their own minds, and can imagine what might be going on in the mind of another person. Theory of mind includes imagining the mind of another, while empathy goes farther. Empathy includes having feelings for what one imagines about the feelings of another. It is a skill that develops in most of us outside of our conscious awareness and very gradually. An example from early childhood is the well-known behavior of one baby or toddler crying when he or she hears another cry. We can't really say that the second crying child is actually feeling sorry for the first, but it does appear that recognition of distress is at the heart of the second child's crying.

A little later in development, you might see a child beginning to understand when another child needs a special toy, or blanket, if she looks upset. Children learn about pain and remorse and shame by hurting themselves and each other during play and, in their way, analyzing how it feels. Many boys say they learned not to fight after only one experience of being hurt or hurting another boy. Men relate stories of learning that they didn't like to kill animals through the experience of accidentally, or intentionally, killing a bird or small animal when they were young. They vividly recall feeling sad and remorseful, and knowing they would never intentionally do that again. Interestingly, few women report that experience; they seemed to know they wouldn't like killing animals without experiencing it. I mention this, not to add to the overdone practice of one gender sniping at the other, but to question whether empathy may develop differently in women and men.

An adult who doesn't experience empathy seems very odd when the deficit is exposed in a real situation. In my population, the clients behave as if they don't have the capacity for empathy while some of them actually do and others really don't. The difference is significant because those who can "get" what empathy is will belatedly feel it following the incident in which they demonstrated a failure of empathy. When questioned, they will be able to state, with belated feelings, how they imagine the other person felt. Others, typically those with Asperger's, don't get it at all, before, during, or after an incident.

The following example illustrates how empathy is interdependent with self-monitoring. In conversation, a non-empathic response to someone who is upset—the response exhibited often by my clients—is to ridicule the distressed person, or to point out that the distressing incident was their own fault in some way. Hurt feelings and anger generally follow that response. Then the non-empathic critic will usually get angry back at the person who got angry at her, stating she was "just being honest." Neither participant has the capacity to stop the escalating pattern of anger and hurt feelings because they can't engage in self-monitoring at the same time as they carry on the primary behavior, which is talking. With third-party intervention, redirecting both participants to think about the feelings of the other, empathy can be seen, felt, and expressed by those clients who have primarily executive deficits.

Self-monitoring deficits can lead to behavior that appears to be garden variety selfishness. As seen in my clients, self-centeredness combined with failure to self-monitor will present as selfishness. For most of us, self-centeredness waxes and wanes, depending upon circumstances. When we are getting ready for a job interview, for example, we may seem obsessively worried and self-focused; we may ask people the same worrisome questions over and over. But at other times we put our own interests aside to focus on the needs of others. We are somewhat controlled by our preoccupations, but at the same time, most of us can take control of our own behavior to present a desired attitude, *even when we might wish not to*. The perceived demands of the situation compel us to self-monitor and override our self-centered preoccupations. My clients are very unlikely to have this ability.

Some of this very important interpersonal behavior comes down to a simple inability to do two things at the same time. Executively impaired individuals are not good at shifting their focus from one thing to another, and they are not generally capable of doing more than one purposeful thing at a time. Whatever pulls their attention gets their entire attention. That's the inherent difficulty with self-monitoring as a skill. By definition, self-monitoring has to be done at the same time as some other behavior. *We monitor whatever else it is that we are doing, to evaluate how it's going, while we continue to do it.* To make matters more complicated, as we self-monitor, we are constantly making adjustments in the monitored behavior based upon the evaluation of the ongoing effect on oneself and others. So if I am speaking with great enthusiasm about a favorite subject, it may take me a moment to notice that my listener is not sharing my enthusiasm. But eventually I'll see that I'm being boring! I may then change the subject, or ask the other person a question I know is of interest to her. Or I may, through instant self-monitoring, notice that my feelings are hurt and I want to get away. But I don't want to reveal my sensitive feelings so I might manufacture an unrelated reason to end the conversation. In normal brains, all that mental and emotional evaluation goes on *at the same time that the conversation continues*. It's quite an amazing capacity when you think about it, and it all depends upon the executive functions of the brain enabling us to do more than one thing at a time.

My clients, on the other hand, are not able to do two self-conscious things at once, and so we see rude conversations not monitored, impulsive grocery shopping not monitored, and unawareness of little things like scratching private parts in public.

Summary of judgment, self-awareness, and self-monitoring combined with the other executive functions

It's important to remember the inseparability of the executive functions. As noted with the analogy of a swimmer, we are able to blend and combine all elements of executive functioning with fluidity and flexibility when our brains are intact. Individuals with impairments have different degrees of impairment in the various executive skills. The combinations of deficits and the way in which they are expressed in everyday life cause those on the autism spectrum to have different skills and limitations, even though they all have executive function deficits.

Judgment is critical in almost all aspects of daily life, and self-awareness may truly be the pinnacle of human functioning. But some of our clients are more able than others to avoid the pitfalls of poor judgment. How do they do it? Without realizing it, they rely on other attributes to help them avoid situations where they would need to use good judgment. First and foremost, living according to routines is safer than seeking a lot of novelty in daily life. Many individuals on the autism spectrum love routines, rituals, and habits; novelty makes them anxious. Those clients whose parents raised them with deeply ingrained habits are generally safer and more functional in adulthood than those without good habits. Second, having a nice disposition allows one to be less likely to go through life annoying others, then having to analyze situations and repair hurt feelings. Having a strong need to avoid anxiety-provoking situations can also be a protection.

Judgment interacts with planning skills in a crucially important way. I've said these clients are not good at planning, but they spend quite a lot of time pursuing what they want. The role of judgment in planning makes the difference between a plan and a scheme. We use a word like "scheming" to emphasize the absence of good judgment that would turn a scheme into a plan. Our clients scheme for things they want desperately that will ultimately cause trouble for them or that they cannot afford or manage. Clients want to spend their money on fun instead of necessities. They want to experiment with drinking and "clubbing;" and they want to own the best electronic games and gadgets, like their non-disabled peers. All of which is completely understandable. With judgment and the ability to delay gratification, they could plan to have and do many of the things they want to do. But in the absence of judgment, they plunge ahead and make a grab for things in ways that are inefficient, dangerous, and sometimes comical. The essential difference between a plan and a scheme is the difference in attention paid to the consequences.

The story of the young man who used the internet to seek sex exemplifies the difference between a plan and a scheme. But the saddest story I know to illustrate a poorly conceived plan, and the interaction with judgment, is a story about some hamsters. Two clients moved away from the program to live as a couple, but remained close by. They lived in an apartment complex where they were not allowed to keep pets. But they both loved to hang out at the pet store, and one day they just "forgot" that they couldn't have pets, and bought five hamsters just because they were so cute. When they arrived in the parking lot of their building they "remembered" that they couldn't bring the hamsters in. For many people, the next step would be to sneak the hamsters into the apartment and keep them until discovered. But that's not our story. Our young couple set the hamsters up in their car. Their intention was to move the car frequently, thinking that would make its use as a home for hamsters less likely to be noticed. But then the man accidentally locked the keys inside the car and became very worried that the hamsters would suffocate. He spent 90 dollars to have a locksmith open the car. He discovered that one hamster had died, and at that point he was overcome by the difficulties of the whole enterprise. He called his father who solved the problem by taking the hamsters back to the pet store. The whole venture represented a loss of 400 dollars and a lot of hurt feelings.

To be clear about what this story is meant to illustrate, it was a scheme, conceived in impulsivity, dominated by poor reasoning and poor judgment, with no use of hindsight, foresight, or insight (what's happened before, what's likely to happen), avoidance of facts held in memory, and no attention paid to likely consequences (the death of a hamster, the waste of money, and the sorrow of having to give the pets back).

Analysis of the hamster story leads to another extremely important point about the combined executive skills: the way in which they relate to moral behavior. Many of our clients appear to be amoral or immoral at times. Their parents react with distress and cannot understand how and why they seemed to forget all they were taught at home. I believe the failures of morality stem from the most important clinical observation about impaired executive functioning: *much of the impairment is a matter of not being able to do two things at once.* As mentioned earlier, these individuals live primarily in the present. They don't stop and think before acting. They can't think about how to get what they want and also think about the consequences of pursuing what they want, at the same time. *Therefore, they don't think about the morality of their actions unless directed to stop and think by another person who serves as the missing executive function. In that event, they often make the right moral choice.*

Then why, you may ask, aren't they entirely immoral and out committing crimes all the time? There are many reasons. First, there are no absolutes in this population. Some individuals, particularly the anxious ones, *are* more likely to remember the moral lessons they were taught by their parents. Anxious people tend to ruminate and to imagine the worst, so they are, in a sense, protected by their fearfulness. Second, individuals with executive deficits do many things poorly, including their schemes, so they are often discovered and thwarted before they complete them. Third, once caught, their disability is usually detected, as they cannot explain their behavior and they start to seem helpless. This outcome generally leads to a higher level of supervision in one way or another. Unfortunately, as mentioned earlier, many of the "higher functioning" in this population do commit crimes, get caught, and are not identified as disabled. They appear in prison populations at a rate that no one has clarified exactly, but is certainly high.

It is a mistake to characterize our clients as immoral. But their behavior certainly lacks moral direction or choice in many instances. Our legal system recognizes that impaired individuals cannot be held to the same moral standards as the non-impaired. It is a matter of common sense, then, that if these individuals cannot overcome their disability, they deserve to be protected from their own poor judgment.

Real examples of immoral behavior

The following is a list of typical things my clients have done that exemplify the points made above, particularly about moral failure.

- Edward was seen throwing a large bundle into the dumpster. Later the same day, his roommate reported his collection of model airplanes missing. The airplanes were found in the dumpster and Edward was baffled that staff assumed he had put them there. Edward has Asperger's and doesn't understand how other people make inferences. He wondered if a camera had been installed in his apartment or near the dumpster.

- Clients eat out together frequently. When one suggests that they leave a restaurant without paying, those who go along with the plan say they are not guilty because it was not their idea. But when told their parents must be contacted, they instantly see that their parents will judge them to be guilty, thus casting doubt on their "genuine" feelings of innocence.

- Two clients ordered more food than they could pay for at a restaurant. When presented with the check, they mumbled and acted incompetent, apparently hoping the management would allow them to leave without paying. They had not planned to cheat the restaurant, but after they miscalculated what they could afford, they were unable to solve the problem and would have felt relieved to be allowed to leave. It did not occur to them to offer to return with the money. Once allowed to leave, they would have felt no obligation to the restaurant because the incident would be over.

- Shelley knew that Kirk was interested in her as a girlfriend, but she didn't have those feelings for him. Kirk had a car and Shelley liked to get rides for errands and to her swimming lessons. She accepted rides from Kirk on a regular basis, promising to go on dates or "hang out" in return. But she reneged on all promises.

- Clients at our program who have cars are allowed to charge others for rides, but they are supposed to charge a certain amount. They often exceed the amount set by staff when they see an opportunity to extort money from their peers, their friends!

Part Three

Reaching Adulthood

This part will describe the most typical living arrangements for adults with disabilities. By far, most adults continue to live with parents and other family members throughout their lives. This can be a choice that results in a safe and happy life. Or it can represent overwork by aging parents and dissatisfaction for the adult with disabilities, who continues to function as a child in the parents' home. Group homes and other specialized facilities are other options that will be described. If parents hope to facilitate their children transitioning to adult lives outside the parental home, there are issues to be considered and preparations to be made. The next chapter explores how children can be prepared to function as adults who expect to leave home.

Chapter 10

Preparing for Adulthood

Regardless of whether adults with disabilities live in the parental home, a group home, a program, or an apartment with someone functioning as case manager, there will be issues that require understanding and help. Before discussing how we teach and train adults who come to our program in need of specific remediation and ongoing support, let's turn our attention to how children can be raised and taught with an eye toward the best possible preparation for adulthood.

Every parent should have a support group in which to discuss these issues openly; a place to offer suggestions and reality checks to one another in an atmosphere of mutual trust. Support groups provide a place to consider the kind of future for which your children are being prepared. Where will they live? How will they occupy their time? Will they be safe from unscrupulous people and confusing situations? Will they be employed? Will they know how to care for their own belongings and their environment? Will they drive or use public transportation? Will they understand what constitutes an emergency and how to deal with it? Will they understand medical care? Will they have a social circle? Will they be sexual? All these questions should be on parents' minds during the childhood years because that is when the necessary skills and habits will or will not be developed.

Issues to tackle in childhood

Deciding which issues to focus on in the life of a child with disabilities can seem to be a difficult question. It becomes less difficult if the family issues discussed in Chapter 2 have been negotiated successfully. Recall that we discussed acceptance of the child's disability, joining a parent support group, and taking a reasonable approach to self-education about the disability. If those issues are being handled and re-handled as life goes on, there is only one logical conclusion to reach in terms of how to raise the child with disabilities: he or she should be raised as much as possible like any other child. The expectations a parent should have, that her child will be safe; that he will be confident of his place in the family and then in the larger world; that he will know the accomplishments of learning and being ambitious; that he will grow more and more interested in his friends and his community as he gets older; that he will respect the laws of the land and the cultural expectations of his community—these are the things that amount to "the pursuit of happiness" that we have been told is our birthright. These are the things we want for all our children.

What can go wrong then? Simply put, I think most mistakes come from either *underemphasizing or overemphasizing* the disability. What I mean by underemphasizing the disability is more or less like being in denial. In denial, people choose to avoid the evidence of a problem and distract themselves from seeing the problem clearly. They rationalize and make excuses to avoid dealing with the very real facts they should be facing. The same can be seen with parents who convince themselves the signs of disability in their child are not serious, or not permanent. They insist the child is just "quirky" or will outgrow the problems in time. When the child cannot engage in age-appropriate activities, when he misses milestone after milestone, these parents tell themselves the child will catch up at a later time. I dislike the term Developmental Delay because it fosters the belief that the child will catch up without making any reference to how or why that would happen. This kind of thinking can lead to a waste of valuable learning time for the child with disabilities. Sometimes a window of opportunity can be lost forever.

Overemphasizing the disability causes a different problem. Some parents focus on the disability more than on the child as a whole person. Perhaps they haven't been able to deal with the disappointment of not having a more normal child. Because they don't see the child's strengths and her potential to learn many things, they focus instead on feeling sorry for the child. Pitying a child, thus not allowing her to develop her potential, is just as devastating as denying the disability. She may not be entirely normal, but she has many functional abilities to draw upon and she need not have a dysfunctional life. In both scenarios, underemphasizing and overemphasizing the disability, the result is a child with disabilities who does not learn all he or she could. Or, worse still, a child who learns to feel self-pity and who seeks sympathy rather than respect from others. There are a few things that are absolutely necessary for a normal life. And those few things are definitely within the capability of everyone who has the disabilities discussed in this book. It's not a matter of whether they can learn; it's a matter of how they learn. And one job of the parents is to figure out how to teach and train them.

Raising the child with disabilities like any other child means that basic skills and values, life lessons, should be taught. And the expectations for good behavior should be as close as possible to the expectations for the typical children in the family. It's not that the child is the same, and it's not that the way she learns will be the same. But with creativity and persistence on the parents' part, the end result can be the same or reasonably close. You can raise a child with disabilities who has some measure of self-control, who has manners, age-appropriate ability to take care of her body and her belongings, participation in maintaining the household, and the ability to be part of everything that goes on in the family.

Hygiene and manners

The importance of dealing with these two issues well before kids with disabilities grow up cannot be overstated. One argument I've heard for not dealing with these issues is that it's too hard to spend time on them during the all-important school years. For many parents, getting their kids to school and through school is so daunting that they can hardly focus on anything else. But this is short-sighted thinking. A child with disabilities who will not bathe will become a young adult who will not bathe. He will become an adult who will not have the opportunity to use his hard-won education in any meaningful adult setting. I imagine this is hard to believe if you are the parent of a small child. He or she is still cute when playfully dirty. But I have seen adults who refuse to bathe, or they stand under a shower but don't wash themselves. Their peers tease them and they get stared at in public for having an offensive odor. Yet when told, with sympathy, that it doesn't have to be that way, they fight all efforts to be taught a routine for personal cleanliness. It is difficult for them to accept that they must learn new personal habits so late in life. Like all of us, but even more so, it is difficult for adults with disabilities to learn new habits when the childhood habits are already deeply ingrained. Childhood is the time for parents to teach these important skills and to require that they be done habitually.

The second answer I hear when kids have poor hygiene and poor skills in cleaning their own surroundings is that the parents figure they will learn to do those things when they develop their own motivation. Generally these are parents who have an older "neurotypical" child, often a son, who somewhat avoided bathing properly until he developed an interest in girls. Then nothing would stop him from buying the right products and spending hours in the bathroom. Similarly, he kept his bedroom a mess during high school but at college he was exposed to young women who looked down their noses at a man who seemed incompetent ("lived like a pig!"). He learned to keep his room clean because he wanted to achieve a new image in the eyes of young women.

I cannot overemphasize how misguided it is to think that this will happen with an executive function impaired child. To be really clear about this, note that the older son in the story above "somewhat avoided" bathing. A normal child may be a little resistant or a little stubborn about bathing as often as you, the parent, would like him to. But he doesn't go to war over it as the child with disabilities will do. And as to cleaning his room, he may practically go to war over that, but he will have the ability to clean when finally motivated. The child with disabilities, by the time he is older, will devote more energy to defeating you than it would have taken to do the chores or take the bath in the first place. And he will not be capable of organizing the steps to completion of the task, when or if he finally wants to do it. In fact, sometimes the war is carried on to disguise the fact that he has no idea how to complete such tasks as shaving and showering.

What works best is to teach those skills so early that they achieve the status of a habit, well before puberty. Following the well-known advice "choose your battles," I would always advise choosing hygiene. Habits are wonderful. But an older child with poor habits will be embarrassed by your attempts to correct his skills in very personal areas, like toileting and bathing. You will both be thinking this skill should be in place already. A better plan is for small children to learn that they can do something they enjoy, like watch TV or play video games, after they have bathed. Or reading stories and going to bed right after a bath can build in a positive association with being clean in bed every night. If you're lucky, your child will become an adult who doesn't like the feeling of going to bed dirty. Imagine how much of the war is won when the child actually prefers the feeling of being clean. If you're facing a really determined kid, connect being fresh out of the bathtub with dinner. "Dinner after your bath" works very well as a recipe for a lifelong habit. (Some kids have a fear or hypersensitivity to getting wet. Special problems like that are dealt with in many other books, so I won't address them here.)

In puberty when additional grooming habits have to be learned, like shaving or managing menstruation, the expectation that the child can and must learn to take care of these tasks personally will be in place. A parent might say, "When you were little you had to learn to wash yourself and now you have to learn this. It's difficult but you can do it." In families that take a lighter approach, a parent might even say, "I hope you don't think you're ever going to have a girlfriend if you shave like that!" The actual teaching should be based upon task analysis of even the simplest tasks, with each step demonstrated patiently by the parent. Flexibility is an asset, as you observe that your unique child has his own way of doing things. If it works, and it's safe, let it be done his way.

Manners will be just about as important as hygiene in your child's adult life. Even a small child can be taught how to be introduced to strangers, to say please and thank you, and how to end a conversation or visit. In addition there are several things all children must learn *not* to do, like interrupting adults and picking up items in other people's homes. Table manners are so relaxed these days that it will be adequate to teach your child to use silverware and a napkin, to keep the food inside his mouth, and not talk while chewing. That's probably enough in these informal times for a child to appear well-mannered. If your child doesn't speak at all, you will have many other issues related to that problem, but I would still suggest that he be taught very simple gestures that anyone could interpret as friendly. He might be able to wave instead of saying hello when introduced. I guarantee that he will elicit sweet smiles from adults he meets, which may help motivate him toward other efforts to achieve a positive connection. I realize that some children, particularly those with autism, will not be able to do all the things I'm describing. As mentioned above, there are many books that devote more space to these special problems.

Manners are discrete, concrete bits of social behavior that can be taught and learned. Social behavior, in the broader sense, is a much more complex concept. It is a network of conscious and unconscious perceptions and responses. We manage and adapt our social behavior at all times, except when we are alone. People who are perplexed by social behavior often prefer to spend most of their time alone; but ultimately human beings are social creatures, so social behavior should not be ignored in children with disabilities. If your child shows early signs of disinterest in others, that may be different from misunderstanding the rules of social behavior. Those who seem disinterested in other human beings are considered to be "more autistic." But we really don't know if what appears to be disinterest is actually some other internal experience for the child with autism. It is probably best to assume there is some level of interest in other human beings and provide opportunities to all kids with disabilities to socialize with their peers.

For those with executive deficits, their interest in socializing is obvious; they just don't know what to do to be socially successful. If they can learn the concrete bits that allow them to *appear* to exhibit correct social behavior, it will increase the number of normal experiences they will be able to enter into. Somewhere between the extremely autistic and the executively impaired are those with Asperger's: they may be oblivious to social behavior, but will want human contact. Their biggest social problem is their rigid conviction that they are always right in the way they want to do things.

An experience we have far too often at our program is represented by the following story, combining elements from many individuals and families. We'll imagine a young man with Asperger's named Seth. Seth visited our program with his parents to see if he might want to apply. He was disheveled and poorly groomed, with greasy hair falling into his eyes. He wore two different shoes instead of a matched pair. He would not sit down when offered a chair, and he made no effort to engage in normal conversation. Seth listened to our description of the program and he objected to most of it. He did not want to get up at a specified time in the morning and he didn't want to follow a schedule. He liked the idea of having his own apartment, but he would prefer to stay there and work at his hobby of collecting baseball cards. That was the way he spent his time at home in the two years since he had finished high school. When we persisted in describing the benefits of attending the whole program, Seth became quite anxious and clearly wanted to end the interview. His parents then tried to negotiate. They made the point that Seth was bound for college in the future so maybe the classes and groups, actually the whole program schedule we wanted him to attend, was not important for someone like him.

To me, these situations are tragic. *Parents such as these have no ability to see their children as they appear to others.* These parents were accustomed to thinking of Seth as bright, which he probably was, and therefore nothing was more important than getting him into college. Normal requirements, like sitting down and talking politely, or even being clean and presentable, were not important to his parents. Seth was being allowed to disregard important parts of life in favor of doing only what he enjoyed. And if he kept going the way he was, not meeting the world even halfway, he would end up so socially disabled that his college education, if he ever achieved it, would be wasted. In such cases, I encourage the parents to place their young adult child in a group home for a while. I feel that the experience of group home living helps these unaware young people see how others follow rules and take care of themselves and their personal belongings. Seth would learn to socialize in at least a rudimentary way. It could be expected that he might come to care about having friendships with his peers. If he could accomplish that, then he could certainly still go to college. Unfortunately, I usually don't find out whether these parents take my advice.

The situation of young people like Seth illustrates another important feature of social behavior that dovetails with manners. It could be called going with the flow. It is the ability to adapt to what others are doing even when it is not one's own first choice.

Going with the flow

Families who have a child with disabilities have to choose in which instances to adjust to the disabled child and when to have him or her adjust to the parents' preferences. Many families describe children who won't eat certain foods and will only wear certain clothes, or certain colors, and have all kinds of idiosyncratic behaviors. It will always be a balancing act to decide which behaviors and preferences to fight and which to live with. But it is important to always be thinking toward adulthood when choosing these battles. Those issues that will be most important in making your child likable to others should be approached with the most conviction and perhaps creativity. If he only wants to eat white foods or crunchy foods, teach him how to shop for those items and how to prepare them. Eating oddly will not be problematic to others as long as he can manage his meals himself. On the other hand, if he needs others to fix his meals in adulthood it will be unlikely that he will be allowed to demand idiosyncratic foods all the time.

The same reasoning can be applied to managing medical procedures and tasks that may be part of the package of a particular individual's disability. If a child has to be catheterized or to take insulin by injection, or any number of other lifelong procedures, the more independence that can be achieved the better his chances to live successfully as an adult. Respect for his ability to manage these tasks will lead to self-respect for him. Individuals with intellectual ability in the mentally retarded range can learn to do things, even complex or troubling things like self-administered injections, that must be done the same way over and over, every day. So can kids who may be better able to express how much they don't want to learn these self-care skills.

The same principle applies to thorny behavioral issues like chronic bed-wetting, seizure management, tantrums, and many other issues of disability. The ideal is to foster a matter-of-fact attitude toward the management of the issue, and to require that the child manage it herself as much as possible. The bedwetter should wash her own bedding every day; the child who tantrums should be led to his room or a special place to ride out the tantrum in safety and without attention being paid to it. Respect should be shown for successful management of the issue even though parents would much prefer for the issue to be gone altogether.

There is room for much creativity and experimentation in the management of behavioral issues. The first question is always whether the behavior is purposeful or beyond the child's (or adult's) control. That is, is it a manifestation of a clinical deficit? For example, tantrums generate heated arguments in families about the level of control the child does or doesn't have. Generally, someone who is a close observer of repeated tantrums will note that there is a build-up of frustration and agitation that leads to loss of control and inconsolability in the child. They will often say that no matter what they do the tantrum has a time limit of its own that must be endured. But there is no reason that you as a parent can't experiment with rewards for improvement in incremental management of tantrums. You could give a reward on a day that there was no tantrum (not food, please!); or you could reward a tantrum that lasted a shorter time than the one before, or one in which no toys were destroyed. Even if the child has not previously experienced self-control, he might try harder to gain control in order to please a parent and to earn praise and a treat. As long as the variable you choose to reward makes sense, you certainly won't be making the behavior worse, and you may be helping.

Many children display issues of control, bossiness, or trying to take charge of others. When raising a normal child, parents can do a variety of things to deal with this tendency. They might consider it a spark of leadership and hope for the best; they might insist on periods of sharing and turn-taking in a very organized way. Whether parents take a hands-on or hands-off approach, chances are the child will be most affected over time by his peers. If he finds that other kids get angry at him or don't want to play with him, he will likely modify his behavior to keep his friendships. Or he will find a sidekick-type best friend who doesn't mind that he is always in charge. The child with intact executive functioning will not be undone by this personality trait.

But the child with executive function deficits will be more extreme in his need for complete control. He may insist on doing what he wants to the point that he has no playmates and doesn't seem to understand or care why. Parents may find themselves drifting toward irrational family accommodations, like being told where to sit and which lights to have on or off and many similarly odd adaptations. They hope that the child will gradually not care so much about these idiosyncrasies. They may believe that the demands stem from anxiety, and if the conditions are just right the anxiety will diminish. But children with disabilities who are allowed to win these contests in the family grow up believing that they should continue to win in all settings. Why would they think differently? And if the need for control is linked to anxiety, the pattern will only get worse in situations where the child is not permitted to be in charge, and the parents aren't there to mediate. Children with this trait tend to end up devoted to solitary activities like television and computer games.

It is not functional for children with disabilities to be allowed to persist in such rigidity. It is important they learn they are not supposed to control the adults in their world. All kids must learn they have to accept what others want some of the time. And it is especially important to learn they must generally obey authority figures like teachers and police.

How can this behavior be managed? Routine is the ally of the household dealing with disability. A child who lives for his computer or video games needs to know under what conditions he will be allowed to go back to his favorite activity; he needs to know what chores or outdoor play are required to earn computer/game time. If anxiety is at the root of the problem, he will be comforted by reliable routines. And gradually he must be exposed to exceptions to the rules and routines. It is important to learn that when exceptions happen, one's world is not shaken beyond repair.

An anxious child must learn that his anxiety is something *he* will have to manage in his life. Of course caring parents will seek treatments. Some parents are comfortable giving prescribed medication, some prefer more naturalistic approaches like biofeedback, movement therapies, use of music, and so on. When the child is older, cognitive therapy may be helpful. But if anxiety seems to be a prominent part of your child's temperament, it is likely it will be with him for the long term. *It is important to identify anxiety, and not to validate idiosyncratic beliefs.* For example, if a child believes something terrible will happen if family members don't sit where he dictates, he can be made to sit through the "wrong" seating arrangement as long as he can stand it, and then find out that the bad outcome didn't happen after all. As always, you must pick your battles. If it seems easy to sit where he prefers at the dinner table, so be it. But if you find yourself rationalizing and accommodating each and every one of his demands, you are probably headed for trouble.

Anxiety is an element of mental illness that is best met with direct challenge. Depression, on the contrary, is not easily contradicted by logic. When one is deeply depressed, there is no obvious counter point of view that can be compelling enough to make someone actually feel better. Similarly, paranoid beliefs are so intractable that no amount of argument can talk a person out of them. But anxiety actually weakens with exposure to the feared situation. (There are many books that deal specifically with exposure treatments to anxiety and phobias.) You as a parent can tell your child that you understand how frightened he feels when things don't go the way he wants them to, but that if he will take deep breaths and pay attention to what happens next, he will find that his fears don't come true. Each time the feared event does not happen, the belief is weakened.

But suppose your child remains anxious and transfers the anxiety to a new feared situation each time you overcome an old one? This is why your child must learn to manage his own anxiety. This is when you explain that he must have his own methods to calm and soothe himself. As an experiment you might put him in a quiet room, read stories, or play his favorite music; you must watch and see which tactics work best. Perhaps he will be an avid reader and find escaping into stories the best refuge. The important thing to remember is this: you will do the best you can to help him, but if he is to be an anxious person all his life, it will be his job to figure out how to manage his own feelings. Ultimately, you cannot do that for another person, even your child. You can help him understand that this is his particular cross to bear, and that we all have our own. No one has a trouble-free life and you shouldn't waste too much energy worrying about whether your child with disabilities has more to bear than others. Perhaps he does; life isn't fair. Too much pity and self-pity are counterproductive. It's important to get on with life.

Moral behaviors

As important as I believe hygiene and manners to be, social behavior in the broader sense, including moral behavior, will be even more important to your adult child's safety. It is difficult for those with executive deficits to make on-the-spot moral judgments about their own ongoing behavior. Why? Because moral behavior is dependent upon intact brain functioning. Without strong moral habits we would have to think about the correctness of our behavior while simultaneously pursuing the many desirable things we want every day. We do this all the time in the sense that we have thoughts about things we might want to do, and then we almost automatically talk ourselves out of them. The most typical examples of this kind of behavior are probably social and ethical considerations rather than actual moral choices. For example, if a clerk in a store is rude to me and I consider being rude back, but then I decide not to, is that a moral decision? It might be to me and it might not be to someone else. But if I get a passing thought to steal something from a store and I simultaneously talk myself out of doing it, that is definitely a moral decision. What if you could only think about one thing at a time, and you were likely to act on the most compelling thoughts passing through your mind? You would be at serious risk to do all kinds of things that upset others, including being rude to store clerks and maybe even shoplifting. This is what it means to say that moral behavior is dependent upon intact brain functioning: one must be capable of thinking of more than one thing at the same time, and of making correct choices based upon instant analysis of the situation. This is judgment.

Children with disabilities may not be able to exercise judgment on the spot, so moral habits can be taught that will be invaluable in adult life. Such habits may actually make the difference as to whether your child ends up in the legal system in adulthood. The moral behaviors I will discuss are lying, stealing, physical assault, and exploitive behavior between individuals.

LYING

Virtually all young children lie before they are capable of understanding what it means to lie. They lie to get material things and they lie to avoid culpability for things they have done; they lie to avoid disapproval or punishment by their parents. Sometimes they lie because they are delighted by their own imaginations. Eventually they go through stages of moral development related to lying. When children are old enough to know that lying is wrong, and they still lie, it is of great concern to parents. Most parents will do whatever it takes, from lecturing and explaining to punishing, to make sure their children learn not to lie, especially to them and to other authority figures.

When young people enter adolescence, there is a second developmental period related to lying. Adolescents will lie to protect a fragile new sense of their right to privacy if parents don't anticipate this stage and negotiate it. For example, most children under 11 or 12 years of age will talk on the phone to a relative or a school friend in front of their parents. They are not offended if mom asks who that was on the phone. But when they turn 12 or 13, they don't want to tell mom, dad, or nosy siblings whom they talk to on the phone. They may become irritable when questioned because they themselves don't understand why they suddenly find the questions intrusive. They just do. So they may refuse to answer, or they may lie. The wise parent sees that this is a normal developmental stage and reconsiders her own need to know many things about the private life of her teenager. If parents don't validate the right to privacy, the teenager *will* lie to maintain it. I do not advocate a complete hands-off policy at this stage; instead, I believe parents continuously have to adjust their need to know balanced by their child's need to take on more and more self-determination. This is the development of independence.

These examples describe developmental accomplishments of non-disabled young people. For those with disabilities the picture is much more complicated. It is most important to notice whether your child ever moves beyond the early moral stage related to lying, which is the stage of concern only about getting caught. If your child can appreciate higher and more abstract values, like respect for the rights and feelings of others, you can teach him not to lie the same way you would your non-disabled children. If, however, they are stuck on the lower moral stage, which is likely, then you must deal with moral issues on the level the child does understand. Fear of punishment may be the best deterrent, and one you can live with.

A number of my clients do not function at the more abstract stages of moral behavior, but only understand the concept of getting caught or not getting caught lying. The effective way to work with that level of moral behavior is to take something valuable away from the child as punishment for lying. This must be done consistently and with enough sternness to ensure the lesson is learned. It is important to express serious disappointment and disapproval for the behavior at the same time that something valuable is taken away. The combination of the toy or privilege and the approval of the parent must be used together, as you want to uphold the expectation that your approval is part of what your child cares about.

Some parents believe they should not show anger for fear it will hurt their child's self-esteem. On the contrary, if you employ punishments without showing emotion, the child tends to mimic the lack of emotion. If parents don't think the infraction is important enough to be emotional about, why should the child give it emotional weight? The child may adopt the attitude that it is permissible to do the crime, over and over, if he can tolerate the punishment. It becomes a deal or a trade rather than a moral lesson. To be perfectly clear, I'm advising that a parent should say things like, "I'm very angry with you when you lie. And you should be ashamed of yourself." Shame has a negative connotation in popular psychology lately, but shame is the evidence for appropriate feelings of guilt following bad deeds. One should feel guilt when doing bad things and a clear conscience when doing good things. This kind of concrete simplicity provides an efficient short-cut to decision-making for those with executive deficits, and all the rest of us, for that matter.

STEALING

Stealing is an even more important issue than lying because in adult life it will, of course, be regarded as a crime and not just a moral failing. I believe it is important to demonstrate to children with disabilities the utmost shock and horror at the idea of stealing. Most parents would express extreme disapproval toward a child above the age of about six or seven who stole from a friend at school. Once the child is old enough to understand stealing is wrong, the conscientious parent will want to explore why the child is stealing. When a child is clearly too old to be stealing, the reasons for the behavior are generally thought to be related to psychological distress of some kind: low self-worth related to not having attributes or skills that other kids have, or emotional deprivation at stressful times like divorce in the family. It is always good to explore the reasons for stealing, but the child with disabilities is most likely to continue stealing for the reason that younger kids steal, because they want something they see and the opportunity presents itself to take the item. It is hard for parents to realize and accept that there may be no deeper reason for the impaired child to steal; in any case, whether the reason is deeply emotional or just age-inappropriate, the behavior must be stopped for the future safety of the child with disabilities.

The parents' emotional reaction toward stealing should be geared to the level of comprehension of the child, but at all levels it must be very emotional and dramatic. A lecturing or compassionate tone of voice does not stay in memory as an important message. Stealing must be dealt with seriously each and every time it occurs. If the child shoplifts, she should be made to return to the store with the item and apologize. If it is an item taken from a friend, the apology should be made to the friend and her parents. No second chances should be allowed to postpone the consequence. Nor should any lingering (guilty) feeling that it's really "not her fault" because of whatever emotional events might be going on in the family. Parents are well-advised to think seriously about the possible psychological causes of stealing at a particular time in the child's life, *but the way to deal with the stealing should not be modified based upon that thinking.*

I know some parents will be thinking at this point about the use of positive reinforcement rather than punishment. You will be disappointed if you expect that positive reinforcement for good behavior will eliminate bad behavior in those with executive impairments. That theory requires that the child be capable of making a connection between the behavior you rewarded and the other behavior you don't like. The executively impaired child cannot make that connection. Instead, she will continue to do the good things you are rewarding and will also continue to do the bad things you thought she could recognize as bad. For example, if your child grabs a toy from another child and you decide to change his behavior by waiting until you see him share a toy, reward the sharing behavior and hope he will know to stop the grabbing, you will be disappointed. He will share when you are watching and grab when you are not watching. I know this because many of my clients still function that way as adults. They have bad habits now because the behaviors were not stopped early enough in their lives.

If this sounds harsh, it is because I have seen the long-term results. I've seen adults who end up in jail because they have no appreciation that the rules of society apply to them. They have been allowed to grow up believing that someone will save them from the consequences of their behavior. If a child with disabilities makes it to adulthood expecting to be saved from his own bad behavior, it tells me that a parent has, indeed, stood between him and all consequences. If this is what you are inclined to do, you are not doing your child a favor. Remember, you will not always be there to run interference. Be proud of doing the hard work early, knowing you will have prepared your child to live by the rules of his community.

To summarize, the most important moral behaviors to instill in children are prohibitions against stealing and against lying to authority figures like police, doctors, teachers, and other adults. Lying to their peers, if they have peer relationships, will be handled by surprisingly effective social means, like shunning, teasing, and even forgiving.

PHYSICAL AGGRESSION

Hitting and otherwise physically attacking others are also serious moral issues that must be addressed with some children with disabilities. I don't know why this would be, but, thankfully, I don't see physical aggression in very many clients of our population. Certainly there are a few who have dysregulation of their emotions, who occasionally hit others when suddenly angered; but I find this to be fairly rare. Perhaps it is because this behavior is so universally abhorred by their peers and has no tangible reward, like stealing does. Those who genuinely have trouble controlling their emotions are, in my experience, very grateful when their peers understand it's a problem they can't help. Peers with disabilities will accept angry outbursts pretty calmly, especially after they come to understand that the sudden rage will not be accompanied by hitting. They learn that it is like an emotional flash of lightning, rather than a whole storm, that the person will apologize later, and that it really doesn't hurt anyone. This is just another of the many benefits of socializing with one's true peer group.

Unfortunately, I have nothing very helpful to say about that population of individuals who grow to adulthood without learning how not to be physically aggressive. I don't see any way they could live at the level of independence I'm intent on promoting in this book. In other words, it is probably the case that an individual who hits and can't learn to stop will likely always need a level of containment and control that precludes living even semi-independently. There will always need to be different levels of care for various kinds of disability.

EXPLOITATION

Mistreating one's peers represents a sad irony for this population. It is ironic because of the inability to learn from personal experience, that is, to use empathy. Being teased throughout childhood does not result in these children learning not to tease others, even in adulthood. Nor do they learn to think abstractly about the rights of others without specific training toward that end. Children and teenagers with disabilities do not have much opportunity to exploit their non-disabled peers while growing up. It is more typical that kids with disabilities spend their efforts trying to be accepted and finally giving up. Regarding exploitation, they seem to have had their proving ground in manipulation of parents and other family members rather than their peers.

As with so many other issues, habits can be instilled early in childhood that will enable your child to live with others without becoming the exploiter or the exploited. Habits that promote acceptance of boundaries between individuals and respect for the property of others will be invaluable in adult life. It will probably be more difficult for your child with disabilities to learn to live with others if you have a loose interpretation of boundaries and of who owns what in the family. For example, a family that doesn't close doors when using the bathroom while the children are small may find it difficult to teach a different behavior to the child with disabilities as he grows older. He won't naturally or easily see the point for changing the family rule now that he's in puberty, and you may be surprised because your other children take to that change naturally; some even demand it before their parents think of it. With disability in the family, you may see the wisdom in living with more concrete rules from the very beginning.

Closed doors should mean one must knock and wait for an answer. Items in a sibling's room should be off-limits to other siblings. Mom's purse or dad's dresser top should not be places to "find" loose change without asking. Even how and when children have access to family food is a matter to think about. Am I being judgmental about family styles here? Am I trying to dictate against a climate of openness and trust in anyone's particular family? No, absolutely not. All styles of openness and firmness can be normal and effective for any given family. But if you have a child with executive deficits, you must always be thinking about how your individual family culture will prepare your child for the expectations of others. Your child will be unlikely to think abstractly about the ways that different families can have different styles and different concepts of boundaries. And he might not anticipate that he must adjust to others when he goes out to live among them. Your child will, instead, operate as though his family is correct and therefore he should be allowed to continue doing things the family way. Especially if your child has Asperger's, he will see the world through a network of rules; he is comforted by rules. So you are best preparing him to live with others if your rules are closest to what will be generally expected by others.

Exploitation in adult life is accomplished by manipulation. If you allow your child with disabilities to talk you out of your own reasonable rules, you are setting him up to be a manipulator. You may be tempted to believe that a child who can mount a good argument is exercising a skill and should, therefore, be rewarded. Or he may be clever enough to tell you he is confused, or tired, when clearly he is not. Or he may use charm. If his methods consistently get you to bend your rules, you are headed for trouble. Such children become adults who don't follow rules issued by authority figures. They are accustomed to defeating their parents by charm, confusion, or passive resistance, or by intimidation, or by inducing guilt. Such individuals are poorly prepared to live with others.

CHORES AND OBLIGATIONS

Another way to be sure you are treating your child with disabilities like other children is to be sure he has chores and obligations in the family. Neglecting to teach children that they have obligations and responsibilities is a serious oversight, with consequences that last a lifetime. As I've said repeatedly, the reasons for such neglect are easy to understand. Parents feel overwhelmed with the sadness and disappointment that they see as their child's unfair lot in life. Or they focus their time and energy seeking further evaluations and treatments for their child. They spend huge amounts of time managing the child's school work—this important subject will be taken up later in this chapter.

Chores are important, not just in the way they are important for all kids, but also as a kind of ongoing, in-house evaluation process. You have the opportunity to study what your child can do and how he does it. You might start with the requirement that all kids make their beds each day as part of getting ready for school. You can make this chore as easy as you like. Many people now make beds with just one comforter type cover instead of multiple sheets and blankets. Fitted sheets may stay in place for two weeks or more, depending upon your own sensibilities. So making a bed can be as simple as throwing the comforter up and over the pillow. You have the opportunity, though, to notice what kind of organizing principles your child uses. Does he go from one side of the bed to the other to see if the covers that hang over the sides are straight and equal on the two sides? Does he pull up the top sheet separately from the cover or bedspread, or is he content to leave the sheet in a tangle hidden by the top cover? Is he willing to be taught how to do it properly, and if so, does he remember the steps in the order that you demonstrated them? These are all important observations for you to use in teaching more complex tasks as the years go by.

Virtually all tasks have steps to completion. Task analysis is what experts call the breakdown of a task into logical, sequential, and efficient steps. You can train yourself to see tasks broken down into their parts and to notice whether your child approaches tasks with any kind of logic. Very young children resemble those with executive deficits in that they tend to try to get to the end result without seeing the logic or the need for the steps. Small children with intact frontal lobes will begin to organize their approach to tasks with minimal guidance. It is really quite miraculous when you see your child figure something out for the first time without verbalizing what he has learned. It just suddenly looks right to do it that way, and it is right.

Unfortunately, your child with executive deficits may never get to that stage on his own. You can provide a substitute for executive functioning by verbalizing for him what his mind should be "saying" to him. When a very young child wants to dress himself, you might say, "What goes on first?" You might say "Socks before shoes," even though you can't believe he wouldn't see that by himself. You might develop ongoing prompts to encourage his mind to say "What goes first, what comes next?"

Teaching your child how to do chores provides the opportunity to learn about her abilities and deficits, but it is also important in and of itself. What message does it give your child with disabilities if she sees her siblings learning to wash the dishes or feed the dog or mow the lawn and she doesn't have to do those things? Does she feel deficient, or special, or unable to contribute to the family? The rationales that stem from kindness (pity) are just as damaging as those that come from impatience or lack of creativity. And it does take patience and creativity to provide the extra thought, extra help, extra prompts, and maybe extra tools and accommodations that allow a child with disabilities to do "normal" things his own way. It is well worth your time and effort because, otherwise, whatever your child is doing in lieu of these tasks will become his habits for a lifetime.

More importantly, those conclusions he reaches—that he is not required to contribute to the family, or he is unable to do useful things, or someone else will take care of everything—are the messages he will take into adult life. And these are difficult messages to undo.

I titled this section "Chores and obligations" because it is important to note that children reach conclusions not just about the family's assessment of their abilities, but also about what will be required of them as members of society. You want your child to know people will expect him to take care of his physical appearance in certain ways before he goes out among them. Similarly, they will expect him to know how to treat public property and how to live cooperatively in a neighborhood or an apartment complex. Cooperative living includes being aware of noise levels, being clean enough not to attract bugs and rodents, being respectful of the property of others, and so on. If he works, his co-workers will expect him to have a sense of his duties in relation to theirs and to the business in which he works. In other words, he has obligations to the society of which he is a member. He will be expected to have done a kind of task analysis of how his life fits with others' lives. The ability to do this analysis will not come online when needed. He will have to have it spelled out for him, just as in the task analyses of chores. Again, a parent can develop the habit of telling the child what his own brain should be telling him: people are watching you. What do they expect you to do?

TELEVISION, COMPUTERS, AND OTHER ELECTRONIC ENTERTAINMENT

Here is one more area in which habits will be crucial later in life. Television, video games, computer games, cell phones, and all other forms of electronic entertainment have become a major factor in modern life. For the child with disabilities, who is low in initiative and poor at making friends, the electronic world is seductive. Video games are compelling, mesmerizing, and directive. They keep the child involved and entertained; some are useful for developing skills, but where will those skills be used other than in more video games?

Clearly this is another area that should be controlled by the formation of sensible habits. Parents must monitor the types of electronic entertainments available to the child with disabilities. Those that reward violent acts should be avoided because there are no negative consequences following the acts of violence, and this is exactly what you don't want your child with disabilities to believe in. Nor do you want your child to believe there will be so much focus on confrontation and violence in his real life. I think most parents, when they think about it, still believe that playing outdoors in the real world, and having knowledge of the natural environment, are the best parts of childhood play. To that end some parents are still able to let their kids play freely outdoors. Some live in circumstances where that is problematic due to concerns about traffic, gangs, drug dealers, predators, and other unsafe conditions.

Many parents spend great amounts of time taking their kids to various supervised activities, and, depending upon their skills and personality features, kids with disabilities can participate in these activities. For the child who will never be successful in team sports, most experts recommend the more individual type sports. Running, swimming, skating, dancing, martial arts, playing a musical instrument, and many other such activities might suit your child's temperament and skills. Individual lessons with a kind teacher can create lifelong positive memories.

Reading should be encouraged for those who can read, at any level. Reading to your child early in life is most likely to encourage the desire to read. But inevitably we find ourselves turning back to the television and the computer. I recommend that you choose which television shows are permitted and stick to your decision. One program at a time and then the television is turned off. Two activities can be linked as a habit, like one TV show and then read one story, or do something physical such as jump on a trampoline or ride a bike, outside, or a stationary bike indoors. Siblings who may not need this level of control can nevertheless participate without being unfairly penalized. The various kinds of taping and recording options will allow others in the family to keep up with favorite TV shows. When parents are comfortable strictly enforcing common-sense rules, children with disabilities grow up able to accept direction from other firm adults. Accepting advice or direction later in life is a form of support for individuals who have to live with poor judgment.

Computers are even more addictive than television for those with attention problems. In a way, the mind is even more engaged than in watching television because the fingers are also at work. For computer use I recommend using a timer with a benign sound, maybe a ringtone-type jingle chosen by the child, to signal when to take a break from electronic play. A relatively short amount of time should be chosen, say 15 minutes for children under eight years old and a half hour for others, at which time the tone will sound and the child must take a break. He could do a chore in his bedroom, or play outside, feed the dog (not make a snack). Choose activities that will momentarily break the hold computer games can have on a "sticky" brain. This should not be seen as reward or punishment, but rather as a healthy habit for a lifetime. In fact, parents should probably use the same approach to their own computer time to demonstrate their belief in the habit.

Taking away computer time is a useful punishment for a child, but other than reinstating the usual amount of game time, I would not offer extra time as a reward. In this way, you don't contribute to the notion that computer time is the most valuable commodity in the child's life. I cannot advise too strongly that you try to instill a lifelong habit in your child, not just compliance while you are watching.

As your child grows older and talks about computer use with other kids, he will eventually discover pornography. Even worse than pornography are the predators who stalk children by tracking use of pornography websites online. Many parents take a zero tolerance stance on this type of computer activity, imposing punishments immediately, and requiring education about predators, tailored to the age of the child. Of course there are programs that block undesirable websites, but the wise parent keeps tabs on computer use in person as well.

Cell phones present a special problem. Many parents feel they are invaluable for use in emergencies, and they are. But they also offer kids the ability to be in touch with parents and yet lie about their whereabouts. The plans by which they are paid for vary considerably, and children and others with disabilities often can't comprehend why a call made at one time is unreasonable due to cost, but at another time the same call is fine. Furthermore, cell phones now have the capacity to go online, which offers the same dangers as the computer, and they are small and portable and can be misused anywhere.

Nevertheless, they are here to stay, and will become more and more complex and ubiquitous, so plans must be made to manage them. Again, I would take cell phones away as punishment, but would not encourage using them for reward. I would make rules about their use related to cost, and would be concrete and consistent in enforcing those rules. And if they are meant to be used for emergencies only, prepare to have your notion of what constitutes an emergency challenged in the most creative ways. Make a list of emergencies and be consistent in punishing other use, if your intent is really to use the cell phone for emergencies only. And be aware that the cell phone is another way for kids to be taken advantage of by friends with bad intentions.

Another special problem with electronics in modern life is the availability of "virtual friendship." Many kids now spend hours online talking with people they've never met. More and more scams and dangers are revealed every week in the news. Children and those with disabilities have a hard time realizing that something they see on their screen could be a lie. Even when my clients lie online, they think others are telling the truth! Rules that we've already discussed for parental monitoring and oversight should be in place. And if your child wants to meet someone from online in real life, I would encourage you to meet the other child's parents first and then to supervise first meetings.

To look at both sides of the issue, online meetings can have a valuable place in the lives of some kids with disabilities. Those with Asperger's, who are so verbally proficient, are especially likely to enjoy chat circles with others like themselves. Even if they never meet in person, their lives can be enriched by talking with others who understand their preferences and odd interests. However, I would strive to keep a balance in the lives of such kids, always encouraging them to have some experience with face-to-face friendships.

MONEY

Money is one of the quick tools for diagnosis of the population we're discussing. Virtually all individuals with executive function impairments have problems in managing money. They know how to spend money, and they do spend it; whenever they have it, they spend it! In dealing with children with disabilities, money can be handled just about the same way you would handle it with non-disabled children: never allow a child access to an amount of money you can't afford to see him mismanage. The difference is that non-disabled children will gradually display a variety of different ways of dealing with money. Some are just as impulsive in their spending decisions as those with disabilities. But others will begin over time to want to save or to spend on gifts for friends and family members. They might be seen to deliberate long and hard about a purchase. They develop restraint. Don't expect to see these developments in the executive impaired child.

With rare exceptions, the ability to manage money cannot be taught to adults with executive function impairment. Warnings and advice can be memorized; the words can be repeated back to you. The intentions can even be pure. But the behavior cannot be changed, in my experience. Money in hand demands to be spent as quickly as possible. Perhaps if the training were begun early enough, I would be seeing different patterns in adult clients.

Families have different ways of dealing with money. The child with disabilities can be treated as much as possible like other kids in the family. If all children get some discretionary money to spend, then the child with disabilities should as well. But if, for example, he wants to go to the movies and he can't get from home to the theatre without spending his ticket money, what should be the outcome? You could repeatedly give him money for a movie and watch him spend it elsewhere and then be devastated that he didn't see the movie. You could remind him it was his choice. But you'd be banging your head against a brick wall. The wiser and kinder course would be to help him get the things he wants most, even though it means managing his discretionary money, and still give him some opportunities to do it his way. Just don't expect him to learn the lesson. It's not actually about *learning*. It's about managing impulsivity, and most impaired kids cannot manage their impulses. Money seems to have particular force toward impulsivity. Money is different from anything else in life. It sits in your hand and begs to be turned into something else. It promises pleasure. It is wish-fulfillment, immediate gratification, and it works every time.

The greatest difficulty with money occurs when kids reach 18 years of age. They feel they should be regarded as adults. Society says they are adults. Adults make their own decisions and they manage their own money. Often these kids don't have money to manage, or maybe they have a part-time job that provides a little pocket money. They want to spend all their money "independently" without any thought about rent and groceries that are still provided by the parents. This is no time to expect logic to kick in where it has not been operating so far. Ideally you have already found ways to talk with your child about his difficulties with money. You certainly have helped him to label his other disabilities throughout his life. Money should have been discussed calmly all along. When he reaches the stage of applying for benefits, it is imperative that you explain, in simple terms, that he will not be expected to control his own financial decisions. He will have a payee who will set up a budget. He will be given the amount of spending money that is left over after all his budgeted needs are accounted for. In all likelihood this will be the milestone that will most impact your child. He will see that adulthood doesn't magically alter his disability. It doesn't solve the problems of childhood.

FOOD

Food and its inevitable connection to health is a huge issue for this population. Eating is probably the most ubiquitous pleasure in our society; it's fun to eat and it's necessary, so it would seem to be a simple issue. However, as with the population at large, our clinical population is experiencing a great deal of illness from obesity, high cholesterol, hypertension, and diabetes, and they're encountering all of those ills at younger ages than the general population. Why? I think it's partly because, in the broadest sense, the issue of food and families has changed so dramatically over the last generation or two. I don't want to glorify the past in terms of knowledge about nutrition, but the value in cooking balanced meals and eating together as a family was unchallenged until recently.

Many things have changed. Women have gone to work in large numbers. Children have learned to forage in their fridges, and the culture has embraced fast food. Parents began to allow children to make more decisions for themselves, including those that have so much to do with healthy habits. I imagine this is partly due to guilt about not being home as much, but it also stems from changes in beliefs about whether parents should be authoritarian toward their own children. Also, families have developed the habit of eating while watching television to the extent that it almost seems the dinner table is obsolete. Even meal planning by adults in the family is slipping away. I can't tell you how many parents I've heard say, "My kids won't eat what I cook, so I let them fend for themselves."

Schools are also implicated in that they have allowed fast food to replace cafeteria food. Whereas milk was the drink that accompanied school lunches in "my day," soda is the beverage of choice in schools today. No child I knew was ever allowed to drink a soda without permission from a parent. It would be like eating a candy bar whenever you wanted to: it was not considered healthy and it just wasn't done.

On the positive side, recently there has been a proliferation of fast-food options that focus on healthfulness, appealing to the conscientious but busy parent. Parents who work can buy a completely cooked, balanced meal to bring home every evening. I see this as the beginning of a compromise and a turnaround that I hope will be a good thing.

But what factors are most important for the family dealing with disability? As with each of the issues discussed here, habit is the most important ally of the parents of these special children. Many children with disabilities have quirks about food. They may want to eat the same thing every day or have the same meal routine each week. They may not like certain colors, textures, and tastes that make it problematic to cook for them as well as the rest of the family. As with so many other issues, you the parent may find it more trouble to teach your child than simply to continue to do everything yourself. I know many parents don't find the time to teach their typical children how to cook, so how would they make time to teach the child with a disability?

It is undoubtedly important to teach all kids to eat well, but even more so the special child. If your child continues to eat impulsively it will become a habit perhaps impossible to break later in life. By eating impulsively I mean eating what he wants when he wants it, and in the amounts he wants to eat. In addition, the habit of rejecting foods for impulsive or silly reasons should also be confronted. Requiring a child to try one bite of a non-preferred food can be an easy routine to employ. When a new food tasted this way is found to be a pleasure, you can make a big fuss about how smart the child was to try it.

The skills necessary for adult life will be difficult for the child with disabilities to learn later on and this is as true for food issues as it is for any other important issues. Unlike his non-disabled counterparts, he will find it especially difficult to try new things, including foods, when he is away from home for the first time. The more idiosyncratic your child's tastes, the more and the earlier he should begin to share responsibility for his own food.

Remember, all children benefit from learning how to prepare their own food. Let's talk about the nuts and bolts of learning about food. The first rule is the sooner the better. Let a child wash a piece of fruit, or pick out a box of cereal from a shelf he can reach, or get the two slices of bread out for a sandwich just as soon as she is capable of doing those simple things. Try not to be impatient if she is slow or spills things; your goal is to have her enjoy learning about food.

You will need to do a task analysis of things you have previously done without thinking about them. How many steps are there to making a sandwich? You will have to figure this out so that you can name the steps and put them in order. Which tasks are more difficult and which easy? Which ones involve safety issues like the use of sharp knives? The important thing to keep in mind for the child with executive deficits is to be concrete about the task. Break it down and do the same steps in exactly the same order every time. Put the dry cereal in a bowl, then pour the milk, then put exactly one spoonful of sugar on top. Or if you prefer to put the sugar on before the milk, do it that way, but make up your mind which way and stick with it.

When making a sandwich, analyze the steps and do them in the same order each time. As you watch your child doing these things you will learn very interesting things about his motor control and motor planning, his dexterity or clumsiness, his ability to remember from one day to the next, and so on. If you find this interesting, you will be well on your way to learning about his strengths in areas that both you and he can build upon. You will also learn about his limitations and what kinds of accommodations fit his needs. As often as possible, make a game out of any aspect of the task that is difficult for the child. You might make up a rhyme or mnemonic that the child thinks is funny. Praise her for the steps she learns readily, and remind her that she will be able to learn the whole task if she keeps at it.

Plan to teach your child up to three different kinds of breakfasts, such as cold cereal, hot cereal, and scrambled eggs. Or he could learn to make toast, or toasted bagels or muffins, and try items like yogurt and cottage cheese for breakfast protein. Lunch could be a variety of at least three different sandwiches, canned soup, and hot dogs or hamburgers that could also be made for dinner. Fruit should be eaten every day, and cheese and crackers can be eaten as snacks. Dinners are of course the most complicated meal because they typically consist of several foods that should end up cooked and hot at the same time. This is more difficult than many people realize.

The first step is to notice what dinners your child likes enough to eat them for the rest of his life. Teach him to fix his favorites and try to simplify the preparation if possible. Perhaps you would never use instant mashed potatoes but he will be fine eating them when on his own. A good trick is to engage him in food preparation when he is hungry—not starving, but hungry enough to have the good experience of anticipation of something he really likes. Salad should be promoted as something to be eaten virtually every day. For ease, the new bags of pre-washed mixed greens are convenient with bottled dressing, again perhaps not the best choice, but certainly not the worst.

Some of the statements I'm making about food represent value judgments about which people have a wide range of opinions. There are vegetarians with a live-and-let-live attitude. Others think about food from a political perspective and think everyone should be vegetarian, or everyone should eat only organic foods. Some people feel fine about eating fast food on a daily basis; and some know they will change their food habits over the course of their lives. Thinking about food for a lifetime, with a disability, is complex enough without introducing political and value-laden concerns. If you knew what adults with disabilities typically eat when left to their own choices, you would see that the compromise of ease and general healthfulness I'm aiming for is actually quite ambitious.

Once you have gotten your child to be comfortable in the kitchen and competent at making his several different meals, you should be sure he practices making the same meals over and over, rather than focusing on adding more dishes to his repertoire. Your goal is for the skills to be so over-learned that they will last a lifetime and be transferable to a new set-ting. Transferring the skills to a new setting is probably the trickiest part. As we learned earlier, individuals with executive deficits do not generalize well and they certainly don't improvise well.

Suppose you have a gas stove and your son moves to an apartment with an electric stove. Suppose you have certain kinds of pots and pans with heat-resistant handles. You'll need to make sure he has the same kind of pots and pans when he moves out on his own. Part of your task analysis should be to develop a list of exactly what utensils your child uses when making her favorite meals. You will need to duplicate those items when she sets up her own kitchen. Don't be surprised if the salient feature of the can opener is the color of the handle, not the way it operates. Of course it must operate the way yours did, but it won't be right unless the color is the same as well. These idiosyncrasies should not be too disturbing when you realize they are a small price to pay for seeing your child accomplish important adult responsibilities on her own.

This may sound like a lot of work. It will be. But it can be a relatively easy and fun way for you to learn important things about your child's abilities, as mentioned above, and it can be a way for you to do something together that will last a lifetime. Besides, consider the alternative: if you allow your child to eat an unhealthy diet in your home, she will eat an un-healthy diet forever. And if you allow her not to learn to manage her own food, she will be dependent upon others long after you are gone.

MANAGING THE INTERACTIONS AMONG FOOD, HEALTH, AND MONEY

I feel compelled to draw attention to the interactions among food, health, and money because they are so difficult for parents of small children to anticipate. But they must be anticipated if you are to prepare your child for a healthy adult life. I'll try to show that what seems normal in family life will not prepare the child with disabilities for independent living on a fixed budget. If you anticipate your child never having to live on a fixed budget, some of what follows will not apply to your child. But the interaction be-tween food and health exists for all of us.

Picture your ten-year-old darting into the kitchen from playing in the back yard and asking for a soda. Perhaps you know this particular child plays with enough physical exertion to burn the calories contained in a soda; you also know you only allow this on Saturdays. When the same child asks for a soda after school you may have no difficulty insisting she drink milk instead. You might mention your reasons for limiting the sodas in her diet. She accepts your reasoning or she doesn't, but you maintain control of the situation.

Now consider the same circumstances in the life of your child with a disability. He asks for a soda while playing, but he isn't physically active, and he argues about your rule for soda on Saturdays only. You may feel sorry for the many times he has to endure limits he can't understand. So you allow sodas every day for this particular child. Maybe as he approaches puberty you notice he's overweight. Now would be a good time to focus on improving his diet. But he's so unhappy with his social life; eating is such a comfort to him. As you can see, following this reasoning, sodas and other junk food can easily slip into the life of a child with disabilities and no time will be the right time to backtrack. As you see food habits forming, it is easy to see the connection to health issues in his adult life.

What about the interaction with money? If your son attempts to live away from you, he will either be buying his own groceries or he will have assistance. If he shops on his own and he has no firm nutritional habits, he will spend his limited amount of money on junk food. If he has assistance, he will then have to be retrained to eat a more nutritional (and less expensive) diet, or it may be the issue over which he goes to war. Food management in conjunction with the food budget can make the difference in whether your young adult with disabilities lives in a group home or can live more independently.

I have a suggestion that seems shocking, even to me, but I think it's a good one. In order to teach a child the cost of foods that should be considered treats, like soda, candy, ice cream, pizzas, and cookies, you could charge him for those items when he wants them more often than what you allow for everyone else in the family. For this to work, he would have to be receiving an allowance on a regular basis. He would be given, say, five dollars for the weekend to spend as he pleases. But if he wants a soda on Friday evening after dinner, and this isn't what you allow, you could charge him one dollar of his weekly spending money. That way he would learn that certain foods require a decision, a choice, between competing luxuries, so to speak. If his health and weight are more at issue than his grasp of the cost of junk food, you could similarly put a price in calories burned on various junk foods. So when he wants an extra soda he would be required to walk on a treadmill or ride an exercise bike to burn a certain number of calories. Your goal is to make a connection between "luxury" foods and health and money. The concept of paying extra money, and having to burn the extra calories, would be valuable habits to carry into independent adulthood. Or, even better, he will decide it is just easier to drink water, milk, or tea, which is really what you were striving for all along.

SCHOOL

Many readers will be frustrated at this point and will think that I don't comprehend the time it would take to deal with all these issues, especially the management of food. The time crunch has a lot to do with the amount of time spent in managing school issues. I'll bet you're saying, "There's no way I can do all this when just getting my special kid through school is such an ordeal!" I have an answer for you, but get ready to be surprised. I would encourage you to rethink your priorities. *School will not be the most important achievement for kids with the disabilities I'm discussing.* No, they are not mentally retarded and, yes, they are capable of learning many things. But they are not going to have careers in fields that are dependent upon a quality all-round education. They are more likely to be highly skilled in idiosyncratic areas or easily trained in general areas. They are not going to end up managing people or systems because of the disorganization inherent in the brains of people with executive function deficits.

Therefore, it is not as important as most parents think to push their children to accomplish what others are accomplishing in school. If your child can read, encourage him or her to read as widely as possible. You never know when an interest might be stimulated that could lead to a lifetime of productive work or, at least, pleasure. Perhaps you can steer much of his school work toward his quirky interests so that he enjoys school and continues to learn about what is interesting to him. If he can't read, try to focus his school program on mechanical skills, physical skills, and oral presentation, and use visual materials that can be utilized without reading. This will require some ingenuity on your part and on the part of a tutor or other special teacher. If your child has the aptitude for a marketable skill, especially anything using computers, try to design his school years with a focus on that endeavor. And no matter what his aptitude, be sure to include computer literacy.

What I would encourage most strongly is that you *not* manhandle your child through the school years in such a way that he appears to get by, but doesn't actually accomplish anything meaningful to him. You probably know many parents who do this; they do their child's homework and micromanage every assignment way beyond the time they realize *he's not really getting it.* To what end? None of my clients who work have ever been asked if they have a high-school diploma! If they look nice, can speak with confidence, and can follow directions, that is sufficient for most entry level jobs that are appropriate to this population. The special jobs, those related to your child's quirky skills, will occur without reference to a balanced high-school education.

There is another reason why the school years are so difficult for families who are managing disability. Generally speaking, these children are not able to make friends very well. They are the teased and the bullied and the exploited, the children shunned by their non-disabled peers. Just attending school every day can be an ordeal. The choice most families face is whether to take advantage of special education or to try to stay in the mainstream for the entire 12 years. The disadvantage of special ed for this population is that they usually don't quite fit in there either. They are generally more intelligent than the special ed kids who may be mentally retarded. In addition, the special ed classroom is more and more likely to be a catchall for every kind of psychiatric and behavioral "problem child." Our population of kids are likely to learn odd, even dangerous, behaviors from children with other kinds of disability or disorder. Yet in the mainstream, our kids continue to be seen as odd and continue to be teased, abused, and exploited in many cases.

I think the solution, albeit difficult to achieve, is for parents to be involved in designing their child's school experience each year. Sometimes a wonderful teacher can be found who makes all the difference for at least one or two years. Some parents opt for small private schools, or schools designed for kids with Asperger's or other learning disabilities. Home schooling in small groups is an option. I predict there will be more creative options in the coming years as these disabilities become more well-known.

In the meantime, the highest priority should be to minimize the misery of the school years for our unique kids. Opportunities for friendship with similar kids should be sought relentlessly. Use your parent support group to establish a friendship network for your child. Plan homework evenings in groups and approach the curriculum as a group to minimize feelings of isolation in your efforts. Engage your special child in individual sports such as swimming, jogging, bowling, weight training, and martial arts for building self-esteem. Team sports should be avoided unless your child has a real ability to contribute to the team and enjoy the endeavor. If your child is interested in learning to play a musical instrument, by all means have him try more than one or two until he finds the best fit. Clubs that focus on your child's special interest can be found or even started by your family. Sometimes such clubs, like model train clubs, are for adults but they will allow your child to participate if he has a high level of interest and knowledge. Relationships formed in such clubs can be extremely important for the child with disabilities.

Summary

In summary, all the advice above is based on understanding the major difference between children with executive disabilities and typical children. The child with disabilities has many normal abilities mingled with her disabilities. But the neurotypical child has something like a blueprint, or you might prefer the image of wiring. The blueprint or wiring in the brain is designed to acquire the skills, including social skills, needed for adult life. It leads the child through developmental stages, proactively heading toward a certain result. Whether "normals" receive poor training or the best, whether strict or lax teaching of healthy habits, as young adults they can decide what they want to learn. They can choose to be different from their parents in fundamental ways. They may want to be looser or less rule-bound than their parents would prefer, or they may choose to be more grounded in structure than their parents are. They grasp social behavior without having to analyze it; the building blocks of social behavior just come on line without effort. They learn from friends and teachers and the culture because they can *think about things* at the same time that they are doing what they are learning to do. They can develop their own preferences and values. They develop judgment. They anticipate consequences. They learn from experience.

The individual with executive deficits cannot engage in analytical thinking unless guided from outside. In effect, another person in conversation acts as the organizer of thoughts, the frontal lobe, of the person with disability. A helpful conversation might go like this: Wow, that didn't seem to produce a very good result. I wonder if you'd be happier if you did something different in this kind of situation. *Well, what else could I do?* Let's think about it…it seemed to annoy the interviewer when you said you wanted different hours. Maybe you should ask what the hours are and not say what you want right off the bat. *OK, I'll try that next time. Will you remind me at the right time?*

The last remark, about needing to be reminded, seems like a joke, but it's not. This type of conversation has to be repeated many, many times before any change in behavior is likely to occur. Can you imagine the kind of internal monologue you would have if you couldn't accomplish that kind of thinking without help? If you, the parent, cannot be there for every necessary conversation toward introspection, and you certainly cannot, then habits are the best preparation for adult life.

Chapter 11

Living with Parents

Most adults with neurodevelopmental disabilities live with their parents. This may not sound surprising or problematic, until you think about what it implies for the middle and late stages of parents' lives. Also, from the point of view of the young person, if you believe in the importance of peer relationships, in friendship, love, and sex, and in the feeling of independence as an important stage in life, then you begin to see this fact as something to be given serious consideration. The following stories are descriptions of real adults who have lived their lives at home with their parents. All of the personal stories in this book have been disguised for the sake of privacy.

Kenny: a life of music

Kenny is a trumpet player, a diminutive man in his mid-fifties, who loves music and enjoys the adoration of an audience. He has played with many orchestras, at various levels of sophistication and professionalism, not breaking into the very highest ranks, but into perhaps the next tier. When Kenny has the opportunity to be a featured soloist with the orchestra, his performance is very good, touching in fact, and he receives huge ovations, partly because people are surprised by the combination of his appearance and his talent. He adores being in the spotlight. In addition to playing with orchestras, he has his own band that plays Dixieland jazz around the large metropolitan area where he lives.

Kenny has disabilities that can be seen immediately in terms of his small stature, the shape of his head, and his movements, which are hesitant and indicate poor vision. He wears glasses and has small hands with short fingers, and very small feet. If you talk with Kenny, you notice very soon that he prefers to discuss himself and his music. His father died recently, at 95 years of age, and when I spoke to Kenny to offer condolences, he changed the subject to his music without awareness that his behavior might seem inappropriate. Nevertheless, his mother tells me that he does seem to miss his father at times, although they had a hard time being close.

Kenny was born into a family of his parents and two sisters, older than Kenny by four and a half years and almost two years. The first girl was a bit hyperactive in childhood, but Catherine, her mother, said she just considered her firstborn bright and active. Kenny's father was 12 years older than his wife; he was a research chemist whom Catherine describes as "not a children person." However, she was quick to point out that many families break up when there is a child born with disabilities, but that was never a consideration in this family. Kenny's father lived a long life in good health and spent time in retirement learning to use a computer. He also played the piano.

When Kenny was born it was not known immediately that he would have disabilities. "He had a perfectly round little head," Catherine reports, focusing on this detail, I assume, because he would later turn out to have hydrocephalus. At seven months, Kenny had a fever and cried for most of 24 hours. Upon taking him to the doctor Catherine was asked, "Did anybody ever tell you this baby is spastic?" Catherine still sounds shocked as she reports this comment. She absolutely didn't believe the doctor and thought he was "crazy." Many labels start out as medical terms, only to get co-opted in common language as terms of ridicule. "Spastic" is one such term, as is "retarded." Catherine's story of raising Kenny is replete with misunderstandings and muddled thinking on the part of doctors and teachers. She did know that spastic was a medical term, but she had not thought, up to that point, that there was anything wrong with her baby. She later questioned close relatives, who replied that they had noticed some things that didn't seem normal.

After this episode Kenny's regular pediatrician measured his head and concluded he had hydrocephalus. The blockage of his spinal fluid seemed to have self-corrected by that time, though, and Kenny never required the surgery to install a shunt. No one seemed able to predict to what extent there would be residual effects on Kenny's brain development. Catherine found out soon enough. Kenny's language development was late and impaired, and he was diagnosed to be aphasic. In addition, he was clumsy, had poor balance, and impaired vision, with one wandering eye.

By the time Kenny was six years old he started to go through puberty. He also seemed to have sensory sensitivities that his mother couldn't fathom. Of course this created a demand upon Catherine's time and resourcefulness that the other children had not presented. Later in their lives Kenny's sisters expressed some resentment over the disproportionate amount of time Catherine had spent with Kenny, a problem mentioned frequently by the siblings of children with disabilities.

One event in Kenny's childhood stands out in Catherine's memory. All the children had chicken pox, and Kenny was only two years old. He had been crying interminably, and in desperation Catherine put on a phonograph record and placed it close to Kenny. He was immediately mesmerized by the music, and he stopped screaming. Catherine began to play all kinds of music for him, using the local library to get stacks and stacks of records. Eventually, in conjunction with the soothing effects of music, and by listening to recorded stories as well, Kenny began to understand language and to communicate.

The stage was set for Kenny to begin his relationship with the school system. His first school was a nursery school for retarded children. Kenny eventually attended many different schools, some "special" and some in the mainstream. It seems to me, in listening to Catherine tell these stories that are quite old by now, that the quality of her experience depended upon whether the teachers had an understanding of Kenny's abilities and disabilities that was in sync with her own understanding of her son.

Unfortunately the earlier and better educational situations came to an end and Kenny had to move on. In grammar school there were some bad experiences, including times when Kenny was teased, bullied, and hit by other children. Finally he landed in the public high school in his neighborhood, where he had a good experience. He participated in orchestra and band, and was able to take his physical education credits in learning massage. He still likes to give back rubs, and he still considers some of his classmates to be lifelong friends, although his mother recognizes that he isn't able to conduct friendships in the way that "normals" do.

Asked if she knows Kenny's IQ, Catherine explains that the testing never made sense to her since she knew Kenny didn't understand language. He first tested in the 50s, which is pretty deep in the mentally retarded range. However, another evaluator said he seemed to be "a damaged genius."

When Kenny converses about music, the listener does not feel he's with a mentally retarded person. But turn the conversation to any other topic and the experience is like talking with someone with Asperger's Syndrome. Kenny prefers topics related to music, including which radio stations he listens to, requests made to hear specific music on the radio, the dates of his upcoming performances, and so on. The level of vocabulary and complexity of sentence structure are not those of a retarded person.

Kenny was introduced to the trumpet at nine years of age. His first teacher remained his teacher and friend for over 20 years. He happened to be a man who wouldn't give lessons to young children unless their parents were completely committed to the endeavor. Catherine attended every lesson and established a pattern that continues to this day: Catherine goes everywhere that Kenny performs. In fact, Catherine attended almost every music class offered at the University of California (Berkeley), with Kenny, after fighting for him to be allowed to audit the classes. As usual, some teachers were happy to have him—one gave him a B for the class, which Catherine still cherishes; others seemed to be unnerved by his presence. It's difficult to say how Kenny feels about those classes now, but more than once he has told the story that he pointed out something about Beethoven's music that the Beethoven "specialist" didn't know.

Regarding music Catherine is, I think, very realistic about Kenny's abilities. He is a good enough trumpet player to be first chair in a community orchestra. He is good enough to have been a paid member of several municipal orchestras. His abilities are varied enough that he can play Dixieland jazz as well as classical music. He has played with over 20 organizations of varying levels of professionalism. Having heard him play many times, I can say he has a sweet tone and rarely makes mistakes detectable to the general audience. Most striking, given his poor appreciation of the way normal people interact, Kenny is capable of improvised accompaniment to a singer. I recently heard him play with a band whose repertoire was based on swing era jazz. The singer employed a charming style, with subtle emotional shadings expressed in song. Kenny was able to interpret, on the spot, the style of accompaniment that enhanced the emotions of the song. I asked Catherine how she understood this ability, and she replied that Kenny has been listening to all kinds of music for about 50 years, so it is an over-learned skill for him. She believes Kenny understands emotions, but it seems to me his easiest access to them is through music.

On the more objective side, Catherine expressed some frustration that Kenny can be difficult to direct. He is stubborn about accepting her interpretations of what the conductor has asked of Kenny. He warms up exactly the same way every time he plays, and there are some kinds of music he isn't interested in. Catherine does not believe his ability is a savant gift, but she does emphasize the special connection he seemed to have with music from the time before he could speak. He has acute hearing and perfect pitch, and to Catherine this makes a "born musician."

Most of Kenny's acquaintances are other musicians. Catherine says that when Kenny joins a new band, either there is a strong leader who maintains control, or else Kenny takes over. He has been fired from two orchestras and his executive function deficits were probably at issue in both cases, but Catherine is certain prejudice against the disabled also played a part. Kenny likes to talk. In some orchestras, either the conductor or the other musicians didn't feel they should have to make adjustments to work with a person with special needs. I have seen at first hand, however, that a conductor who is kind but firm has little trouble managing Kenny's spontaneity. Kenny's life would have been inestimably less satisfying had his mother not provided this path to self-esteem and joy he obviously feels when he performs. And his gift to the overall spirit of tolerance and open-mindedness is incalculable.

From the point of view of an outsider, Catherine, who is well into her eighties, appears to be in good health, is trim and energetic, and seems almost untiring in her support of Kenny. But in intimate conversation she reveals her concerns. Catherine, like most mothers of the disabled, would be relieved to outlive her son. She knows that others have opinions about the kinds of plans she should be making. All the time spent driving and waiting while Kenny rehearses or performs is time she might spend on hobbies or activities of her own. What of her time for friendships, or to visit her other children and their families? She has two grandchildren who live two states away. Both her daughters ended up living in the same town, and they encourage her to relocate there. But she says the weather would be bad for Kenny. Besides, he has his music. And he has lived in the same house every day of his life.

I tried to imagine Kenny's life without his mother. In terms of self-care skills, Kenny manages his hygiene almost independently. On one day that I went to interview his mother, he had just cut a lock of his hair with his razor. It made a barely noticeable short patch in his haircut. Catherine seemed troubled by this, and she and Kenny bickered about it for a moment in the way that overly interdependent relatives sometimes do. The moment passed easily, suggesting that there are many such moments in their life together.

Could Kenny have learned to cook and do household chores? He does fold and put away laundry for the family, he can empty the dishwasher, and he keeps his bathroom sink clean, but he doesn't take an interest in most of the chores required to manage a life. He can make phone calls related to his rehearsal and performance plans. He thinks of himself as having friends, but he never goes out independently with a peer. He doesn't use public transportation or schedule and attend medical appointments on his own. He doesn't shop.

Catherine is not reluctant to discuss the inevitable plans that must be made for Kenny's future in the event that she might die suddenly. She feels that his sisters would not be willing or able to care for him the way she has. After all, they are already in their late fifties; taking on Kenny's care would be almost like having a baby at that age. Like many other mothers of adults with disabilities, Catherine knows there are differences of opinion about whether the care she has provided was really the best thing for Kenny. Catherine cannot second guess herself at this stage, but she imagines that others do. On the other hand, many people who know Kenny through his music think of Catherine as a saint for the way she has cared for her gifted son. She simply points out that the relationship is not entirely one-sided; she finds Kenny to be a truly interesting person.

In terms of his attachment and dependency on her, Catherine feels that Kenny will be lost if she dies before he does. Given the amount of time they spend together, one cannot imagine that Kenny would be complacent about his mother's death as he appeared to be following his father's recent death. Also, one must acknowledge that his feelings may be different from his outward behavior. Catherine has discussed with Kenny her eventual death. Sometimes he says he should get married so he'll have someone else to take care of him. Kenny does not have a community of people with disabilities from which to seek relationships. Could he live alone?

The answer to the last question is no. Catherine cannot picture Kenny living alone. When she and I have discussed this, I've made the suggestion that she have someone come to live in the family house now, before the inevitable and painful changes must take place. A caregiver, who would "audition" by joining the family now, could give Catherine peace of mind for the future. In order to trust that such a caregiver would take the responsibility seriously and for the long term, I would think a substantial payment well into the future would have to be arranged. Perhaps one of the siblings would be in charge of the estate of her parents and would oversee a trust set aside for the caregiver following Kenny's death. The trust would provide for more payment the longer he lived. One wonders if Kenny's sisters understand that they may have the choice of caring for Kenny themselves or relinquishing their inheritance to such an arrangement.

Another choice would be for Catherine and Kenny to move into assisted living together, even before Catherine needs such support. Kenny would become accustomed to eating his meals in a dining room with the other residents. He would learn how and when his laundry would be done; how to get help with medical appointments, and so on. Catherine sees the positive side of such an arrangement, but the negative for her is the loss of her home and her privacy. And she would still be expected (by Kenny) to drive him to his rehearsals and performances unless she could persuade herself to hire someone else to do it.

Does a mother in Catherine's position ask herself if it's all been worth it? She has clearly provided Kenny with a wonderful life and Kenny is an inspiration to all who see and hear him perform. But perhaps Kenny's life has come at a cost to Catherine and to her relations with her daughters. Would things have been very different if Kenny's musical ability had never been discovered? Did Catherine deliberately choose for Kenny to focus his life on one activity, or did it happen by chance? Does Catherine feel fortunate to have had this delightful but completely dependent son? Catherine has not told me whether she asks herself these questions, but I can say she does appear to be a happy and fulfilled woman.

The story of Madelyn and Butch

Unfortunately, not all stories are as charming as Kenny's life with music. And no one really knows how many stories of families with disability are satisfying and how many should be regarded as a national shame. Madelyn and Butch's story is one of the latter. Madelyn had a son, born after her daughter, whose disabilities were not known to her, at least not definitely, until he started school. The story is like so many, filled with visits to doctors who said nothing was wrong, and later, that he would outgrow his boisterousness. Hyperactivity hadn't been labeled as a diagnosis when Butch was a boy, in the early 1960s. This was a working class family without extra money for special camps or programs. But even if there had been money, not many services were available that a family could locate on their own, at least not the kind of family with little education and limited emotional resources. The Learning Disabilities Association wasn't even created until 1963. Who knows how much Madelyn would have been able to benefit from the support of a group of other mothers for the mutual betterment of their children?

Madelyn and her husband both worked outside the home. The boy, Butch, was punished for the many reports of misbehavior at school. His sister served as an example of a child who was doing well within the same family, so the parents concluded it wasn't their fault their son was doing so badly. At least they tried to convince themselves of that point of view. As the school years went by, Butch's difficulties only increased. He had no friends, but occasionally fell in with groups who were up to no good. He was exploited and was always the one who got caught; then he would be rejected even by the boys who had enticed him into trouble. Throughout these years, Butch was not labeled as having disabilities because, as we see time and again, his intact verbal abilities caused people to judge him to be intellectually normal. The formula seemed to be: if not obviously retarded, then not disabled.

By the time Butch's older sister had finished high school and left the family home, Butch's father and mother were headed for divorce. There can be many pressures in any marriage, but disagreements over how to handle a troubled child can erode a relationship beyond recovery. And, sad as it may be to employ this generalization, the mother is most likely to remain to protect and care for her child with disabilities. Madelyn was no exception. After the marriage dissolved and her daughter had grown up, Madelyn and Butch were left with one another, and they were left with even fewer resources than they had had before. Madelyn worked as a waitress. She worked long hours and it was hard work. She imagined that as Butch grew older, and he no longer had the pressures of school since he had dropped out, surely he would see how to be helpful around the house.

But this was an unrealistic expectation. Butch was disorganized and hyperactive, though less so than he had been. Madelyn was somewhat hopeful that he would outgrow some of his quirks as he appeared to be outgrowing the need for constant movement. Butch was not capable of seeing the world through his mother's eyes. He was a young man without friends, without a girlfriend, without a job or a driver's license. He was resentful and unable to comprehend why he had so much less than the other boys he knew. And his father had left him as surely as he had left his wife.

Eventually Madelyn was able to find jobs for Butch. But she was amazed to find that he fought her every attempt to help him. Sometimes he would take a job and seem to do well for a while; other times he wouldn't even go to an interview she had carefully negotiated. While Madelyn found this hard to understand, it really isn't when you think about it in terms of developmental stages. Butch was at the age that he should be achieving separation from his parents. Even though he had poor self-care skills, he had a concrete understanding of independence. He knew what his eighteenth birthday was supposed to mean. So it didn't feel right to rely on his mother to find jobs for him. At the same time, he couldn't do it by himself. He was afraid he would fail, and he was right to be afraid. He remembered the many times in school when he couldn't follow instructions, when he seemed to miss parts of what others easily understood. But of course he never admitted he didn't understand. He didn't want to be regarded as mentally deficient.

The failure to gain employment persisted for several years, and all the time, Madelyn hoped Butch would spontaneously learn to clean his room or do the dishes or the laundry while she was at work. Instead, he played endless computer games and watched TV. He overate and became obese. He stopped shaving. Inevitably, a young man who experiences his life as hopeless, miserable, and boring will eventually discover drugs. Butch began smoking marijuana and drinking alcohol. To obtain these things without his mother's help, it was also inevitable that he would fall into a rough crowd of young men.

Several years went by with Madelyn alternately trying to convince herself that Butch would "find himself" and threatening to throw him out of the house if he didn't shape up. Many times he did things she had thought she would never tolerate. He stole from her. He lay around her house in a drunken stupor. He became fatter and fatter. And still he didn't know how to cook a meal, wash the dishes, or do the laundry. He had never bought groceries or fixed a meal by himself. What would happen to him if she didn't continue to take care of him? Was he grateful for her care? Of course not, because Butch was humiliated by his dependence on his mother. He tried to tell himself that she was "holding him back." He was verbally abusive toward her, and then one day he hit her.

Madelyn had her limits after all. She called the police and Butch was arrested. Madelyn was counseled to seek help for herself and for Butch. She found that Butch qualified for financial support in the form of Supplemental Security Income, known in the system as SSI. But as long as he lived with his mother, it was an amount of money that actually made things worse instead of better. Had Butch been on his own he would have been entitled to something like $830 per month to be used for shelter, food, and other necessities. While supported by someone else, he was entitled to about half that much. Since Madelyn couldn't turn her back on him, and she couldn't convince him to spend the money on their household needs, Butch ended up with his own source of money for drugs and alcohol.

Madelyn had by this time learned much more about disabilities than she had known during Butch's childhood. She applied for assistance from the Regional Centers, the organization that provides for children and adults with developmental disabilities in the state of California. But Butch could not qualify for those services because his school years were characterized by failure and bad behavior, but not by a documented developmental disability. His records showed that he was not mentally retarded and not autistic. The term autism spectrum was many years in the future. This was the fate of many young people who grew up before the neurodevelopmental disabilities were even as well-known as they are now. The diagnosis that would come closest to fitting Butch would be Pervasive Developmental Disorder—Not Otherwise Specified. To get that diagnosis, Madelyn would have had to pay minimally around $1500 for a neuropsychological evaluation of Butch. And it is not a foregone conclusion that an evaluating psychologist would make that diagnosis by this time in Butch's life because of the intervening years of drug use. Drugs do damage to the brain. An evaluation cannot show how the brain functioned before the drug use.

You've probably anticipated that this story does not have a happy ending. Butch continued to live with Madelyn, and though he never attacked her again, he withdrew even more into sullen inactivity, helplessness, and drug use. One night he staggered into the path of a car, sustaining injuries including further, serious brain damage. Now he is truly incapable of learning to care for himself. His diagnosis will never be understood; his family's life, especially his mother's, has been dominated by his condition. Someday he or his mother will die. If Butch outlives Madelyn he will most likely be left to his own inadequate self-care until he too dies. In the event a social services agency would become aware of his plight, his best outcome would be placement in an assisted living or convalescent care home for individuals on government benefits.

Other lives

There are countless other stories of adults with neurodevelopmental disabilities who live their whole lives in the parental home. Certainly not all of them are as sad as Butch's story. For many, probably especially for women, life settles into a routine that includes helping around the house, participating in activities arranged for the disabled, and having a social circle composed of relatives and friends of the parents. Perhaps this routine comes about after some years of struggle. Typically, there are struggles for independence, usually sometime soon after the eighteenth birthday. These may revolve around the young adult wanting to go out alone, learning to drive, wanting personal spending money, taste in clothing, music and movies, dating, sex, and many other issues. Generally young adults will know the significance of the eighteenth birthday as a marker for independence and they will want the rights of decision-making but will have no concept of the responsibilities most adults take on simultaneously.

Efforts to continue with higher education may take a few years to be exhausted. Remember that school was a miserable experience for most people with autism spectrum disabilities; they were teased and rejected socially, and they were largely unsuccessful in their studies. Nevertheless, many parents think the best future lies beyond some form of higher education or trade school. So the young person gets signed up and heads off to school, often to the local community college. To my knowledge, few such stories end up with even one semester of school successfully completed. Furthermore, the students usually end up lying to their parents. They may be frustrated or bored by the classes, or the old intimidations of school may be awakened in a new setting, or they may stumble over the simplest social requirements. Unable to explain their feelings, they find it easier to leave the house at the scheduled time and hope for the best. Executive function deficits include being unable to predict or manage consequences that are far out in the future. When the deception is exposed, both student and parents feel frustrated and angry and misunderstood. The parents are only trying to help and the student is unable to explain why he can't fulfill his end of the bargain.

Following the acceptance that school isn't going to work, many parents go through a period of years in which they try to set the young person up with a job and a place to live. As in Butch's story, too often they fail at the job, or they reject the job as not what they had in mind for a career. They may have grandiose fantasies and no idea how to make them a reality.

Time after time, the young person will return home, usually with unrealistic explanations for her failure. Blaming others is typical of those with a disability that precludes self-awareness and introspection. Finally, if the parents are able to give up their expectations, most of these young adults will settle into the routine of life in the parental home.

Some will be luckier in the job market. If they find a job that suits their skills and one in which they will not be pushed to take on more and more responsibility, perhaps a job with a relative or friend of the family, the outcome can be very good, like the story of Howard, who worked as a school janitor for 30 years and retired with a pension. Many adults with disabilities are pleased and proud to continue at the same job longer than anyone would expect given the simple nature of the job skills and the lack of opportunity for advancement. Doing the same things over and over can lead to a feeling of mastery and competence, a welcome achievement for this population.

After the routine of daily life emerges from chaos, there can still be struggles around issues of friendship, dating, and sexuality. Friendship is always hoped for but is a difficult thing for parents to arrange, unless there is a known group of other adults with disabilities. Generally the groups for adults with disabilities are either for those with Down's Syndrome and other mentally retarded individuals or, more recently, for those with Asperger's Syndrome. Those on the autism spectrum find a better fit with the Asperger's groups, but there are the rare few who will happily socialize with the mentally retarded. Any path toward socializing with other adults with disabilities should be welcomed, especially when you see signs that they are experiencing the group members as a peer group.

Once a routine is established a family can go along for many years with an adult with disabilities being cared for by her parents. Gradually the young person will give up certain dreams, like the dream of marrying and having children. It will be clear that no one thinks that is possible or is a good idea, in most cases. Sex may be an issue that is never dealt with to the satisfaction of the young adult, but gradually that too becomes a dead issue. Obesity is a chronic problem for many with executive deficits. Medical problems may crop up sooner than they would for the non-disabled peers.

From the parents' point of view, the routine of caring for the adult as if he were still a child can be fulfilling for some parents. After the years of struggle and worry, it may be a relief to know he is safe under the same roof every night. Invariably, it is not the picture of adulthood anyone dreams of for their child, but then they've known this particular child would be different from very early on. It is not a surprise at this point. But one nagging worry persists, if only in the back of the mind. What will happen when we die?

Parents either have a plan or they don't, and the reasons for approaching the future the way they do are numerous and complex. If there are other children, siblings or cousins of the adult with disabilities, they may be expected to take over the care of their relative. But sometimes this expectation has not been clearly discussed among all parties. Many siblings and other relatives harbor the suspicion that the disabilities could have been managed differently and the outcome would have been better. In other words, they fault the parents for contributing to the poor outcome of their sibling or relative and this allows them not to commit to providing the same level of care. Instead, they may vaguely intend to care for the relative, but don't picture themselves providing the comprehensive care the parents have provided all those years. This can be a sad situation. If the parents live a long life and continue to care for their disabled adult child in the home, like Kenny, the question of whether a different kind of care would have created a different outcome will be moot. The now middle-aged adult will likely be bereft upon the deaths of his parents, and undone by the sudden changes in where and how and with whom he will live. This is no time for him to be expected to learn a lot of new skills. Or to have to hear that his parents coddled him all those years and things are going to be different now.

If any argument will convince parents to seek adult care situations outside the family home, this should be it. There is no better time to move a young person to relatively independent living than the time when he or she naturally feels like moving out. And there is no worse circumstance under which to have to move than when dealing with the deaths of one's parents.

Chapter 12

Living in a Group Home

Many people are aware, if only in a vague way, that there are group homes for children, adolescents, and adults with special needs. Most people think of group homes as emergency services to meet unforeseen needs in terrible times. Adolescents who become so mentally ill or behaviorally impaired that their parents can no longer control them may have to live in a group home for a time, until they are well. Specialized group homes exist for the mentally retarded who also have medical conditions that require 24-hour care. Those diagnosed with schizophrenia, with little hope of becoming self-sufficient, often live in board-and-care homes, a specific kind of group home. It seems natural to think that there might be group homes designed for the population under discussion in this book.

Unfortunately, because this population has been so poorly understood and defined, there are no group home options designed specifically for them, but rather for the larger groups of which they have been seen as a subgroup. The two larger groups that subsume our population are the developmentally disabled (DD) and the traditional autism group. In thinking of the DD group, we think of the familiar Down's Syndrome mentally retarded and those with cerebral palsy, epilepsy, and other lesser known syndromes like Fragile X, Turners Syndrome, Rett's Disorder, Williams Syndrome, Prader-Willi Syndrome and others. Generally, these disorders are accompanied by mental retardation as a component of the syndrome.

The autism spectrum has recently been given much attention; and an important finding for our population is that mental retardation may or may not be a component of the disorders on that spectrum. Those with

Asperger's and high-functioning autism are likely not to be mentally re-tarded, but to have significant anxiety and impairments in social behavior. Those with PDD-NOS are somewhat different from both the other groups, and I've made the case that it is primarily in the area of frontal lobe, executive function deficits that we find their defining symptoms. How does this relate to care in group homes?

Individuals from the population I am discussing are generally not well served when placed with the mentally retarded. They may have below average IQs, but still be well above the range of most mentally retarded individuals. The difference of 10 to 15 IQ points on paper makes a huge difference in real life.[1]

Our adults, who may need to spend their whole lives in supported care, are nevertheless not content to live and socialize with those who are mentally retarded. Similarly, our population has trouble mingling with the autistic population unless they are not immediately identifiable as truly autistic. The misunderstanding of social requirements, and failure to make a normal presentation in public, are embarrassing and offensive to those who can do those things pretty well. That is, they can go to stores and restaurants and other public places and pass for normal; they are very proud of that ability. They are embarrassed when publicly identified with a whole group of disabled individuals. Unfortunately, both the developmentally disabled group and the more severe autistic group can generally be identified at a glance.

Group homes designed to serve the higher functioning autism spectrum clients would fill a great need, as they would ideally be able to keep the adults safe and well cared for in terms of nutritional, medical, dental, and financial needs. And they would also have to provide vocational opportunities and a social network. Are there such group homes?

There must be group homes here and there that serve this population, but I know of no network of such homes, or referral service that would direct a parent toward such a specialized service. If you as a parent or social worker were to search for a group home for your adult child or client with neurodevelopmental disabilities, I would advise paying attention to a number of factors.

Factors to consider when choosing a group home

- *The staff.* Do they speak the same language as their clients? Are they committed to learning about the disabilities? Are they working in this field by choice or by default? Are they paid well enough to take pride in their work and stay with it long enough that your adult child doesn't have to live with constant staff turnover? Do they receive training toward a clinical approach to understanding your loved one? Will you have access to staff to participate in decisions that are made about your adult child's care?

- *Food and exercise.* Are meals nutritious, appealing, and varied? Will your adult child take part in preparing food, or be able to make any decisions about meals? What if he doesn't like to exercise? What will be the level of supervision? Will he take up smoking? Drinking?

- *Money.* Of course you must be able to trust the financial arrangements and be assured that your child is not being exploited. This field is shamefully under-funded and service providers as well as clients often fall below the poverty line. Will your adult child have access to adequate resources and still have some amount of spending money?

- *Daily activities.* Will your child be left to sit around the group home all day doing nothing meaningful? Will he be required to leave the house for the day regardless of where he might go? Who will provide the motivation and planning of daily activities that your child is not able to do for herself? Are there vocational services available to your child? Is there a day program of activities associated with the group home and do both staffs communicate to provide coordinated care?

- *Personal safety.* What if your adult child leaves the group home, claiming to have scheduled activities, but you know he lies about such things? What level of supervision will be provided? What about exploitation by people in the greater community in the form of enticements to engage in crime, substance abuse, sexual behavior, traveling or wandering, and responding to misunderstood financial offers? Will there be oversight of all these dangers?

- *Medical and dental care.* What level of care will be provided and who will make decisions about your adult child? Sometimes parents and other relatives can be excluded from all decisions unless you seek legal status as guardian or conservator of your adult child. If he takes medication, will it be monitored? How often will he see a psychiatrist? Will he get medical care only in emergencies?

- *Social life.* With whom will your adult child socialize? Will he have the opportunity to meet others with his level and type of disability? Will he be able to make friends, go out in groups, and date? Will he have a safe and private place to engage in sexual behavior? Will birth control and safe sex be utilized? Will he socialize through the use of computer, cell phone, and other electronic media? If so, what will be the level of supervision?

- *Personal autonomy.* What kind of accommodations will your adult child have to ensure some control over her needs for privacy and solitude? Will she have her own bedroom? Will there be a quiet room or other space for being alone? Will her belongings be secure and under her own control? Will she be able to make her own decisions about fashion, hair styles, and make up? Will there be a balance between personal freedom and assistance with matters of judgment?

- *Parental involvement.* Consider the relationship you will have with the group home and its staff. Will your opinions be considered? Will your participation be encouraged? Will you feel concerned about your adult child being "kicked out" if he misbehaves? What if something happens to you?

Those are a lot of questions and concerns. You can probably think of a few more, especially if your child has idiosyncrasies, behavioral quirks, or special interests. I have heard very few positive comments from the parents of my clients who lived in group homes before they came to our program. Neither do the clients themselves have anything positive to say about living in group homes. *But this could be primarily because the group homes were not tailored to the disability I'm discussing.* Most of my clients who had negative experiences were either frightened by behaviors more common to a psychiatric population, behaviors they had never seen before such as talking wildly to themselves or self-mutilation, or they were bored and dispirited by living with those who functioned at a lower intellectual level than themselves.

There is definitely a need for group homes that would serve the executive function impaired population. My plea would be that they situate themselves within networks of several affiliated homes so that the residents could socialize among themselves, and not be isolated with just the four to six residents who generally live in a group home together. That way they might consolidate other services, like a visiting psychiatrist or medical doctor who would attend all the houses in the network; or a vocational service that would support employment for all the clients. Parents could form a support group and provide extra supervision for recreational and social activities and even travel. Clearly, leadership is needed in the area of ongoing care for adults on the autism spectrum. To that end, I have suggested a new idea for a model of care that parents could set up for their adult children with these disabilities. Please see Appendix I for a full description. Let's turn now to an in-depth look at a therapeutic program with comprehensive services that already exists.

Note

1. An IQ of 70 or below along with other self-care criteria defines mental retardation. The population I'm discussing usually have IQs from about 80 to the normal range, but with significant highs and lows in various intellectual subskills.

Part Four

A Model Program of Supported Independence

I work as the Clinical Director of a program that provides comprehensive services to adults with neurodevelopmental disabilities, increasingly referred to as autism spectrum disabilities. The CAL program (stands for Center for Adaptive Learning) functions as a small therapeutic community rather than as an institution or other set-apart facility. We are located in a mid-size town on the outskirts of the greater San Francisco Bay Area. The locale provides a range of services and experiences such that our clients are not isolated, yet they are protected from some of the greater difficulties of a more urban setting.

I call our program a model because it provides everything parents need to consider, to feel confident about releasing their loved ones to a life of supported independence. It is not the only good outcome for adults with disabilities. Some adults stay with family members and have a good life. Some live in group homes, board-and-care facilities, and even hospitals or skilled nursing facilities. And some will hold out for complete independence, with varying levels of success. But this model is worth replicating. It could provide supported independence for more and more of the many young people on the spectrum who will attain adulthood in the next decade.

Suppose you do not have access to this program or another one like it. There are several ways you will still find this section valuable. You may be exactly the sort of person who will be inspired to create a place for your own child and his friends. If so, you may want to read Appendix I first, and consider my recommendations for parents who want to create their own supported living program. Then, when you return to this section, you will find much more advice on what to expect and how to proceed. Maybe you will become an advocate for this kind of care for adults on the autism spectrum.

Another reason to read this section is to solidify what you've just learned about the behavior patterns that stem from executive function deficits. I will provide many real-life examples of quirky, creative, funny, and dysfunctional behavior, and it should become more and more comprehensible, even enlightening, to see that the behavior makes sense in light of the brain deficits experienced by people on the autism spectrum. Ways to respond to problem behaviors will always be presented, as well. But, first, let's take a look at the upside: the very best reason places like CAL should exist.

Chapter 13

The Value of Living with Peers

Leaving the parental home is the major adult rite of passage. If an adult with disabilities does not leave home, he is likely to reach middle age and have to endure his parents' death while still dependent on them. Genevieve Stolarz, CAL's founder, realized early in her son's life that he would need lifelong support, *and* that it would be important for him to feel like a successful adult. As a result, she has spent her adult life and career providing a therapeutic and supportive environment for her son and perhaps one hundred adults like him so that she and other parents could feel confident allowing their adult children to leave home and to be relatively independent. It has been a success story.

For those clients who anticipate staying at CAL indefinitely, goals can be approached with less pressure to produce change quickly. Clients work toward developing skills in several areas simultaneously, and they are all important. Before employment is attempted, self-care skills and interpersonal relations should be progressing well. Sometimes the stresses of holding a job are such that other newly acquired skills may be neglected or even lost. It is better not to put clients in the position that having a job costs them too dearly in terms of friendships or just plain exhaustion.

Ideally, we take at least six months to one year establishing habits of personal cleanliness, apartment maintenance, healthy eating and exercise, the sleep/wake cycle, and attention to time management and schedules, before we attempt employment. When good strategic choices have been made, it is wonderful to see the pride of accomplishment in individuals who have jobs they can perform with confidence. When young men and woman can work *and* maintain their other obligations and friendships, something wonderful has been accomplished. Then, naturally, we like to see them enjoy the life they have gained, using all the skills and having all the rewards of life at the highest level of independence they can achieve, with support.

Those who choose to make a permanent home in the program do so, generally, because they have friends for the first time in their lives. As discussed elsewhere, it is a powerful developmental event, and the same one that operates in the lives of normals, to leave the closest relationship we've known, with parents, for new ones with peers. To enumerate the benefits, let's begin with the feeling of independence, and the fact of semi-independence. The clients have an address in an apartment complex. There is nothing in their address to indicate they are categorized as dependent adults. If their parents have thought it best to obtain conservatorship over them, then they are not legally allowed to enter into contracts or make other specific decisions about their lives. But nothing in the way we provide services indicates who is and who is not conserved.

Another appealing aspect of independence for our clients is their ability to decorate their apartments as they please. They can bring their favorite possessions, including computers, video games, televisions, music, photos, posters and knick-knacks to their apartments, just as anyone else would when leaving home. They have keys, like other adults. If they or their parents have the means, they can own and drive a car. But those are just some symbols of adulthood.

The developmental task of separation

Most young adults have practiced identifying more and more with peers by the time they are ready to leave home. *From early adolescence, separation from parents is the psychological developmental task to be accomplished.* It is programmed into our species. This means that the young person begins to consolidate a personality of his own. At first he may exaggerate the differences from his parents in order to feel truly separated. Later, a balance is achieved in which he acknowledges the deep connections based in familiarity and in values and aspirations shared with parents, while at the same time recognizing differences from parents that we share with our peers. Separating from parents can be painful, and adolescents often dwell in defiance and anger to overcome the pain of this developmental stage. Separation also produces exhilaration and a feeling of accomplishment. Considering how frightening this stage can be, there would have to be major rewards built in to keep us all moving forward. The anticipation of a social and romantic life, a family of one's own, work, and mastery of the tasks of adulthood are the rewards.

As life goes on, we expect to go through the same stages that our parents went through. That provides an ongoing connection to them, but also ensures that we are never in the same place psychologically and developmentally as our parents. The people we will feel most similar to, in the middle years, are our partners in primary relationships, our peers. This is an ingenious plan, developmentally speaking, because it propels us to seek the company of our peers and thereby to find mates, to procreate, and keep the species going. Sexual urges certainly have a large role to play in demanding independence from parents, but other aspects of social behavior are just as important.

Given the disability of our clients, and given that some of their behaviors make them seem like perpetual children, it is logical that parents have a hard time seeing them as adults. But inside those adult bodies are the same hormonal urges as in their non-disabled peers. Moreover, the drive toward an independent identity also occurs, much the same as in their non-disabled peers. And most difficult to comprehend is that these young adults, who have never had friends in school, far from being adjusted to that condition, by late adolescence experience another wave of longing for peer relationships. They want romance and sex and companionship, just like their non-disabled peers. When viewed as an important developmental stage, this is entirely understandable.

Here is the most optimistic part of my message to you: when you gather together a substantial number of young adults with similar disabilities, you observe that they go through the stages of autonomy and accomplishment that are driven by normal developmental milestones, only they do it in their own way. This is the very best feature of a program such as ours. It is a joy to see people who have never had a real friendship finally talking casually and comfortably with their friends. Hangin' out! Any day of the week I can look out my office window and see clients sitting at the picnic table. Some are talking and joking, some are playing chess, one presides over the barbecue. It looks so normal.

Granted, there are differences from the world of neurotypical adults. Our clients are likely to tease one another and to lose their tempers abruptly; they gossip endlessly yet feel wronged when they become the object of gossip. I can hear some of you saying, "My normal kid and her friends are exactly like that!" True enough, perhaps, but there is a qualitative difference, otherwise our folks would be friends with normal kids. But they are not. The differences don't matter in our community. Our clients are not normal in their social behavior, but they are normal for one another, and that is what matters.

In addition to the easy friendships they finally enjoy, our clients have the opportunity for romantic and sexual relationships. Again, these relationships are adapted to the level of social abilities our clients can manage. Some couples spend as long as a few years in relationship without engaging in sexual intercourse. They can be very devoted to one another and seen by their peers as a couple, yet one of them is not comfortable with the idea of sex, and the other accepts that limit. Another couple declared they were just friends but behaved in every way as a couple. They insisted they were not being sexual, but everyone knew they were. When, under pressure, they decided to declare themselves a romantic couple, something went wrong and they broke up very publicly. Subsequently, they went back to their own adaptation, which was to say they were just friends, but to be exclusive sexual partners all the same. We see no reason to intrude upon this arrangement.

I don't want to leave the impression that sex is the most prominent part of the adult lives of our clients. I think members of this population actually pursue sex less than the general population does. But the *possibility* of romance and sex seems to allow them to feel normal, and they appreciate that. Some other milestones of adult life, particularly marriage and babies, are talked about by our clients. But they tend to conceive of those stages or achievements as being always in the future. Our clients adjust pretty well to keeping things out in the future as eternal possibilities. Motherhood is the most heart wrenching (to me) of these future possibilities. None of the women in our program would be capable of caring for a child. Some of them know this and have accepted it; others hold it out as a future possibility, along with marriage to a "normal person." But with the executive deficits such as they are, the future never comes. Our clients live in the perpetual present. To the extent they have a sense of time, it is related to the schedule we provide them, or to their work schedule, or to upcoming events like concerts or birthdays. The passage of time and the way it relates to stages of life, and the feeling of doors closing, is too abstract for our clients to grasp, and that is a blessing.

Here are some things our clients do on a regular basis: they hold down jobs and use public transportation to get to work. They walk to the bank or the grocery store on Friday afternoons to cash their checks. They eat dinner out on the weekends, or bring food in and eat together. They shop at discount stores together. They buy tickets on their own and attend major league baseball games, traveling together by public transportation. The women trade clothes and help each other with make-up and hair styles. They also critique each other's appearance pretty harshly at times, and then they apologize. They are invited out for social occasions by parents who visit from out of town. They invite one another to family weddings, birthday parties, and holiday celebrations. A few clients who like to cook will make dinner for a small group. They don't expect this to be reciprocated, and it isn't. Perhaps most importantly to their continued safety and relative independence, they call staff when they perceive that someone among them needs help.

Finally, an aspect of our clients' lives that is essential and might not be anticipated by parents is the importance of their relationships with staff. Unlike parents, who will always have a hierarchical relationship with their kids, as well as positive and negative emotional histories, staff can be seen as benign service providers. Just as anyone may employ a tax person or housecleaner, the clients feel that staff are their service providers. We provide solutions to problems and we devise accommodations to overcome ongoing limitations. In truth, we are also authority figures because we have to manage some aspects of the clients' lives against their preference. But we strive to be logical and use real consequences when we must intrude on their autonomy. And clients like the staff; at first their affection is directed toward staff as an amorphous group, rather than toward us as individuals. That protects them from the pain of loss, as staff move on and are replaced. Eventually, staff who stay many years emerge as individuals and can engender genuine affection from some clients. The important thing from a parent's point of view is to know that the staff will treat their loved one with respect and care, and that the client will feel safe and respected. The mutual affection that can occur is the icing on the cake.

Chapter 14

The Structure and Goals of the Program

This and the following chapters will provide a description of the nuts and bolts of the model program as it has been designed to provide comprehensive services to adults on the autism spectrum.

Structure

The building in which one lives can be important in providing a feeling of independence. The CAL program (Center for Adaptive Learning) has an office building for administrative services and for the day program. Adjacent to the program building is a small complex of two-bedroom apartments. Each client has his or her own bedroom and a roommate with whom they share the common areas of the apartment. This arrangement encourages basic social behavior; but we do not expect roommates to be best friends.

The program day is structured to keep the clients occupied with meaningful learning opportunities as well as social contact and accomplishment of the usual errands that make up life. The day starts when everyone gathers in the program building for Morning Meeting. Each day of the week has a different focus, with the overall intent for the community to convene, say good morning, and preview the day, mimicking what happens in a family. Most of us say good morning to the people with whom we live, and we may go over our plans for the day, mentioning when we will see one another again, and what we are looking forward to or need to accomplish. In this way, we unconsciously remind ourselves of our *interdependence*. Our clients would not do this if it weren't built into the structure of the program.

Following Morning Meeting, there are 45-minute learning groups that focus on various aspects of living. One day's subject is money matters, another is current events, another focuses on habits that promote healthy living. Every client who isn't employed attends these classes. Living skills time follows, when residents return to their apartments to do chores associated with independent living. Some need supervision, some need visual cues, and some engage in a constant battle to avoid these chores. Others, whose limitations lie elsewhere, are able to manage apartment living about as well as the rest of us.

Lunch time follows living skills. Some clients eat lunch on their own, while others attend cooking groups of six to eight individuals who make and eat a meal together, with supervision by staff. Then they return to the program building for afternoon classes and individual appointments for art, computer training, vocational readiness, and counseling sessions. There are group activities intended to demonstrate how to manage leisure time, like poetry, journaling, music appreciation, and a video group, each led by staff. There are no academic classes, although we added Brain Group a few years ago, in which I teach various aspects of brain functioning that relate to the interests and disabilities of the students. The afternoon schedule also includes exercise four days a week, an activity that requires huge enthusiasm on the part of staff to encourage the participation of clients.

In addition to at least one individual counseling session per week, the counselors also lead Men's Group, Women's Group and Relationship Group, as well as counseling for specific needs, like roommate issues or couples counseling. Managing the schedule for over 40 residents and about 20 staff is quite an undertaking in itself.

Great Escapes, a group designed to teach the clients how to plan and complete an outing, merits special attention. People with disabilities often have more time on their hands than the rest of us. They need to have skills in managing their leisure time, and those skills don't come naturally, as you might expect they would. Each Friday for three weeks in a row the Great Escapes group meets to select a destination, discuss the transportation, the options for lunch, the cost, the weather, and all other factors that affect a good plan. On the fourth Friday the group goes on the outing, with staff. The point is to have a good time and to expose the clients to activities they might not select on their own, such as museums and informational exhibits, as well as picnics, hikes, shopping, and parties. The process provides an opportunity to experience, through repetition and the reward of a good time, *the steps that make up a plan.* There is nothing as effective as a concrete experience to build the next experience upon.

At the end of the program day, clients are expected to manage their unscheduled time on their own. They must make their evening meal, socialize or be alone, stay in or go out, and get ready for bed without assistance. There is one staff person on hand from 6 to 9 pm to assist some clients with laundry and other chores that they may not have done during the day because they work. Sometimes that staff person organizes an activity, such as bingo or game night or a video, for those who want to participate. Clients may go out in the evening and many do so. Interestingly, those who are not confident about being out alone or out after dark rarely make the effort to change; rather, they accept the limitation unless someone else persuasively draws them out.

There are major league baseball, football, and basketball teams within reach by public transportation, and some of our clients are huge fans. Concert venues also appeal to our clients, who like to go out in unsupervised groups, just as other young adults do. We've even had some karaoke devotees. About a fourth of our clients have driver's licenses, and half of those maintain and drive their own cars. Despite all these accomplishments that seem to suggest normalcy, these clients have substantial disabilities that may be manifest at any point, during almost any activity. Living within the CAL program allows them to maximize the normal aspects of their lives and minimize the problem areas that cannot be "cured."

At 10 pm on weekdays there is curfew check for all but the most reliable and independent clients. We emphasize that the checking is a matter of safety, not control. When clients complain about being checked on, I have only to say to them, "What if your parents called and I had no idea where you were?" When it is pointed out, they see the necessity of staff knowing they are safe on the premises for the night. But soon enough they will voice the same complaint again, having forgotten the rationale; repetition is part of life at CAL. There is an emergency staff person available—living in an apartment in the same complex with the clients—who can be called in case of emergency during the night.

The program is structured to provide opportunities for families to vacation, have holidays together, and keep in touch about the same way other adults visit their parents. Like a college schedule, we have spring break, summer break, and winter break, totaling four weeks away from the program. Many parents plan vacations like cruises or camping, just as they might with their neurotypical kids who get married and produce grandchildren. In addition, the breaks provide a period of relaxation of the schedule for both staff and those clients who remain in their apartments. We maintain a minimal staff presence to monitor medications and respond to emergencies.

Finally, there is one most special day for CAL clients, families, and staff: the Annual Awards Ceremony, a day to celebrate the ongoing accomplishments of the clients. Each client receives an award related to the goals he or she has been working on for the past year. The awards can be as mundane as Most Improved in Doing Laundry Independently, or as impressive as Longest Time Employed at the Same Job. Parents are strongly encouraged to attend the event, even if they live across the country. Our intention is for this special day to make up for the school proms and parties, graduations and weddings, that our clients will likely not experience to cherish and mark their life's milestones.

Goals

Broadly speaking, the CAL program has one goal: to have each client reach his or her highest potential for independent living. More specifically, there are those whose goals include leaving CAL someday and those who make CAL their permanent home. For both groups, a therapeutic experience that leads to greater self-confidence and feelings of autonomy, membership in a group of one's peers, and the attainment of practical skills are paramount.

Employment is one of the most important practical accomplishments. We believe everyone can find some niche in which to be a meaningful participant in the greater community. Some of our clients are employed full-time or part-time in the commercial sector. Some are employed in enclaves (more about that later), and some do volunteer work, with or without supervision. As clients spend more time in employment, naturally they spend less time in the program day. This leads to a feeling of a more normal, unsupervised life, and our clients are very proud of making that transition, although many of those who are employed still keep one weekday free to attend the program, because it continues to be their best opportunity to receive assistance and to socialize with their peers.

There are many other goals that have to do with independence. Social behavior is an issue for most of our clients. Consistent with diagnoses on the autism spectrum and with the self-monitoring deficits described earlier, our clients have odd interpersonal behaviors. Some are dominated by impulsivity, which means the filter between thoughts and speech isn't activated quickly enough, or at all. These individuals say what they think without taking time to *decide* whether they really want to express each and every thought that flits through their minds. On the other end of the social spectrum, some of our clients are isolated and lonely because they have such a poor ability to connect with others. Generally, the mix of the community provides friendship for even the oddest members of the population.

Safety may be the most important goal of the program. There are so many ways for our clients to endanger themselves. Only a parent of this kind of child understands that statement. I know many professionals who complete comprehensive evaluations of these clients in a clinical setting, but I only know of one psychologist who, as part of his evaluations, goes out in public with the clients to observe how they behave in stores, on public transportation, and in other daily living situations. This kind of observation is invaluable. How else would you know that our clients might ask anyone on the street for a cigarette; or that our young men might walk up to a girl or a woman and make a sexual request in the crudest possible language? This is information that will never be provided in an interview—the clients simply don't know it's important enough to be mentioned.

Safety is a multilayered concept. There is personal safety in public on the streets. There is the safety of knowing how to assess one's own medical needs. There is financial ruin waiting around every corner for our clients, as they are offered credit cards, and goods and services on the internet. They are not aware when they've entered into an agreement to pay for something on the phone or via credit card, because the contractual language is presented so breezily and quickly, and they don't want to admit that they've failed to understand what's being asked of them. Bills that come in the mail intimidate them, so they often throw them away.

Even eating can be an unsafe activity in the lives of our clients. Junk food and soda—consumed all day long instead of water—can lead to early onset of diabetes, hypertension, high cholesterol, obesity, and tooth decay.

No discussion of safety can be complete without reference to drugs and alcohol. In the CAL program we do not allow drugs or alcohol on the premises. Our adult clients cannot be forbidden from drinking, as it is a legal activity. Drugs, of course, are illegal. We don't describe our approach as zero tolerance, but we do take strong action against drugs. If a client cannot give up drugs, even after repeated efforts, he has to be expelled from the program. Drug use is too destructive to the community as a whole. Over the years, we've expelled only a handful of clients due to drug abuse, probably because it requires planning and management of one's money to secure drugs on the street, not just once or twice, but to become a pattern of use. Our clients are not organized enough to be successful. In addition, they tend to be frightened by the people they meet in the world of street drugs. If not, they would likely not be candidates for our program because they would already be lost to the drug culture.

We go to great lengths to prevent clients' drinking and driving. Generally, there is a parent behind car ownership, and that parent can be enlisted to threaten to take the car away if the client drives after drinking. This is very effective and illustrates the way we work as a team with the parents of our clients. Cars serve as leverage, and we use natural consequences related to items that provide leverage, like cars, computers, cell phones, and the like.

The scourge of smoking is an issue of health and citizenship in our small community. Most of our clients are on low, fixed incomes. Cigarettes are too expensive to fit within their budgets. Some of our clients come from more affluent families and have budgets with much more leeway for luxuries. It is inevitable that cigarettes become barter under these circumstances. However, our clients are not really very good at bartering, in the sense of making a fair exchange of something else for cigarettes. So they beg and wheedle and make promises to those who can afford to supply cigarettes; then they usually don't repay the lender. We observe that those who can afford to provide cigarettes to their fellow smokers don't seem to feel exploited. The wealthy don't comprehend the value of money any more than those who have little—maybe even less so. So they give and give, without seeming to experience it as a burden, not understanding where their money comes from in the first place. It falls to the staff to try to stop what we perceive as exploitation of the more affluent clients. We try to teach them to say no to the many requests. We look forward to the day when there will be an easier method to quit smoking, and then we will insist that our remaining smokers quit.

The last issue of safety is one that I take up with some trepidation: the matter of safe sex. Most of our clients are not sexually active. This is partly because they have so few partners to pick from. As you probably know if you are familiar with this field, these disabilities affect males more than females, generally reported at a ratio of 4:1, perhaps 3:1. In the CAL program we currently have a ratio of closer to 2:1 males over females. Many of the clients want to have sexual experiences but they are unclear how to pursue them. Many want to have romantic relationships, whether sexual or not, with "normals," who are idealized; they disparage their own peers as partners. This is particularly sad because, in our experience, normal people will not engage in a romantic relationship with a person with disabilities severe enough to require supported living. The plain fact is that the two groups are not peers in a way that would lead to romance. So our clients go out seeking normals to date and they get rejected time after time. Many of our clients have discovered that people who attend church tend to be nice to newcomers, perhaps nicer than anywhere else. So they attend a church and pick out a woman to ask for a date. Sometimes the woman will agree to meet "as friends," but when she discovers the true intentions of the client, she inevitably finds a way out of the relationship, not even wanting to be friends. Since they do not understand what they did "wrong" to elicit this reaction, our clients come away hurt, confused, or angry. Eventually most of our clients face the prospect of finding a romantic or sexual partner within the CAL community, through leisure services for the disabled, or not at all.

We can only hope for the best in terms of safe sex. We do require that all the women have birth control methods in place, and not those methods that depend upon judgment at the moment. We teach classes on the importance of safe sex for disease prevention as well as prevention of pregnancy. However, we are realistic. We know that most of our clients are not able to manage condoms because of fine motor deficits or sensory-motor integration deficits, or simply because they won't practice enough to become skillful at it. If they are non-conserved adults, we cannot intervene in the management of their sexual activities, beyond the methods already mentioned. This is actually about the same situation as that of any parent of an 18-year-old who is determined to have sex. Many of our clients' parents have anticipated this problem and have instilled in their kids the conviction to have sex only in a committed relationship or to wait for marriage. Some clients seem content with that plan, though they don't really understand that they are unlikely to marry. Others profess to agree with their parents' injunction, but take the opportunity to have sex if it presents itself. Again, this is much the same as the situation in many families with non-disabled young people.

Sometimes our clients find people in the general public who have similar disabilities. They can have meaningful relationships with these individuals if they are presentable enough to be accepted by the parents or caregivers of the new friend. If the new acquaintance is not being cared for but is out on her own, this can be a hazard for our client, who may want to join her in the lifestyle of hand-to-mouth existence or even home-lessness. Again, this is when teamwork with parents enables us to keep our clients safe.

Chapter 15

The Clinical Methods of the Program

I'm tempted to call this section "Troubleshooting," as it seems that much of what we do, besides conducting the program according to the schedule, is strategize how to solve the myriad problems the clients create for themselves. I hope that describing the kinds of problems and the types of solutions we provide will be informative and helpful to those who are just beginning to raise a child with these kinds of disabilities. Also those who may be living with an adult still at home might find some helpful advice in this section. In fact, understanding the difficulties these clients get themselves into is part of learning to diagnose the disability. If your child would never do any of the things I'm about to discuss, the chances are that your child's disability is substantially different from those I'm dealing with. It may be helpful to think about the level of intellectual ability required to come up with the various kinds of schemes I'll be describing, and the level of verbal and other practical abilities required to accomplish them.

The most important factor in the way we as a professional staff deal with problems is that we don't take them personally. *That is, we are not personally affected by the very fact that the clients get into so much trouble.* One of the great stumbling blocks for parents is that they take their kids' mistakes personally. They imagine each mistake could have been prevented, if only…if only they had been more vigilant, or had anticipated more cleverly, or had not taken some time away for themselves. Also, parents hope for incremental improvement in areas that may never show improvement, or may show it at a heartbreakingly slow pace. The saddest waste of energy occurs when parents feel guilty. They feel guilty for the mistakes of their adult kids and then they feel guilty for their own feelings of disappointment, frustration, and anger. If you are reading this as a parent of a disabled adult, and you don't identify with this description, pat yourself on the back. You are the exception to the rule. You are doing your child a huge favor by not being filled with guilt!

Imagine how much better it is for adults with disabilities to know the person who is meant to help them out of trouble is not mad at them. Not mad, not disappointed, not guilty, not frustrated, not hurt. In fact, the main emotions we, staff, feel are compassion, respect, and humor. We feel compassion because it is impossible not to be aware of how difficult life is for these individuals. We feel respect because we know that each day when they get up, they know they are going to make mistakes, and it takes great courage to take on the day anyway. And we laugh a lot because the pre-dicaments the clients get into are so logical from their point of view, yet so dysfunctional at the same time. We feel great affection for the clients, even when they make their own typical mistakes over and over again. And, yes, we do feel frustration when our efforts to help sometimes go awry!

When CAL staff assist clients with the many tasks they can't manage on their own, we want the clients to feel no shame over needing assistance. It is appropriate for them to feel they have "their people" to help with various things, just as the rest of us might have our tax person or our thera-pist or our cleaning service. We don't feel inadequate when we get help. We decide we would rather pay for those services than learn to do them ourselves. Our clients did not have a choice about having a disability, and neither do they have a choice about needing assistance. But they should not have to feel worse than the rest of us who choose to seek help. They should be able to feel competent in knowing what kinds of help they need, accepting it, and using it.

Teaching, training, and protective management

A program that intends to teach and train individuals with disabilities should have interesting and effective methods at hand. Foremost is the need to keep in mind the nature of the disabilities we're dealing with. The execu-tive functions have been discussed in terms of initiation, planning and de-cision-making, organizing and sequencing, abstract versus concrete think-ing, regulation of attention and emotions, appreciation of consequences, problems with working memory, judgment, and self-monitoring. In teaching and training individuals with deficits in all these skills, many difficulties are encountered and must be solved creatively.

Teaching

Repetition is one of the simplest methods employed in teaching adults with disabilities. We repeat the lessons of healthy eating, safe sex, hygiene, avoiding exploitive people, and many others, over and over. With each repetition there is increased ability on the part of clients to *restate what they've heard*. This type of learning is most successful in areas that don't have to be translated into behavior. For example, in my brain class I've been able to teach the clients the names of the lobes of the brain, the basic functions of each lobe, the nutrients the brain needs for basic survival, the names of the five senses, what a stroke is, and many more facts. I teach with a very dramatic, emotional style, to hold their attention. I let them call their answers out loud and I'm emphatically appreciative of correct answers. There is no reason for the clients not to want to learn about the brain in our setting, and most of them are very successful. Many clients watch television shows about animals, cooking, home improvement, crime, etc., and they can learn in that way just like their non-disabled peers.

A second type of learning that is successful with this population involves situations that are inherently dramatic. We can teach what to do in various emergency situations with confidence. We recently had a flooded bathroom (due to poor judgment) that resulted in three adjacent apartments requiring new carpet. The resident of the first apartment had heard the sound of water running, but decided to ignore it and go to bed. The bathtub overflowed all night long. We realized we needed to teach what to do when water is leaking from any faucet or appliance in an apartment. We showed each client where the shut-off valves are located and taught them to turn them off. (Note that left-handers need to be taught by left-handed demonstration. We learned that the hard way.)

Clients who have learned to shut off the water at the valve will know how to do this even if the need doesn't occur for years. First of all, the occurrence of a leak or an overflow is dramatic enough to pull their focus forcefully; second, there is no motivation not to do the right thing. In many more mundane situations, the clients have learned what to do, but are motivated to do something more gratifying, like buying candy instead of groceries.

Rote learning in a stimulating setting, and recalling emergency responses, are successful areas for teaching and learning with our population. But what happens when we try to teach all those practical things like safe sex and healthy eating habits? Learning and putting the lessons into practice are two very different matters for those who have executive deficits. It is a hallmark of executive function impairment to be verbally articulate and yet unable or unlikely to act upon ideas, even those stated by oneself. Simply put, many times our clients can say it but they can't do it. Furthermore, they lack awareness that most people expect actions to be consistent with words, so they don't understand why parents and others are exasperated by their failure to do what they talk about doing.

How can this be? It seems so basic that a person with normal or almost normal intelligence would know that most people say what they intend to do and do as they say as a matter of course. And that repeatedly not doing what you promise will cause ruptured relationships, anger, and loss of respect. The problem is: the person with executive deficits doesn't link behavior with *discussions* of behavior. Recall that the person with disabilities can generally do only one cognitive thing at a time. When the one thing he is doing is talking, then the action under discussion is not being engaged. When the time comes to do the action, then the talking (and thinking) will not be taking place. *There is a disconnection between talking now and doing later.* So when clients talk in class about the best thing to do in a given situation, they sound smart and correct. But when it becomes time to do that very thing, they often behave as if they were on autopilot toward the most selfish or foolish possible outcome.

Shopping for a gift provides an illustration. We employ practice sessions to help clients buy gifts for family members. The clients are able to learn about selecting a gift that will please the recipient and fit within a budget while they are in class. But once they are in a store and are enticed by many things they would like to own, they are likely to abandon their plans to purchase a gift and instead buy something for themselves. They have not forgotten what they learned in class; they are revealing that the two events, learning and doing, are not connected.

We used to make meal plans in a group. Healthy eating was explained over and over. Meals were planned with emphasis on health and on ease of preparation, as well as personal preference. Shopping lists were prepared to fit the meal plans. The need for the occasional treat was recognized and items like cookies or ice cream were allowed in moderation. Lists in hand, the clients would go off to the grocery store. But once they arrived, most

181

of them would buy whatever they saw that grabbed their attention, completely ignoring the list. Even when staff accompanied them, they ignored the plan, filled their baskets with whatever they wanted, and became angry at staff for even reminding them of the list. We learned, by repetition you might say, that the clients could not hold a plan in their minds that was compelling enough to override their impulses when confronted with so much food that they wanted. Of course, there are some clients who can and do go to the grocery store weekly and buy according to plan, but they are the minority. For the others, we now buy food online. It is a matter of accepting what is pointless to fight.

What, then, is our level of faith in repetition as a teaching tool? It feels important to repeat lessons, advice, and so on because the lessons are obviously so difficult to master. We repeat ourselves exhaustively, and after many repetitions we do see some acquired learning. But the difficulty of teaching to this population leads naturally to the next technique.

Training

Training involves doing. If you want someone to learn to make a bed, you could describe a well-made bed, but you would get better results by going to the bedroom and demonstrating bed-making. Then you would have the student of bed-making do it himself. Many repetitions of bed-making lead to the achievement of a learned skill. Making the bed the same way every day at about the same time is the development of a habit. Training plus willing repetition equals a habit.

Routine is the greatest ally in the management of executive deficits. We use structure and routine as essential shortcuts for training in groups. More than the rest of us, our clients are dependent on routines because it is too difficult for them to think through every step of every day. We promote routine in the lives of our clients in planning the day, apartment chores, food and exercise, medication management, and money.

The CAL program schedule is designed to utilize routine and structure. Each client has a schedule filled with activities, hour by hour. The biggest difficulty is in adequately supervising the living skills time, the attention to chores that keep the environment safe and pleasant. A simple list of chores would be making one's bed, throwing away trash, keeping the floor clear of everything but furniture and shoes, doing laundry and keeping clothing where it belongs, and keeping surfaces reasonably uncluttered and clean. Kitchens and bathrooms have their own obvious lists of chores. Some of the clients, who have a natural preference for a tidy environment, easily learn a routine for doing chores. Others, who aren't good at cleaning and don't have built in motivation, need lots of supervision.

The stages employed in the training of multi-stage tasks like living skills are observation of the initial level of ability, training for improvement or efficiency, cueing to initiate the tasks, and checking to see that the client stays on task. The extra ingredient that keeps the endeavor from being simple is personal variability. Everyone has a personal style in everything they do; those with disabilities are especially variable. So we see some who are pleased to learn how to do things and we see some who balk at any and all suggestions. The art of training is to manage personal quirks so that the strengths of the client are emphasized and the limitations are circumvented or accommodated.

In essence, most of the growth and improvement, achievements and accomplishments of clients with executive deficits amount to the replacement of bad or inefficient habits with better habits. Because of poor ability to initiate and to think analytically, clients cannot be told what *not* to do without also being told what *to do*. In the world of normal adults, we can often proceed as if the solution is implied by a description of the problem: don't leave your socks on the floor, please, implies that the one spoken to will be able to figure out where to put his dirty socks. With a small child, you might be more specific about the solution: don't wipe your nose on your sleeve, please. Use a tissue. This is the way it must be with our clients, only even more concretely than with a child: if you (an adult) wipe your nose on your sleeve in public, people will be disgusted and will make fun of you, so you must always have a tissue with you. Eventually, the client who carries tissues and uses them will have replaced the bad habit of wiping his nose on anything handy with the good habit of using a tissue. This is one way we see progress in our population.

Teaching and training, building habits, repetition and the use of routine and structure, take us as far as we can go with each client according to his or her abilities. But what happens when we hit the limits of any given client's ability to learn and to exercise self-control? The method we use at that point is protective management.

Protective management

Perhaps because we are speaking of adult clients, it makes some people uneasy to contemplate clients being managed (controlled). The helping professions, particularly psychotherapy, stress that people should be helped toward making their own choices. Empowerment is a popular concept, stressing each person's right to make his own decisions and to be in control of his or her life.

It is important to remember, when thinking about management, that our clients are adults with intellectual abilities in the normal or borderline range, but with severely impaired logic and judgment. That means they have the intellectual power to maneuver themselves into all manner of trouble, far beyond what the mentally retarded could do, but they don't have the judgment to solve the problems they create for themselves. When children do the types of things our clients do, parents take control of their lives. As adults, our clients don't look as if they should be managed; but in many instances their safety depends upon just that.

Money is the first issue most people will concede must be managed. After many incidents involving money spent foolishly, most family members of adults with disabilities are adamant about the need to take control away from the individual. Actually, the expectation for management by another party is built into the system whereby persons with disabilities receive government benefits. Most social security checks issued to the mentally retarded, the mentally ill, and others, including my clients, are managed by a designated payee. The widespread use of designated payees indicates that persons with disabilities are not expected to be able to manage finances. The need for help—protective management—is obvious in this instance.

It should not be difficult to imagine other aspects of life that can be truly dangerous when mismanaged. Our female clients all use birth control. We cannot force anyone to use birth control, but they may not live in the CAL community if they (or their parents) don't agree with the value of preventing pregnancy. Using their own judgment, many would have numerous unplanned pregnancies. Similarly, when they drive a car, we feel a moral imperative to make sure they don't drive while under the influence of alcohol or drugs. Do they have the right to make their own choices and suffer the consequences of their behavior? Some might say yes, but in situations of great consequence, we do not.

Interestingly, I rarely encounter parents who object to the management our program provides their loved ones. Parents know their children, and they know that our control over some aspects of their lives allows them the amount of independence, and safety, they cherish for their loved ones. The objection to such management is generally an abstract idea based upon a general notion of personal rights, and is expressed by people with no real stake in the individuals' lives. Mostly, objections stem from the misguided expectation that adults who look pretty normal wouldn't really do things that are so dangerous or unhealthy or illegal. And even if they do make some mistakes, they will learn from the consequences of those mistakes, the argument goes. Unfortunately, our clients don't function that way. They are capable of making the same mistake over and over, and still not coming up with a new strategy. The belief that "hitting bottom" produces change does not apply in the presence of executive function deficits.

Carl is a middle-aged man who has had diabetes for about 15 years. He learned easily how to monitor his blood glucose level, which involves pricking his finger and applying the drop of blood to a meter that then displays a number. He knows which numbers are too high, and he knows, in theory, that food causes the numbers to go up. But he cannot grasp the connection between high numbers and damage to his body. He feels no pain so he doesn't believe anything scary is happening to him. He is aware of the anxiety and frustration of those who love him because they question him repeatedly about what he has eaten to cause his numbers to be so high. After years of watching Carl be unwilling to eat properly and unable to comprehend that damage is occurring, damage that will eventually lead to his death, both his family and staff concluded that his meals need to be managed. But managing every morsel of food Carl eats is difficult and so demeaning to him that we have reached a compromise. We control his food during the week and we allow him some leeway on the weekends. Otherwise he would become so depressed and resentful that his quality of life would be even worse than his health. There are many issues that must be experienced to reach a compromise of this sort.

Leverage is the tool that assists us when we need to manage a behavioral manifestation of the executive function disabilities. We most prefer the leverage to be a naturally occurring feature of the client's life, and not something we have to cook up, like a bribe. Justin is a client who has worked for many years and is proud of owning his own car. His mother is his payee, and she is very savvy about how and when to use the leverage of the car to manage her son's difficulties. Recently he wanted to cut back his hours at his job. In his mid-forties now, he only works two hours per day, and would be completely idle if he were to lose the job by asking for a decrease in his hours. He seemed to be interested in a woman in the program and he probably wanted to spend more time with her, though he would not admit that was his reason for wanting to work less. When our clients become obsessed with a plan or scheme, they find it difficult to pay attention to other things of importance. Justin is quite determined (and rigid), and he could have begun a campaign of missing work and manipulating the situation. Instead, he was told by his mother that if he cut back his hours, he couldn't afford to make his car payment, which he actually made to her each month. One warning that his car could be "repossessed" caused him to recommit to his job.

Justin's mother has told us she will never let him know when his car has been paid for because she would lose that leverage. He will continue to make his car payments to her, and she will save the money for his emergencies. She has been able to pay for very expensive dental care for him, care that would not have been covered by his government benefits, because she had managed and saved his money in this way. She feels no guilt for this type of management by deception; in fact, she worries that no one else will do the same if she dies before Justin does.

Leverage can be employed without involving deception. One female client loves to attend rock concerts. After finding out that she had gotten drunk at a concert and accepted a ride with a stranger, we banned her from concerts for a period of time. When she asked what she could do to earn the right to attend concerts again, we realized we could require almost anything, such was the leverage. It turned out that she had become lax about brushing her teeth, so we required that her teeth be brushed before Morning Meeting every day for a month before she could attend a concert again. Of course, the main goal was that she not get drunk or accept rides from strangers, but she had learned that lesson by suffering the real consequence of fear. The management and leverage allowed us to emphasize the danger of her previous behavior and to achieve something else for her own good.

Adults with disabilities encounter many issues with which they will need assistance. Whether they are living with parents or in group homes, programs, or other supported living situations, they will continue to need help and, in some areas, protective management. Help can be provided through a complex intermingling of the individual's skills and abilities and the creativity and resourcefulness of the various support staffs. Before discussing some specific issues and methods for dealing with them, let's look at counseling as it applies to our population.

Chapter 16

Counseling

At the Center for Adaptive Learning (CAL) we have developed a model of counseling that is similar to cognitive behavioral therapy, but with our own modifications. This adapted method of counseling, tailored to individuals with executive deficits, has been taught to staff and numerous interns who have trained in our program.

The weekly counseling our clients receive is one of the most important and untypical innovations developed by our Executive Director, Genevieve Stolarz. Genevieve realized early on in her son's life that he had all the feelings of any other human being, but that he experienced, processed, and expressed those feelings differently from "normals." It was through her life with her son that she realized counseling would have to be tailored to his ability to use it. Genevieve intuitively knew that traditional counseling, especially the hallmark feature of complete privacy between client and therapist, would not work for her son and for others like him.

After 20 years of refining the therapeutic process, we can say that the executive functions have to be understood as part of any therapeutic endeavor. Insight and self-monitoring, and the ability to analyze the behavior of oneself and others in an incident, and to intuit and analyze the feelings of all participants, are important elements of the typical counseling situation. Since those functions are not intact in our clients, they must be brought into the counseling setting by the clinician. In other words, the clinician must know enough about the life of the client to bring insight and surrogate self-monitoring into the clinical conversations with the client. To do that, she must know much more about the daily life of her clients than any therapist could possibly know without observing them living their lives on a daily basis. For these reasons, CAL employs staff counselors who see their clients in the therapeutic milieu, in various settings throughout the week, in addition to their counseling sessions.

The CAL staff therapists not only provide counseling but also lead some of the scheduled classes, groups, and activities. They come to know all the clients, not just the ones in their own caseload. They know the milieu, the grapevine, the social hierarchy, and the problems and successes the clients are experiencing in all service domains, not just social/emotional behavior. The therapist knows the problems each client faces and what goals they should be working toward. In fact, counseling goals and objectives are explicitly stated as part of each client's Individual Program Plan (IPP) each year. But staff counselors know when clients have a more urgent need than the ongoing attention to the goals and objectives of the program plan, and they can set aside the ongoing goals to work instead on whatever aspect of daily life has become problematic. This is invaluable.

Our way of handling confidentiality is the first departure from traditional counseling or psychotherapy. As most people know, privacy between the therapist and the client is a cornerstone of psychotherapy and most of its variants. There are, however, situations in which confidentiality is modified and limited. Large clinics which serve the same clients for many years, clients with chronic mental illnesses, have charts that are passed on from therapist to therapist depending upon who is available to see the patient on any given day and over a period of years when personnel may change. Similarly, in facilities like in-patient hospital wards, therapeutic group homes, halfway houses, alcohol treatment centers, and board and care homes, there are many issues that are known to all members of the facility because they occur in the milieu. In those cases, confidentiality is maintained between the facility and the outside world, but everyone within the treatment confines knows that confidentiality is not maintained within. The trust issue regarding confidentiality is that there must not be a violation of an *expectation* for confidentiality. When the limits of confidentiality are clearly understood, then there is no betrayal of trust.

All staff are expected to know about each client's relevant history, his goals in counseling, and the methods that will be used to overcome his problems and interpersonal issues with other clients. There is very little focus on privacy in the program because the clients tell one another everything that is on their minds, and are generally incapable of keeping secrets for themselves or for one another. When they occasionally ask their counselor if a bit of information is likely to become known to the community, the counselor is trained to ask them, "Who have you already told?" Invariably, they have told the person most likely to spread the story! The question is on their mind for that very reason.

Here is an example of a therapeutic interaction that exemplifies the CAL method. Recently a client was reported to be shoplifting in stores near the program. The reports were made by his friends, other clients. In session, the counselor brought up that she had found out about the shoplifting and needed to talk with the client about it. So the first difference from traditional counseling was that the client did not initiate the topic. The counselor brought up something she felt needed to be discussed. She admitted she had been told about the problem by another client. The counselor asked if it was true, and the client replied that he was taking things from stores but that it didn't "count" as shoplifting because, well, because of one reason after another. When a store is going out of business you're practically doing them a favor to take things they need to get rid of. When the item is tiny it doesn't count, and when it's extremely inexpensive, say ten cents, it doesn't count.

As you can imagine, this was interesting and, in a way, amusing to the counselor, but she certainly considered it her job to get the man to stop shoplifting for his own safety. So she tried a scare tactic, albeit in a supportive way. She said she was afraid it would be very embarrassing and frightening if the police were called and he was arrested. The client answered, "They don't do that. They just make you sign a paper that you won't come back to the store anymore." That remark revealed, obviously, that the client had been caught and subjected to that process. The client would never have offered that part, in fact any part of the story, if it hadn't come out the way it did, step by step. Finally, the counselor said, "Well, what would your father say about all this?" He replied that his father would definitely be upset. That allowed for the only crack in the insistent reasoning of the client, that what he was doing wasn't really wrong. *Why would your father be upset if it isn't wrong?*

As you can see from this example, the element that led to a therapeutic impact on the client was the lack of privacy surrounding the situation. Privacy would not have led to a positive outcome. First of all, the client's friends reported the shoplifting directly to his counselor. In our therapeutic community we support a notion of citizenship that includes telling staff what they need to know to help others who may be in danger. Sometimes when they tell on one another their motivation is not so high-minded.

Nevertheless, when someone is engaged in a dangerous behavior, staff will hear about it sooner or later. So the client's counselor knew about the shoplifting and was able to bring it up in his individual counseling. It did not seem unusual or unfair to the client that others had told about his shoplifting. If he had expressed anger at the client who told on him, the counselor might have engaged in thinking out loud. This is a process that utilizes the executive functions of the counselor in place of those of the client. She, the counselor, might have said something like, "I know that Ralph is your friend and I think a friend would tell staff what you did so that staff could help you. I don't think Ralph would want to see something bad happen to you."

Involvement in the community also allows the staff counselor to know whether the reporter is truly a friend of the client. If she knew that the two were not friends, and that the reporting was in fact malicious, then she could use that information in the "thinking out loud" process. She might say, "I know you and Ralph don't get along, so he might have been trying to get you in trouble. But you and I can use the information to try to keep you safe." It gives the counselor additional credibility to have gotten that part right, and not to have to guess about the likely motivations of the reporting client.

The absence of confidentiality extends to staff counselors knowing how the client is doing in other domains of service, and they also use this information to the client's benefit in counseling. For example, if a client had not been doing her chores lately and her roommate was upset with her, the counselor would know the real story and not be deceived by a self-justifying version from either client.

Relationships among the clients come into the counseling sessions constantly, with the counselors being privy to everything that is known on the grapevine, so to speak. If a client is having difficulties with her room-mate or her boyfriend, it is beneficial for the counselor to know the truth behind the issues. Knowing the effects of another client's disability may be especially valuable in the sessions. For example, one attractive woman is well-liked by most of the community, but she has a hard time with friend-ship because she doesn't follow through on plans. One by one the clients have befriended her and then become disillusioned with the friendship and angry when she disappoints them. A staff counselor is able to offer a solution by thinking through the problem (out loud); she knows the issue for the disappointed client cannot be solved in a normal way. Those who remain friends with the woman who can't meet obligations do so in spite of her inconsistency, not because of being able to solve it. So the counselor may ask suggestive questions like "How many others in the community have the same problem with Doris? Do you think maybe she just can't keep promises the way the rest of you can? Can you be friends with her without making plans? Maybe she's someone you can just hang out with when you see her instead of making plans with her." (An off-site counselor might spend time suggesting ways for her client to work at the friendship, or she might suggest different interpretations of the other client's behavior. None of this would be helpful.)

Another controversial aspect of confidentiality is the inclusion of the parents or other family members in the treatment team. In traditional treatment of children, it is necessary to keep parents informed in a general way about the treatment without violating the child's privacy. Experienced therapists have ways of balancing the parents' need to know how treatment is going and the privacy rights of the client. With our autism spectrum clients, there are similarities to the treatment of children. The parents have generally needed to manage their adult offspring somewhat like children. They have made major decisions for their kids and have had to take responsibility for many mistakes made by them. Therefore, it would be quite worrisome to most parents to be shut out of their adult kids' counseling. In addition, the parents would expect to be allowed to supply vital information from time to time.

In the program, we encourage all parties to think in terms of a team composed of the client, parents and other family members, and all staff working together. The team counselor isn't any more or any less likely than other team members to discuss the client's issues with the family. The living skills staff may call a parent to explain that the client broke his Game Boy, and the conversation can become therapeutic as they discuss what stressors may have led to his throwing the gadget across the room. Everything that happens in the community is understood to be potentially therapeutic, depending upon how it is analyzed and handled. Nevertheless, there are times when a client will ask his counselor to keep a bit of information secret and the counselor can usually agree to do so. Invariably, though, the information will be circulating on the grapevine within hours or days, and the client himself has spread it, usually telling "only" three or four people.

So, confidentiality is modified in our model of counseling. What about trust and support? Our clients are generally eager to enter into a trusting relationship with any well-meaning adult. Anyone who comes to work for our program is unusual in having an interest in this population in the first place. Often they have personal reasons for choosing this field, a sibling or child of their own with similar disabilities, for example. The counselors I've known and trained have found it extremely rewarding and enjoyable to work with these clients. They like the clients and the clients can feel their regard and their warmth. So trust is not a problem.

Support can be a bit different, as the clients sometimes feel "policed" by the staff. But they tend to be situation-specific when they get angry at staff. In other words, the same person who takes away a gallon bottle of soda may see the client an hour later in a learning group or in counseling. The client will generally enter into the relationship with the emotions that fit the context. However, if a particular client dislikes a particular staff member from the very first meeting, the relationship usually cannot be altered. It is as if a decision has been made on a level that is not accessible to change. This is an effect I saw in acquired brain injury clients as well. It simply has to be worked around. There are plenty of counseling match-ups, and flexibility is built into our system.

I've mentioned several techniques that are employed in counseling with this population. Questioning in a step-by-step manner helps the clients see how to think through a situation; thinking out loud by the therapist helps the client see how one might feel about the motives and behavior of oth-ers, among other things. Following the logic of the counseling goals and objectives can be difficult for the client, even when they are his goals. For instance, a client may be very clear that his goal is to have a girlfriend. The counselor helps break the goal down into tasks that will achieve what he wants. She may suggest learning how to talk with a woman you like. The client will agree to this in the moment, but later will forget why making conversation relates to his real goal of having a girlfriend (or having sex). He will need to be reminded over and over that he can't just approach a woman and say he likes her and would like her to be his girlfriend and have sex. A staff counselor will be aware of his failed efforts, and may even be able to set up opportunities for him to apologize for mistakes and earn a second chance with a woman.

Having staff counselors allows us to bring together clients who need to communicate to solve a problem. If a client says her roommate stole her food, we can walk a few yards to her apartment and see how the situation looks. We can bring the roommates together and do a session of roommate problem-solving on the spot. We support client relationships by catching difficulties as they are developing, rather than on a certain day at a certain time, when all may be forgotten.

Another goal of in-house counseling at CAL is to help the clients identify and develop feelings that don't come automatically to them. Empathy is particularly difficult for those on the autism spectrum to feel because it requires setting aside their self-focus to focus on the dilemma of another. We encourage the development of those feelings the same way a mother of much smaller children does, by asking them how the same situation would feel if they were the victim. We ask what would you want others to do for you in this situation. If the clients are able to focus and listen to the questions, then they are able to produce the right answers. Whether they respond more appropriately when staff are not around is, of course, the long-term test. As far as I have been able to determine, our program is unique in placing so much importance on the social-emotional development of our clients; the only program to have a licensed psychologist, and counselors in training, on staff, in-house, full time.

Chapter 17

Specific Issues and Methods Employed at CAL

The order in which the following issues are presented requires a word of explanation. The important matter of clients being unreliable reporters of information, in other words often being wrong, and sometimes lying, will be discussed first because it is so central to understanding all the other issues. Having an understanding of the many ways the clients misperceive, misinterpret, and remember poorly will be a key to understanding their behavior in all other areas. I offer this explanation because it seems mean-spirited to appear to pounce on one of their most (seemingly) unappealing traits right off the top. But the only way to view this fascinating aspect of our clients' disability is with a desire to understand, not to be critical. It is in that spirit that I offer the following stories and interpretations. It will help to keep in mind the methods already described in terms of teaching, training, counseling, and management that we employ in general, as a backdrop to the specific methods that will be described here.

Lying and being wrong

It's probably best to admit that we all lie from time to time, and clients on the autism spectrum are no exception. But there are important differences in the way adults with disabilities lie, and particularly in the many other ways they get things wrong.

Being wrong when not intentionally lying is an interesting feature of our clients' disability. *Perceptual errors and dysregulation of attention and emotions, and judgment problems, and memory problems can cause these clients to misunderstand circumstances, including their own role in events.* As seen in the upcoming example of the mysterious traveling check, our clients often focus on a different feature of an event than what we would consider the salient feature. They can only report, then, on the parts of the event that grabbed their attention and were saved in memory.

A member of our community might relate, for example, that his neighbor is playing his music too loud in the middle of the night. But the situation is likely not so clear-cut. If the reporting client has been sound asleep, wakes up, and hears music, he will conclude that the music is too loud just because he woke up and it was the first thing he noticed; and he will conclude that it was the middle of the night, also just because he had been asleep and was awakened. Most of us would stop to try to figure out whether the music, or perhaps something else, caused our sleep to be disturbed. We would listen carefully to determine if the music was truly very loud. And, more importantly, we would make some kind of judgment about the loudness of the music in relation to the time of night. At 9 pm it's more acceptable for a neighbor's music to be a little loud than after midnight. Most of us would actually look at a clock to see what time it is. Our clients would do none of these things. Instead, they might yell through the wall at their neighbor, or they might call the emergency staff.

Staff then have to serve as the frontal lobes in the situation and ask the questions just mentioned: what time do you think it is, does the music really sound so loud now that you're wide awake, and so on. The subject of lying might pop up the next day, as the accused client will say the other was lying because the music was actually not very loud. The notion of a difference of opinion, or different tolerance for noise, would not occur to the clients. Those are abstractions. They could be comprehended by the clients if suggested by staff, but they are not likely to be considered during the heightened emotions of the original situation.

Memory errors that lead to being wrong are very easily imagined. Our clients typically have short-term memory deficits. As mentioned earlier, short-term memory is defined as the time and effort needed to store a new telephone number long enough to dial it. In real life, short-term memory is the kind of memory we use throughout the day in dealing with everyday activities. We might see someone discussing a new movie on television and decide we'd like to see it over the weekend. We make a determination, with our normally organized brain functioning, as to whether we will remember the movie we want to see. We can probably judge quite well whether we will remember the movie when we want to, or if we should make a note and leave it where we will find it at the right time.

Our clients often have deficits in short-term memory because they are not efficient in storing information and, especially, in choosing what to store, purposefully. Because their minds are generally disorganized, and they have difficulty with sequencing the steps toward a chosen outcome, it doesn't occur to them to choose to store bits of information that will come in handy later. Information is accessible or not, later on, based upon concrete images that have stuck without being purposefully memorized. All of this leads to the explanation that clients will give each other wrong information based on these kinds of memory storage and retrieval problems. And then, depending upon various factors in the situation, the client who was given wrong information is likely to call the other a liar.

There is another way of being wrong that is specific to the clients who have Asperger's Syndrome. They tend to be very poor at what is called pragmatic language, including tone of voice, use of idioms, sarcasm, and facetiousness. On the other hand, they tend to have good rote memory, so they may accurately repeat a conversation between two other people, conveying the point to the listener while completely missing it themselves. Those without Asperger's can also make errors in deciphering nonverbal aspects of communication because of the difficulty of doing two things at the same time. If they are attending to the concrete meaning of the words, they may not be able to access another "channel" that could be providing valuable information through, for example, tone of voice. Most of us can take in word meanings and tone of voice simultaneously, but those with executive impairments often cannot do this. This is most obvious when a client quotes others and reveals (to staff, at least) that she has completely missed the point due to failing to decipher a bit of sarcasm. For example, we might question a client's choice of a particular outfit because it looks too tight. The client will quote one of the fashion leaders of our community, stating, "But Mary said this shirt looks really big on me!" In this instance, the woman quoting her friend is not lying, but failed to "hear" sarcasm.

When our clients lie intentionally, they generally lie in the manner of very young children. Some of them lie without any regard for the low likelihood of getting away with the lie. Some lie without consideration of the consequences to others, even serious consequences. They lie to avoid getting in trouble, to avoid responsibilities, and to get things they want. When parents have done a good job of teaching their kids not to lie, especially not to authority figures, it can be seen in the adult's behavior. Their rare attempts to lie are accompanied by fear and fumbling. And they cave in and tell the truth when pressed ever so lightly. On the other hand, those who lie with ease and with no conscience have been lying all their lives. The past can be seen in the present.

So what do we do about the lying we encounter from some of the clients? We get to know our clients individually and learn that their lying, like other aspects of their personalities, has a consistent quality with their other behavior. There are standard lies told over and over by the same clients in the same manner for the same reasons. One wants the day off work to watch a playoff game, so he relies on illness except that he actually says he's going to be sick tomorrow without even pretending to be sick now. Another denies that she begged a cigarette from another client and adds, "You can ask him, he'll tell you the same thing." She doesn't realize she's revealing that the two clients have already discussed telling staff "the same thing" instead of telling the truth. When we say, "You're lying," which we do often, the clients tend to insist they're telling the truth, but not very forcefully. However, when someone is accused of lying who often does lie, but happens not to be at that moment, the righteous indignation is something to behold. You can tell immediately that they were actually innocent that one time because of the difference in the quality of the denial.

Generally, the clients either lie frequently, or they don't have much of a problem with lying. And this difference I attribute partly to early training and partly to the type of inner resources the client has. One client who had exemplary training in childhood, after he was adopted, is one of the chronic liars in the program. I think his lying stems from his early years of deprivation in an orphanage. He was forced to rely on his wits and survival skills literally to stay alive. I believe he doesn't even think he is lying so much as telling a plausible version of events that might make things go his way. He is very offended when accused of lying. And he frequently defends his stories by saying that if someone else tells it differently, that person is lying. It is important to understand that this type of lying does not resemble that of a psychopathic personality type, who lies to gain something material or some advantage over others. It is as if our clients fall into lying instead of purposefully relying on it as a tactic.

We don't really have much trouble managing the lies told by clients, but we sometimes have a problem with the parents of those who chronically lie, or otherwise get things wrong. A few months after their adult kids are placed with us, parents tend to forget some of the daily troubles they had when their adult child lived at home. They knew he lied to them, but after the separation, they seem to think he has become truthful. He calls them and claims something bizarre occurred at the program, and they believe him. We've been accused of some of the most comical things. I will generally say to the parent, "Does that sound plausible to you?" After they reconsider and see that the story isn't plausible, they have a range of reactions to the obvious implication that their child caused the confusion. Some parents just sigh with disappointment upon realizing they unconsciously believed in a greater level of improvement than is possible. Others are too defensive to accept that truth; and some are able to laugh at the situation and at themselves for being both hopeful and gullible.

On the other hand, some parents trust us and work with us to solve the problems of misperception and lying. Suzy was having a dispute with her roommate about the posters each had contributed to decorating the apartment. I suggested that her counselor and the living skills staff person go to the apartment with large pieces of paper with the initial of each roommate on several pages. They placed one large initial on each poster that belonged to that person. I felt that a visual representation would be more convincing than just saying who owned each item. When they were done, there were Ss for Suzy on seven posters and Ps for her roommate on two items. Suzy could then see how unfair the situation was. Staff suggested some ways that the posters could be moved around, more of Suzy's going into her bedroom, for example.

The next day I received a call from Suzy's mother asking for my explanation, as she had heard this: "They're making me throw away all my posters and they told me not to tell you!" I understood that posters were to be moved, not thrown away, but I couldn't explain the part about not telling her mother. I did believe there was a logical explanation, though, and said so to the mom. She agreed that Suzy has a tendency to get anxious about any change, and is then likely to have distorted perceptions. I questioned the staff as to what had been said about Suzy not telling her mother about this incident. Suzy had told the living skills staff person that she needed to call her mother while they were labeling the posters. The staff person had said, in an attempt to encourage Suzy's independence, "Don't you think you can do this by yourself?" Suzy was so anxious about the change, and perhaps about seeing that she had been unfair to her roommate, that she distorted both the plans for the posters and the intent of the remark about handling the problem without calling her mother.

Suzy's mother did not call staff with an accusation, but rather with the full knowledge that her daughter was probably misperceiving and distorting. However, many parents would have called with a real head of steam about staff throwing away their kid's belongings, because that is what their child said. No one wants to have to second-guess their own child for the rest of her life, but that is reality with this kind of disability.

You may wonder what we as a staff do about all this promulgating wrong information, as well as the intentional lying. Well, it depends. It depends upon what effect we think we can have on the behavior. If a client lies about having finished his chores, staff may say, "You know I can go to your apartment and check on what you're telling me." Some of the more disingenuous would say, at that point, "No, don't look, I'm not really finished yet, but I'll do it." They would not then appear to feel any guilt about being caught in a lie unless staff said, "Wow, you just lied to me." Then they might look a little guilty. Here's the interesting part: I believe they really would not know they had lied if it hadn't been pointed out. That is a failure of self-monitoring at the most basic level. Remember, self-monitoring means having awareness and judgment about your own behavior while you're doing it. In this case the primary behavior is the conversation with staff about chores; the lie is an automatic response to avoid "getting in trouble;" self-monitoring would be awareness of one's primary behavior, the conversation with staff including lying, while doing it. Because our clients cannot self-monitor, staff provide an external monitor by pointing out obvious lies. Or we might say, "I'm going to ask you a question and I want you to be sure not to lie." This gives the client a little reminder to think before speaking. With a thousand repetitions, the habit of thinking before speaking might take root.

Lies committed in the service of a scheme are handled, like so much of what we do, with a focus on real consequences. We don't do a lot of moralizing to our clients because we think that implying they have done something "bad" in an abstract theoretical way is not very useful to them. However, if a client lies to another client, we are quick to point out the effects of getting a reputation as a liar or as one who reneges on promises. We paint a picture of a concrete consequence that could happen. For example, clients who have cars are often lied to about favors that will be granted in exchange for rides. When the time comes for the favor and the person reneges, we will say, "Well, I hope you don't expect him ever to give you a ride again." Sometimes the one with the car will give rides repeatedly and become very frustrated about the failure to have favors returned. We will say to him, "I guess she knows how to manipulate you. How many times do you think you'll go through this before you decide to collect the favor first?" We are coaching each client toward a different behavior, serving as the frontal lobes that would, in a normal brain, do that kind of thinking internally and independently.

We rarely punish clients, unless they are behaving in a truly childish manner. Punishment implies an imbalance of power that isn't usual in most adults' lives. Except for punishments meted out by the legal system, most adults have to suffer the consequences of their behavior where and when it occurs. Usually this is at work, in public, or with loved ones and friends. We want the clients to feel as much as possible like their non-disabled peers living in "the real world." So we try to get them to provide consequences to one another in a realistic and fair way. The example above illustrates the way staff tried to shape the behavior of the driver and the behavior of the favor-seeker by predicting the consequences they each might suffer.

The disastrous Friday night dinner is a good example of the clients providing consequences to one another. Gloria was new to the community and she brought some habits with her that were extremely dysfunctional. She was invited to the informal Friday night dinner. This is a situation in which some of the more independent clients eat at a real restaurant, rather than a fast-food place, and they take pride in passing for normal as a group. They don't tolerate behavior that might expose them as disabled. Gloria was asked very pointedly if she had enough money to pay for her dinner. She stated that she did. But when the check came, Gloria said she didn't have any money after all. She was lying, but the others didn't know how to ascertain that. When they insisted she pay her share, and she insisted she couldn't, a standoff developed. The clients who cared about public embarrassment were horrified when Gloria suddenly put her head down on the table and cried. Someone quickly produced Gloria's share of the bill so that they could leave. As they arrived back at the apartments, Gloria admitted she had the money all along. She said she wanted someone else to pay for her dinner so that she could use her spending money the next day. I was actually proud of the clients at that moment for not physically attacking Gloria. In the following weeks they made the point repeatedly that she didn't know how to behave, that she shouldn't lie to her friends, and so on. Eventually, she conformed to their expectations and was invited out again. This exemplifies how living with one's true peers can be so successful. Staff would not have been able to change Gloria's behavior as effectively as her peers did.

There is yet another interesting kind of lying engaged in by people with autism spectrum disabilities that appears to have absolutely no motivation behind it. It most resembles psychopathic lying, but there is a fascinating difference. This kind of lying stems from being stimulus-bound. Of all behaviors that might be misinterpreted, this one really just looks like bad behavior. I want to try to explain why that is not the case.

A few of my clients lie *because the context becomes a more powerful stimulus than their ability to focus on the truth.* Two stories illustrate this phenomenon. In the first counseling session with Alice, she was telling me how difficult high school had been for her. I was letting her lead the conversation wherever she wanted to go, and she seemed eager to let me know her. She told me she had always been teased about her thick glasses, but not her disability. Then she told me there was one boy in her high-school class who was very popular and well-liked by everyone. He surprised Alice by being nice to her. They formed a friendship, and then he killed himself right after their graduation ceremony.

As a sympathetic listener, my face must have registered shock and compassion. So picture Alice telling me about this boy who was nice to her and then killed himself, and picture my face showing sympathy, shock, and compassion. The various expressions that crossed my face were all gratifying to Alice. A part of her mind subconsciously responded like this: "Wow, that feels really good. She cares about me and this bad thing that happened to me. People aren't usually this nice to me. I want more of this good feeling." This response is normal in the sense that anyone who tells a story notices how their story is received. People with normal executive functions can evaluate the reception of their story while continuing to talk and listen, and can remain the kind of person they want to be, including being truthful. Alice could not do all that at once. The response she felt inside, that it was so good to see compassion or shock or any other kind of intense emotional reaction, was so strong that she could not overrule it. She wanted to experience more of it.

Alice proceeded to tell me about another suicide that occurred after her high-school graduation. This involved another young man who shot himself, the only difference being that he had no real connection to her. A third classmate drove himself off a cliff into the ocean in a Mercedes. Imagine my skepticism kicking in. For one thing, no community has three teenage suicides following graduation, without getting some attention in the media. I have lived in the same greater area as Alice's home town during the period of time this carnage would have taken place. I would have heard of these tragic events. So, my on-the-spot reaction was that Alice was "inventing" at least the second and third suicides, and maybe all three. But why? It was at that point I reviewed the interaction between us and formulated the theory of Alice being drawn into the context of my sympathy and being unable to resist provoking more of it.

I have known other clients who are stimulus-bound as part of their disability. It can happen after a head injury. Being stimulus-bound means they cannot resist the pull of a stimulus. A simple example would be seeing a stapler on a desk and being unable to resist the impulse to staple something. Some individuals will pick up everything on a desk and use it or mimic using it, and will not realize they are doing so. I am convinced that Alice's lying (for she was making up the second and third suicides) is an example of being stimulus-bound, with the stimulus being the gratifying reaction of the listener, me! If Alice had the ability to self-monitor while conversing, she might have caught herself lying. She might have asked herself why she would lie to this person who is being kind, this person who will have the opportunity to check on her lies. She will surely find herself confronted about her lying, and what will she say then? But Alice does not have the ability to ask herself any questions while the interaction continues; that is self-monitoring and she is impaired in that executive function.

All my new interns and trainees are told the following story because it is the surest way to explain the concept of a stimulus-bound deficit. When I was very new at my job, I had occasion to take a client named Julie on an errand to the mall. Before we left the program office, Julie and I stopped in front of the desk of another staff person named Hilda. While we stood there, Hilda reminded Julie to talk to a sales clerk about her cell phone. There was a particular question Hilda wanted us to ask. I made note of it in my mind, but intended to let Julie take responsibility for asking the question. We went to the mall and we were never apart. Later, we returned to the program building and ended up in the same spot in front of Hilda's desk.

As we stood in that same spot, Julie brought up the question Hilda had reminded her to ask and then told Hilda what the sales clerk had said. But we had both forgotten to ask the question! I was astonished. There was nothing to be gained by lying about this matter, and no blame for Julie to avoid since she was accompanied by staff. In any case, it was a fairly inconsequential matter and Julie was not lying to avoid a consequence. On the contrary, *she did not realize she was making up a whole conversation.*

Standing there stunned, I decided to just go with the truth, so I said, calmly, "You know, Julie, actually we forgot to ask anyone the question." Julie looked at me blankly and said "Oh." From that day on, my observations of Julie have confirmed that she enters conversations with radar for what the situation calls for. She is pulled to agree with whatever is going on. She is glib and highly verbal, and is the client most likely to be mistaken for normal, and assumed to be staff. Her right to receive benefits for the disabled has been questioned repeatedly. And yet, Julie has caused herself and her friends immeasurable difficulty because she cannot be believed. She truly cannot distinguish what has actually happened from what just seems to fit the occasion.

And to complicate matters further, Julie can and does also lie the old-fashioned way. She has used the death of a grandmother to get off work three or four times that we know of (at different jobs, of course). But the far more interesting kind of lying is the kind that originates in the stimulus-bound deficit and then spirals out of control. Once Julie told a friend in the program that she knew someone in the country music industry in Nashville and that she could use her influence to help him get started in show business. Julie would never initiate such a story, but when the friend talked about wanting a career in country music, that was enough of a stimulus for her to produce the rest. The young man actually packed his bags to go to Nashville to meet a completely fictitious person. Fortunately, staff heard of the story and intervened. Julie is chagrined and unable to justify her actions when these things happen. Before the new interpretation was taught to all staff, she had learned to parrot the many explanations of her behavior, which used to vary with changing staff. When I met her, the interpretation was that she lied to get attention. It's not an inconceivable theory, in behavioral terms, but it is not accurate.

As with all the other stories I've told, the client cannot ponder the consequences at the same time as the scheme, because that would require doing two intentional brain processes at the same time. This is the most important thing to understand about these interrelated functions, the executive functions. Even if these functions end up with different labels, as they most likely will, the nugget to remember is that the disabled brain is operating in a disorganized manner and generally cannot conduct two thought processes, or monitoring processes, at the same time. This is an important difference from the normal expectations of brain functioning.

Hygiene and manners

Most of our clients' hygiene problems are not extreme. Commonly, there may be an issue of clients not generalizing a habit from home to their new surroundings. Or they may be excited by the freedom of having no one to answer to. Eventually staff tell them the same things mom did and they adapt to doing what is suggested, and, for some, continuously cued. This isn't really full independence, but it is the best some of our clients can manage. Some are completely independent as to daily hygiene like showering, shaving, and brushing teeth, but they don't know when to get a haircut or how often to wash their pajamas. Generally, the path to success is similar to that of society at large: you meet a standard and go unnoticed or you miss it and attention is paid until you adapt. Those who never adapt are seen as "not normal."

George's story exemplifies the bad outcome when hygiene does not become habitual in childhood. George, like many in this population, is overweight and more or less oblivious to his appearance. He does not like to bathe or shower and won't do so without being pressured. We suspect that when he does get into the shower, he does not know how to wash himself thoroughly. We assume so because he often smells of body odor, even just out of the shower. You would think that one instance of George being told by his peers that he smells bad would cause him to try to wash properly. But it did not work that way. Because George has a confident and cheerful personality, he handles the criticism by saying he's been teased before and he can take it. He either doesn't want to or can't believe that his peers are doing something different from teasing: they are pressuring him to comply with their standards. Our clients care tremendously about being embarrassed in public by one another. They know they are seen and judged as a group, whether fairly or not, so they try to influence and control one another toward a standard that is strongly felt by all.

They also tell George he smells for a practical reason: because they have to sit close enough to be bothered by his odor. Sometimes his cheerful demeanor fails him and George stomps out of the room; at those times he seems to expect that the others' rudeness will be seen as a worse offense than his smelliness. None of his defenses or his reasoning had led to him finally concluding that he'd rather be clean.

Several things can be surmised from George's situation and they hark back to childhood. One is that George clearly was not taught how to wash all the offending body parts, and to wash daily or at least frequently enough not to give off an odor. The second assumption I make as a clinician is a more subtle one, but very important to our discussion. The way George handles the pressure to wash tells me how he handled his parents' pressure. He does not do as he is asked or told by others, whether by his peers or by so-called authority figures. George doesn't recognize his parents or our staff as authority figures. This tells me that George was allowed to tantrum or argue or flatly refuse to do as he was told by his parents. We have learned that our clients will try everything with us that "worked" with their parents.

Of course I wanted to check these assumptions and I was able to do so, as George's parents are good members of the team caring for their son. Sheepishly, George's mother admitted that every shower George ever took in his life was the result of a battle, and that more often than not she, the mom, just gave up. She admitted that George still yells and screams at her and has even hit her a few times. I offered the belated suggestion that I would have said "no shower, no dinner" and stuck to it; in fact I suggested they do that the next time they had their son at home for a visit. They did and it worked, at least in that one instance.

In order to manage a serious problem with someone who doesn't re-spect authority, you have to have leverage, as discussed earlier; you must have control over something the person cares about (no shower, no dinner). Many of our clients are motivated most of all by money. We do not use a token economy; that method is employed at levels of care that are more institutional than we want to be. But we or parents have control over the clients' money. And we have the leverage of membership in the program: if you don't want to live by our standards, then you can't live in this program. We obviously have control over who stays and goes.

In George's case, we told him he would have to spend his own money to hire an occupational therapist (OT). This was a male clinician, trained in rehabilitation and accommodations for disability, who was able to observe George in the shower and assess what kinds of assistance he needed to achieve an acceptable standard of self-care. The OT was so good at his job that he was able to gain George's confidence and help him be comfortable in a situation that could have been embarrassing. He found that George just needed to be taught how to do a thorough job, and he was given some handy devices that made showering less of a hassle. The money was an important part of the solution, however, because George liked the OT and would have liked him to be present every time he showered. Having to pay for the services made this prohibitive; yet he could be "threatened" with the need for a refresher course whenever he tended to slip back to his old habit.

Problems with manners boil down to two things: either the person with disabilities has never been taught but can learn, or the real problem is one of self-control. As already mentioned, many parents don't think it's important to teach manners to kids with disabilities for a variety of reasons. But those who do teach minimal manners will see the rewards last a lifetime. Those clients who have not been taught but can learn are taught best by their peers. As noted repeatedly, these adult clients hate to be embarrassed by "their own" when out in public. They will do a very effective job of criticizing and letting the offender know what they expect. They achieve impressively good compliance.

Problems occur with those clients whose disability includes poor social judgment and/or uncontrollable impulsivity. Imagine if you had no filter between your thoughts and your speech, or no time to stop yourself from saying every thought that passes through your mind. These are the twin problems of obliviousness and impulsivity. With obliviousness to social expectations, it doesn't matter how much time you have, you just don't see the problem in saying whatever you want to say. This is especially common to those with Asperger's. With impulsivity, it is a matter of time; the remark is out before you have time to decide whether you really want to say it. People with these two problems have an impaired ability to conform; they can scarcely help themselves. Nevertheless, we remind them repeatedly when they misbehave, finding that numerous repetitions eventually help for some clients. It is interesting to observe whether effort is actually brought to bear on the problem, and then whether that effort leads to success. Most clients will make more effort to please their peers than to please their parents or staff.

When the "stop and think" prescription isn't enough, we focus on helping the clients see how the disability impacts their daily life. They may have lost a job because of their blunt or caustic remarks. They may have hurt their friends' feelings. We help them see that the disability caused the difficulty, not using it as an excuse but as an explanation. Furthermore, we help such clients analyze when they owe an apology or some other act of conciliation that might help the situation. And we do these things over and over again, even though, in some cases, the problem is unsolvable.

There are times when we need to persuade the clients of the pervasive effects of this deficit, so they understand that a given job may be wrong for them because of this social behavior aspect of their disability. Perhaps they cannot work in an environment that requires casual conversation with a variety of people. Or they need to understand that friendship with someone who doesn't accept the explanation will be an ongoing series of hurt feelings and anger. The miracle of living with one's peers is that the clients come to understand these things about themselves and each other. It is touching to see how tolerant they are of whatever deficits they can see as real and unchangeable; they accept an apology over and over again. In this capacity they truly achieve friendship in the best sense of the word.

Food and exercise

I frequently say we have a difficult time with food at CAL. It seems we talk about food and exercise, and the way they relate to health, endlessly. But if I am more careful in calculating the number of people who have major problems with food, the picture isn't quite as bleak as it sometimes feels. Our population currently includes 16 women and 28 men. Of those 44 individuals, 8 are obese and another 14 are or have been overweight. Five of our clients currently have type II diabetes, only one of whom must take insulin injections. So about half the population present health concerns that cause us to think a great deal about food and exercise.

If you are beginning to get a good sense of the executive functions in everyday life, it should be clear that deficits in those skills contribute hugely to our clients' problems with food and health in general. Namely, deficits in initiation, impulsivity, the organizational problems, and self-monitoring and judgment all contribute to poor health. Let's review how those functions help us eat well and stay healthy.

Initiation is the ability to decide what to do, moment by moment, rather than being pushed and pulled by stimuli in the environment. We all know how enticing a favorite food, or even just its packaging, can be when we are hungry. Most of us resort to common-sense habits to stop ourselves from eating whatever appeals to us at sight. We may decide to choose from only two or three different breakfasts throughout the week, eating those foods by habit, so that we won't be tempted by more appealing items in a hungry moment. Lunch might be handled similarly, but with a few more regular choices. I eat a large salad for lunch every work day, while I allow myself a sandwich on weekends, with a piece of fruit. If there is a party or another reason for more celebratory food to be served, I am able to eat that and then go back to my healthy habit. If someone started bringing dough-nuts to work every day, though, I would have to make a conscious decision about how often I could eat one. If I ate one doughnut every day—which I would enjoy—I would gain weight.

Dinner probably represents the widest range of choices for most of us. Increasingly, people tend not to cook elaborate meals centered around a meat dish, with a starch, a vegetable, and a salad. There are other options that are healthy enough, like one-dish meals, stir frys, casseroles, and those microwave meals that attempt to be balanced. And there are many options that are disastrous, namely most of the starchy, frozen items that are really not full meals, like pizza. My clients are tired by the end of the day, and not likely to put together a healthy meal. We try to solve this problem sensibly, rather than fighting a losing battle.

Habits are the best tool to override poor initiation, as well as impulsivity. In the absence of good habits, impulsivity goes along with poor initiation in leading my clients to eat whatever they see, without stopping to think about making a conscious decision. Even when the clients have succeeded in establishing habits for breakfast, for example, we have to make sure all food preparation is extremely simple, for the majority of the clients. The organizational problems of our clients cause them to be unable to manage complicated recipes or even, generally, two-stage preparations. A bowl of cereal can be prepared by all of our clients, but adding a piece of fruit might be problematic. It's not that they can't peel a banana, obviously, but they may forget to add the banana when they see the cereal in the bowl with the milk poured over it. The complete bowl of cereal provides a stimulus to start eating. The most interesting part of this problem is that in the health classes all the clients would be able to describe a good breakfast, and all would state that they knew how to prepare it. And they are not lying. They don't have the insight to realize that they don't actually do the things they say they will do.

Judgment, another executive skill, in this case would be the ability to think about the reasons for eating well in the face of competing motivation to eat what is appealing. This occurs in the kitchen where there may be "good" food and "bad" food available. But it also happens at the planning stages. Many of our clients cannot shop for their own groceries because they can't resist all the tempting foods in the market. Most have to shop on a tight budget, so if they don't buy what is on their shopping list, it represents a whole week of eating badly. As we have moved toward purchasing the clients' food in bulk rather than having them go to the grocery store, better groceries are available to them. But there is still the matter of whether they will cook and eat according to a plan.

Generally, the simpler the meal the better. Most clients prefer to use the microwave to prepare frozen meals. But again, there are frozen junk foods and frozen balanced meals. We have found that most clients will eat a well-balanced frozen meal if they are hungry and nothing else is available. But if there are chips, or cereal, or canned soup, or hot dogs, or frozen pizza around, they will opt for those first. Salad has become a little more desirable now that we have bagged lettuces as well as bottled dressings. No matter how many heads of lettuce we might buy, there are very few clients who will take the trouble to prepare a salad "from scratch." Other vegetables suffer the same fate: they are bought, stored in the refrigerator, and then thrown away a week or two later. Fruit is a bit different. Because fruit can be left in a bowl on a table or countertop, it is eaten impulsively by some clients, as an easier choice than, say, making a sandwich. Apples and bananas are the fruits most likely to be eaten on impulse.

We consider our program a work in progress, and flexibility is our best problem-solving device. We now buy food in bulk and try to be realistic about providing only what clients will actually prepare and eat. We used to follow the traditional model of the largest meal being the evening meal; we'll call it supper for this discussion. Then we learned that the clients' suppers were probably their worst meal of the day. The clients were tired at that time and their functioning was at its worst. So we initiated dinner at lunch time. With staff supervision for those who need it, clients prepare a fully balanced meal in groups of eight or so at a time. They learn to prepare easy recipes and they do the work. Each day each participant has a different job: one sets the table, one makes the salad, one prepares the vegetable and two may work on the main dish. We feature a lot of chicken and fish at these meals. There is usually a small dessert, like jello or pudding, also prepared by the clients.

We know that with enough practice the clients learn by doing. There is a fascinating corollary to their discrepancy between what they say they will do and what they actually do. The corollary is that they can learn to do something without consciously realizing they have learned it. So if we want chicken tenders, we put a chicken breast on the cutting board and a knife in front of the client, and he will cut the chicken even after saying he doesn't know how. Again, this is not a matter of lying, but stems from the confused brain of the executively impaired individual. (The same thing has been observed in those with Alzheimer's; they may not remember that they play the piano, but if you seat them at the keyboard they will play.)

Those clients who eat a full dinner at lunch time eat some kind of lunch-type meal for supper. They make a sandwich or soup, or microwave a TV dinner. Overall, this is a better pattern than we were seeing previously. Besides being easier for them when they are tired, this arrangement moves the greater consumption of food to the middle of the day, which is better for weight control.

In addition to implementing dinner at lunch time, we have gone farther in establishing a program for the obese members of our population, and those with diabetes. For this modification of our services we had to hire additional staff, and the parents of those involved have had to pay for this extra service. I mention this arrangement because it highlights the continued involvement of parents in both supporting independence for their adult children and helping them to be as healthy as they can be. Clients must be willing to make a substantial commitment to be part of the "food group." To implement this extraordinary service, clients keep no food in their own apartments. They are given their breakfast food daily and they eat lunch, two snacks, and dinner as a group, with meal prep supervised by the two staff who implement this service. In addition to controlling all their food, and managing their exercise program, we limit the discretionary spending money of these clients. Otherwise they would spend the weekend—when they have spending money—undoing what they accomplished in weight loss through the week. Their money is, of course, still theirs and is saved for other chosen purchases.

We have experienced a bewildering range of reactions to this very tightly managed service. The first client, whose family sponsored the service, was successful in losing just about 100 pounds in a little over a year. But as she approached that milestone, she balked. She began to find ways to get extra food, and she remained a few pounds short of her goal for many months. We realized that her place of employment was a source of extra food, but she needed to keep her job because it provided her health insurance. She couldn't be without health insurance because she had multiple medical problems related to her obesity. The job, the insurance, money, and health were interlocking forces in her life. Finally, as it became clear that she had defeated the food plan, the family member who was paying discontinued in frustration and with regret. Today, still in her thirties, the client weighs over 300 pounds and continues to have medical problems.

But we also have great success stories. Howard, whom you met as the client who came to us at 50 years of age, has diabetes. He comes from a family in which all the siblings are overweight. Howard has had open-heart surgery and a subsequent small stroke. It was imperative that his weight be controlled. Howard responded very well to the controlled food program, because fixing his own meals was a burden. He occasionally would like to eat more food than he is given, so he goes out to dinner once a week and chooses anything he likes. He has lost about 70 pounds and is maintaining his weight very well. His diabetes is controlled with oral medication. It is unlikely Howard will ever be able to prepare his own food again due to cognitive losses following the stroke. Luckily he can afford to pay for the extra care thanks to his small pension. He is an inspiration to others in the food program.

A third outcome of the service is the ideal: those who reach their goal weight and can maintain their health independently. Currently, three women are very close to achieving this. They have lost about 140 pounds among them. Of those three, one is a very good cook and will likely be successful in the maintenance phase. Another is very poor at self-control and compliance, and may have a similar outcome to the client described earlier, if she is allowed to go back to managing her own meals. The third is Sharon, whom you met earlier. Sharon seems to thrive in the food program partly because it feels like childhood to her. A "grown-up" tells her what to eat and helps her prepare it, and she doesn't have to take responsibility for herself. She has lost over 30 pounds and is delighted with her new clothes and image, but it remains to be seen if she will be able to enter a maintenance phase in which she takes responsibility for her own food management. The outcome will be tied to the question of whether she will ever consider adulthood preferable to childhood.

In any weight-loss program, exercise is almost as essential as diet. As you can imagine from the way the general population deals with it, exercise is not easy for our clients to manage. We all know people who seem to love to get their bodies moving. They thrive on being outdoors and being active. They run and play tennis and cycle and swim and dance and play pickup basketball games. Many more people, it seems, have to prod and force themselves to undertake the advised 30 minutes of aerobic exercise three to five times a week. Isn't it amazing how difficult most of us find just walking, a few times a week? I'm probably similar to most middle-aged American women: I know walking is good for me and I enjoy it when I do it, but the habit of walking five times a week can just slip away for months at a time. So our clients, with their disorganized brains, are certainly no better than the rest of us at compliance with an exercise plan.

For most of the clients, we attempt to combat their reluctance to exercise as we do with ourselves. Again, habit is the ally. We build exercise into the schedule four times a week. Besides walking, we use exercise tapes, and outdoor activities, like shooting baskets. Some of the clients participate in organized sports through Special Olympics, although most have a prejudice against socializing with the mentally impaired. (This is understandable in an odd way. My clients are aware of their status in society, specifically because they are not mentally retarded and can interpret curiosity, ostracism, and rejection from the general public. They don't look the same as the mentally retarded, so they don't want to mingle with them and increase the likelihood of being stigmatized.)

Those in the special food program have more scheduled exercise. Currently the women are finding great satisfaction in going as a group to one of the commercial exercise programs; they seem to enjoy the camaraderie within their own group and with others they've gotten to know at the gym. They feel normal in that situation, as they are doing the same activity as the "normal" patrons, albeit with staff assistance.

Those clients who are not in the special food program are completely independent in managing their food on the weekends. Most of them eat dinner out on Friday nights, some going in groups to neighborhood restaurants where they actually order from a menu and deal with paying and tipping. Most opt for fast food for a variety of reasons: it's cheaper, quicker, portable in case they want to take it home, and it doesn't require worrying throughout the meal how much it will *really* cost. (Many clients cannot add up random amounts found on menus and then figure out how much to tip.) The rest of the weekend is more or less the same in terms of food. The clients eat fast food until their money runs out, then they eat the foods in their apartments that are easiest to deal with. There are exceptions; there are a few women and men who actually like to cook, and even bake, and can be found any weekend preparing good meals. But they are the exceptions, and they generally brought those skills with them, having learned them from their parents. The takeaway message here is to see how much better and easier these individuals' lives would be if they had developed food management habits before they left home.

Health care

Related to the subject of food and exercise is the subject of health care, including visits to the doctor. In the same way that our clients are impaired in their management of food, so are their perceptions of feeling ill distorted by their executive deficits. First of all, many members of the autism spectrum population have non-normal perceptions of pain. Generally, they do not report pain as readily or at the same intensity as a normal person. Parents have reported this fact, and I have repeatedly heard doctors ask our clients, "Doesn't this hurt?" or "Why didn't this bother you before it got this bad?"

On the other hand, many of our clients are excessively gratified by having something "wrong" and going to the doctor. They don't present like a normal person with a complaint, however. They will mention a disease they've heard about on television, speaking with a cheerful and positive demeanor about the possibility of having, say, spinal meningitis or diverticulitis. They present without worry or discomfort, but will definitely want to go to the doctor.

I think the positive attitude toward medical visits in this population may be due to doctors being among the few people who were kind to these clients throughout their lives. Memories of teachers and various other adults, like schoolmates' parents are, unfortunately, not generally positive. Doctors tend to be kind and respectful to our clients. But they, the docs, usually have erroneous expectations. Invariably, when I accompany a client to a medical appointment, the doctor will ask questions the client cannot answer, and will give complex explanations, anticipating that he or she will remember and follow directions. Some doctors seem not to even wonder why the patient is accompanied to the appointment; and they are reluctant to believe that the client has not understood what they've said. The clients are so normal-sounding in their social talk, and they want so much to pass for normal, that they pretend they understand, and the doctors tend to go along with the pretense.

Because we need a reliable exchange of information, staff accompany clients to almost all appointments. The client would not explain his complaint thoroughly or accurately (again, not lying, but misperceiving). Then the doctor would give instructions that staff would never hear of. There are innumerable difficult decisions to make in medical care. Given the difficulty of these decisions, we generally err on the side of caution, which increases the overall number of medical appointments we attend. Each client is required to have a physical, an eye exam, and a dental exam once a year, as well as lab tests for those on psychotropic medications. Some take medications, like blood thinners, which require more frequent monitoring. Others get repeated infections related to physical/medical aspects of their disability. Most of our clients are clumsy, as part of the disability, so falls are more common than in the general population of those their age. In addition, some clients cannot cut their own toenails, and need to see a podiatrist regularly. One young man, newly away from home for the first time, failed to remove his dental retainer for over two weeks, and then found that it had grown into his gum tissue. It had to be removed by a kind, non-judgmental dentist.

Medication

Most of our clients are already on medication, sometimes several, when they come to our program. Clients' and parents' attitudes vary, but generally clients have gone through the rigors of finding the most beneficial medication or medication combination with guidance and, often, trial-and-error. Most of our clients have adjusted to the anxieties, stigma, and side effects related to taking medication. Most are very accepting of them and are able to discuss the ways their lives are better with medication. If a client wishes to change or discontinue a medication, we respond as an interdisciplinary team, respect the request, and incorporate past medical history and the memories and opinions of parents as well as the client in formulating a new plan.

We have a wonderfully dedicated psychiatrist who comes to the program twice a month and prescribes and monitors the medications of most of our clients. He is knowledgeable about new medications, psychiatric research, and non-medication resources like sleep studies and smoking cessation methods. Sometimes the clients need to meet with Dr R (as he's known to them) and ask questions so that they feel they are in charge of their own health concerns. Recently, for example, a new client who experiences severe anxiety asked Dr R at their first meeting to increase her anxiety medication. He explained that it was normal for her to feel increased anxiety when beginning a new phase of her life, and that her medication was at a good clinical dosage, so he'd rather not increase it until she had spent some time making the adjustment to her new program. She was pleased to have his attention and she accepted his advice. In other instances, staff may be the first to see the need for a change. The process is a collaboration between client, doctor, parents, and staff, with staff having the role of daily observers.

It is beyond the scope of this book to discuss medication in depth. But I would like to mention the kinds of meds that are most typically prescribed for our clients and how we use them. The selective serotonin reuptake inhibitors (SSRIs)—Prozac and its chemical cousins—are probably the most frequently used medications in our population. Severe depression is not seen often in our population, but mild to moderate depression and moderate to severe anxiety are common, and often respond, at least partially, to the SSRIs.

Mood dysregulation is often a symptom of a major psychiatric illness, Bipolar Disorder. Occasionally a client who has a deficit in emotional regulation will have been diagnosed as having Bipolar Disorder and will be on medications typically prescribed for that disorder. Even though the history and the course of the disorder present differently in our population, the medications are often beneficial, and discontinuing them can lead to increased symptoms. Although there can be different explanations for these observations, it is clear that regardless of diagnostic uncertainty, some clients benefit from mood-stabilizing medications such as lithium, Depakote, and Tegretol.

A class of medication that can be very helpful but is, perhaps, more puzzling and troubling to parents is the atypical antipsychotics class. A term that includes "psychotic" troubles parents because they've already been through such a maze of diagnoses without encountering schizophrenia, and that is the disorder that comes to mind when we hear the word psychotic. The calm and positive explanation is that the atypical antipsychotic medications can be helpful in quieting a confused mind or a mind spinning with ruminations caused by poor thought regulation, focus, and mood instability. This class of medications includes Zyprexa, Risperdal, Geodon, Seroquel, and Abilify. Over the last several years, we have observed that these medications have caused decreases in bewilderment and confusion, an increase in pro-social behavior, and, to date, no significant side effects.

The medications for attention deficit disorders are by now familiar to us. They target poor concentration, impaired focus, and impulsivity. Some of our clients take Ritalin and some take a newer, non-stimulant medication called Strattera. In our experience, the distractibility and hyperactivity seen in the attention deficit disorders are not always successfully treatable.

Our wish list for medications is topped by the wish for a better medication for anxiety. We tend not to use the benzodiazepines in daily drug regimens because of the potential for tolerance and abuse. We do use Ativan as a PRN medication, which means it can be taken *as needed* for situations of unusual stress, or for mood dysregulation resulting in extreme emotional outbursts. A few of our clients use Ativan PRN very responsibly and independently. By this I mean they can sense when an outburst is about to occur, and they ask for a PRN. Shortly after taking it, they become calm but not too sedated to continue their daily activities. Nevertheless, anxiety remains the challenge for which we have the fewest tools to help. A handful of our clients are anxious virtually all the time. It is difficult to watch their daily struggle to do the things others do so easily. For some, the best accommodation is to live the circumscribed life afforded by a therapeutic community that provides tolerance and friendship with very little effort on their part.

We are currently experimenting with the use of relaxation, breathing, and meditation techniques to assist our clients with anxiety disorders, hyperactivity, and mood dysregulation. We employ these techniques in small groups of six to eight clients who are compatible. Several clients also have individual sessions and use relaxation in the form of a five-minute relaxation message tailored specifically to the individual and saved on a CD. Soon we will have clients trying neurofeedback, a biofeedback technique based on quantitative EEG findings. All our efforts are based on the search for pragmatic solutions and the commitment to remain open-minded and dedicated to unbiased observation.

Money management

It is almost universally true that our clients cannot manage money. But there is always an exception. Those who are on the tightly focused or obsessive end of the attention continuum are more likely to be obsessively protective of their money as well. Also, those who are anxious as part of their emotional dysregulation are likely to bring anxiety to issues of money. In their anxiety they tend to worry obsessively about every possible expenditure, or they may be indecisive to such an extent that they never make the decision to spend, or even to go to a store or to an activity. Due to these incapacitating factors, they appear to function as better managers of money than those who spend freely and with no judgment.

But the general rule for this population is that money is like water in their hands. It probably goes without saying that money is both concrete and abstract. The concrete function of money is so easily understood that shopping is probably the most favored activity of our clients. With money in hand and an understanding of price tags, they can shop. And, significantly, having the social skills to pass for normal during the brief and pleasant exchanges that happen while shopping makes this an especially gratifying part of life. *The fleeting experience of feeling normal is an unconscious reason why shopping is so enjoyable to my clients.*

The deficit in understanding how to manage money cannot be resolved by teaching and learning unless the individual also has exemplary self-control, which my clients rarely do. Consider the story of Bill and his checking account. Bill has insisted on working toward the goal of managing his own checking account for over six years. He has learned to write checks, which to him means spelling the words correctly and putting each item in the right place on the check. He has learned to write the amounts in the register and to know when to add and when to subtract. However, it has become clear to us that he will never understand how a checking account works.

Let's say Bill purchases something not in his budget, like a pair of shoes, and pays for them with a check. His father receives his bank statement in the mail, including the cancelled checks, so he knows exactly what Bill has done. By the time his father confronts him about the check to the shoe store, several weeks may have gone by. Bill cannot understand why this is coming up *now*, so he denies having written the check. Bill is so convincing when telling this kind of lie that you begin to think something went wrong at the bank and he really did not write the check. But his father has been down this road many times. He pulls out the cancelled check and shows Bill his odd handwriting.

Most people would realize it's time to come clean. Not Bill. His strategy at this point is to continue to deny everything. He wasn't in that store, doesn't have the shoes, and that isn't his handwriting! And indeed, while persisting in his denials, Bill achieves a level of righteous indignation in his demeanor. He can do this because he does possess a kind of innocence. The innocence stems from the fact that he can't figure out how the check he wrote got into his father's hands. It seems so unfair! It's his check from his checkbook that he carries around with him at all times. He was alone in the store when he wrote the check. He handed it to a sales clerk. How did that check end up in his father's hands?

In telling this story I'm reminded of my nephew when he was about to turn three years old. He was still in diapers, and he was definitely getting a sense of how adults felt about the contents of diapers. One day his father smelled a telltale odor and asked if he had a "poop" in his diaper. The boy answered, "No, and don't look!" Compare the child's answer to Bill's response to seeing his check in his father's hands: the three-year-old already had some notion that he could be found to be lying. He said "don't look" because he understood that his father *might* look. Bill was more at a loss, more innocent, than the three-year-old in that he was unable to anticipate what part of his story would reveal his lie. He didn't understand the processing of a check, and moreover, he didn't understand that handwriting can identify a person. He might as well have said, "I didn't write the check and don't show me any proof that I did!" The only humane way to handle Bill's problem is to try to keep him out of such humiliating dilemmas.

How, then, does the CAL program handle money? Each client has a budget. We want the clients to understand the reality behind their budgets, to know that real facts determine the amount of money they have to spend, and not simply the generosity of their parents. Most of the clients receive government benefits, and those funds are legally regulated in terms of how they can and cannot be supplemented by family members. For those clients who can understand the concept of income and expenses—not all of them, by any means—we emphasize that getting a job will improve their financial picture. We go over their income and expenses on paper or on a computer so that they can see what comes in and what goes out.

For those who cannot comprehend a budget, we are more concrete. We explain that all their monthly income has been used to pay their expenses, except this amount which is left over for them to spend as they please. We give them their discretionary money on Fridays, in the afternoon. We used to call it "weekend money" until we realized we might be endorsing the habit of spending it all before Monday morning. Now we call it "weekly money," in hopes that the label will suggest making it last through the whole week. Generally though, the clients spend their discretionary money on the weekend, rarely saving any for the rest of the week.

When they complain of having no money through the week, we make every attempt to respond with calm, reality-based answers that draw from the real world of actions and consequences. We also don't hesitate to point out just how and when their disability impacted their decision-making. We are deliberately not squeamish about acknowledging the effect of disability in the clients' lives, and I recommend that every family develop non-judgmental terms for this necessary type of discussion.

A typical conversation might go like this:

Sally: I wish I had enough money for a pedicure!

Me: What did you spend money on over the weekend?

Sally: I ate out and rented a movie and bought some stuff at the dollar store.

Me: Are you happy with the stuff you bought?

Sally: I'd rather have a pedicure.

Me: Maybe next weekend you can remind yourself that you'd rather have a pedicure before you go off to eat or to the dollar store. Would you like me to remind you when you get your money?

Sally: Yeah. I hope I'll do it, though. I'm so impulsive when I think of something I want to do.

There are other, very serious issues concerning money. Our clients are smart enough to fill out applications for credit cards that come to them in the mail. They are offered on-the-spot credit cards in department stores, as we all are from time to time. When the clients get credit, they generally go out and use it immediately, their favorite purchases being clothes for the women and computer games and other electronic toys for the men. As mentioned earlier, they also succumb to offers online, on television, and in magazines. Staff try to stay on top of these schemes, but a few get through from time to time. So, what do we do then?

We have four options and we make our decision based upon which option we think is the best fit for the client and the situation. We can pay the debt from the client's account and deduct payments from his weekly discretionary money, until he has paid himself back. We can write a letter to the company explaining the disability and asking for the debt to be excused, or substantially reduced. Or we can let the system work without interference, which can lead to the client's credit being ruined. The fourth option is to ask the parents if they want to pay the debt for their adult child.

In addition to choosing one of the options, we employ our specific way of talking about the problem with the clients. When we think we are at the beginning of something that could become a very bad habit, we use concrete language delivered in a serious emotional tone to criticize the behavior. We point out that the client didn't have the ability or the intention to pay for the items when he ordered them. We say that purchasing with no means to pay is illegal and could get them in serious trouble. We tell them that repeated instances of the same type of fraud could be tracked and would be considered more serious with each new incident.

We do not consider these responses "unfair" or cruel to the disabled. Our clients desperately want to live in "the real world" and not be known as disabled. To that end, we describe their behavior to them in the way it would be judged in "the real world." In this situation, with a client who is just beginning to engage in a bad behavior regarding money, we would probably require the client to repay the debt from his discretionary money over time. Interestingly, the clients who end up with this consequence rarely understand the amounts of money at issue. They may not comprehend the difference between $40 and $400. They do understand, though, that their "weekly money" of $25 has been cut to $15 for a period of six months or more, though they need frequent reminders that the reduction of their spending money was caused by their own behavior and not due to meanness on the part of staff or their parents. Most interestingly, many clients will come to us after a week or two of reduced spending money and make the case that they've learned their lesson and they'd like the discretionary money to go back up now. *They don't understand that a set amount of money really has to be repaid to someone in order for the incident to be over.*

In some cases we like to divide the responsibility between the client and the company who offered the credit or goods and services. Depending upon the amount and the client's ability to repay the debt, we may write a letter to the company explaining the circumstances and asking for some portion, usually half of the debt, to be excused. We then have the client repay the other half by deducting it from their discretionary money week-by-week, just as in the situation described above. We make this choice when two conditions are met: we think the amount is too large for the client to tolerate repaying and we feel the offer was made irresponsibly by the company.

Another option, when a client proves to be better at securing credit than we are at stopping him, is to let the market act on its own behalf. One young woman is a whiz at using the internet to order products. Without a credit card she somehow secures credit temporarily, just long enough to order things. When the items arrive, if staff become aware of them, we discuss with her the idea of returning the goods as an alternative to docking her weekly money. Eventually, this woman ordered so many items that were neither returned nor paid for that she began to be "flagged" as a bad credit risk. The item that finally was not shipped because of her poor credit rating cost hundreds of dollars, and would have been impossible to hide. The ethics of allowing an adult to ruin her credit rating could be a hotly debated issue. Our view is that our clients would be out of control and in true danger if we didn't step in. They would be safest with no autonomy at all, but we prefer the middle ground: relative safety and relative independence. In some cases, ruined credit is a means to safety for the out-of-control individual.

It is unfortunate that shopping can be so frustrating for those who have too little money and various disorders of self-control. For those who are too impulsive to follow a plan, a grocery list for example, it ends up being a better solution to do their grocery shopping online. Parents tell us their kids enjoyed shopping with them and they want them to maintain that skill. But they may not have realized they controlled every moment of the time spent in the grocery store, and managed every decision about what to buy. We make informed decisions. Those who can demonstrate good shopping skills—that is, buying according to a list derived from menu plans that conform to a budget—are certainly encouraged to continue shopping for themselves. Others are allowed to make independent shopping a goal, but they must follow steps that include self-control in the face of temptation. For some of our clients it is too difficult, and we encourage them to think of online shopping as an accommodation, just as using a computer is an accommodation for those who have poor handwriting.

Making purchases in stores illustrates the concrete aspect of money. What about the abstract aspect? Money, checks, ATMs, credit cards and debit cards, phone cards and gift cards, all stand for the ability to get stuff. Most of our clients are unable to think about money abstractly. The difficulty with money is that the concrete understanding of it—go to a store and buy stuff—is so compelling that the clients can't slow down and focus on looking at it a different way, such as saving for a bigger purchase.

Here's my explanation of how a check works: A check is a little note from you to your bank. In this note, you are giving your bank an order. You are saying, "Hi, it's me and I'm writing to you on this date to tell you to give the Fun and Freaky Shoe Store $32.75. You don't have to know why I'm telling you this, just do it. I know you'll take the money out of my bank account and I'll have that much less, and that's what I want. Signed, Me."

Of course I do a lot more explaining and writing and dissecting real checks to illustrate where each of the components of "the note" appears on the check. Confusion arises because the check—the note—is left at the shoe store instead of the bank. How does the "order" get to the bank? How does the money get back to the shoe store? The answers to these questions take us far from the information the clients actually want to know about writing checks. Some of the clients can grasp this kind of explanation when they are not actually at a point to use it. But once they find themselves in a store, impulsivity makes it difficult to use checks appropriately because

221

it's just as easy to use them inappropriately. No one knows whether you really have that amount of money in the bank when you write the check. "Wow!" they think, "I wrote the check and I got the shoes and nothing bad happened." It could be days or even weeks before a confusing item comes in the mail, and they just throw that away. With better tracking technology, this scenario is becoming dated, and that's for the best.

To summarize, we see a variety of patterns regarding money, like the many other issues I've discussed. The adjustment to money management relates to personality issues and to the way the client was raised, again, like so many other issues we've covered. The client with a calm or sunny disposition generally makes an easy adjustment to having money for the weekend, spending it more or less the same way every weekend, and having empty pockets throughout the week. For others there is a constant feeling of not having enough money and wanting to blame someone. With those clients, we emphasize understanding the reality of the math. If the numbers don't add up to allow more spending money, then those are the facts and it isn't anyone's fault. We then stress the connection between being employed and having more spending money.

For other clients, scheming becomes a way of life. They seek to take advantage of their parents, their peers, and even strangers. The rights of others are hard to keep in mind when one has a disability that affects judgment. Those clients must be dealt with creatively. Once they achieve employment, it is sometimes possible to divide their increased spending money over several days of the week, so that they never feel completely deprived. Parents are our ally in coming up with creative ways to help these clients live with the limitations of their circumstances. They may take them on shopping "sprees" to buy needed items that the clients would neglect. Or they take them on family vacations that give them a break from their routines and expose them to sights and places they wouldn't otherwise experience.

Some clients are content with an amount of money that is scarcely more than the amount they were miserable with. In other words, what they want to do in their leisure time might cost $25, week in and week out. So, given $20, they felt frustrated and unhappy, but with a five-dollar increase, they are perfectly happy. For the majority of clients with this disability, the amount of money they feel they need is directly connected to the amount of leisure time they have. When they are busier, say with employment that may also be tiring, they accept being at home for more of their leisure time, so having less spending money doesn't matter. When they have more time on their hands, naturally their thoughts turn to going and doing, and that leads to the perceived need for money. Just like the rest of us, the clients are better off financially, mentally, and emotionally when they have the opportunity to fill their time with meaningful activity, including employment.

Employment

Individuals on the autism spectrum achieve the proud feelings of adulthood by belonging to the community through employment. We believe almost all our clients can find a niche where their unique skills will be valued. We see time and again that having a job or being a volunteer, even if only for a few hours a week, enhances feelings of self-worth and normalcy. For some clients being paid is the ultimate reward. But for others the rewards vary as they do for the rest of us: being appreciated for our contribution, having somewhere to go every day where co-workers talk and joke with us, and accomplishing the required tasks with confidence. All of these outcomes can be experienced by adults with executive deficits, as long as someone with intact frontal lobe functioning is standing by to manage the inevitable mishaps.

Our success stories are heartwarming. Ralph, a client in his early forties, has worked for a major hardware chain for over ten years. He is a member of the union along with his co-workers, and he receives benefits just as they do. Ralph generally completes his work week, working full-time, without much help from CAL staff. He knows his duties and he is friendly with his co-workers. Their friendliness does not result in friendships outside the workplace, but Ralph doesn't seem to feel sad about that. We can expect Ralph to stay employed at the same job until he ages and needs to retire.

Ralph's only difficulties on the job have to do with the interaction of his tendency toward hypochondria and the Workers Compensation system. Ralph has had two Workers Comp claims in the past four years. The first was straight-forward: he smashed his finger with a hammer. The result was an injury that required time off and physical therapy. Eventually he was judged to be permanently partially disabled, as the finger was never restored to normal functioning, though Ralph was able to resume his usual tasks.

The next Workers Comp claim was clearly affected by Ralph's executive deficits. He complained of pain in one knee and asked to leave work. CAL staff took him to a doctor who said he probably had torn cartilage and asked if anything had happened at work to cause the injury. This was the point at which no one could provide an accurate account of what had happened, and Ralph was likely to make a mistake. He couldn't remember an exact moment when an injury occurred, but he does lift lumber and tools as part of his job so it was reasonable to suppose an injury happened in the course of his duties. Ralph was uncertain and so were his doctors. He was told to take time off, and a Workers Comp claim was initiated. By the time he saw a specialist in knee repair, Ralph had missed three weeks of work and was running out of money. The surgeon who finally saw him could find no tear to operate on.

This was a problem because Ralph could be seen as faking an injury to get time off, or to take advantage of the Workers Comp system, which would cost his employer money. In this case, the fact that CAL staff had attended his medical appointments and could verify that the first doctor did diagnose a torn cartilage, and did believe the case to be a valid Workers Comp claim, made the difference in getting Ralph through the scrutiny of his supervisor and his union. But Ralph couldn't report whether any particular tasks, like lifting, continued to cause pain in his knee. And he doesn't realize that his inability to be accurate and believable about physical problems may someday jeopardize his employment. For these reasons, he needs staff to intervene and help make judgments whenever he has physical complaints. For Ralph, reporting physical symptoms and calling in sick would be frequent occurrences, if not for staff intervention and encouragement.

Wendell's employment is another success story. Wendell's parents made good decisions during his school years. He was in special education classes but his parents insisted he be trained to use computers when they became available to the school system. Wendell learned to type correctly, back when it was still called typing, and developed good speed and accuracy. After he completed high school, his mother helped him get a full-time job in data entry, which he held for about ten years. His employment ended because he worked at a military facility that was eventually closed. Losing employment through uncontrollable factors can be a difficult outcome for our clients, as they are not necessarily likely to find another job that is such a good fit.

Wendell adjusted almost too well to unemployment. Since our clients do not understand money, and they are accustomed to being dependent upon others, they can sink into unemployment without worrying, as we would, about the repercussions. They continue to have an apartment and a grocery budget, so life goes on. In Wendell's case, however, there was another powerful motivator for him to seek money. He had a car. He was proud of being a driver and he knew he had car payments, insurance payments, and the cost of gas to deal with. His mother, being a wise woman, talked with him immediately and forcefully about what would happen to his car if he didn't get another job.

Very soon, Wendell was employed again, but in a job that would have been too menial for him a few years earlier. He worked in a noisy restaurant that used video games and clowns to attract families with small kids. For Wendell, this environment was too stimulating and confusing, so he soon left that job. His next employment was in janitorial work, which he liked, but he was hired for only a few hours each morning. He was home by noon and had no other commitments to keep him occupied, other than the CAL program day. Wendell had been away from the program day for many years as a worker, so it didn't appeal to him to return to it. Again, his mother had the best idea. She insisted that he update his computer skills and go back to clerical work, which she was sure he could do. At this point, Wendell is enrolled in a computer class, while keeping his janitorial job. We fully expect he will be employable in a job that utilizes his computer and keyboard skills.

For various reasons most of our clients are unable to work full-time. In the first place, there are not so many jobs that can be done by people with executive deficits. They may be able to complete a type of task, but not be able to sustain concentration for as long as the rest of us. They may be capable of doing the task but incapable of doing it in the environment of the job. They may be unable to incorporate the social aspects of employment, even when those are peripheral to the actual job duties. In addition, they are overly stressed and tired by the efforts they make to appear normal. We also notice that our clients tend to lose other self-care skills if they spend too much time at work. For all these reasons, we find that the best accommodation, for most clients, is to seek employment at a number of hours per month that will not cause their benefit checks to be terminated. The client who is employed always comes out ahead, even when benefits are reduced.

Some of our clients can manage only a few hours a week of volunteer work. Some work at various charitable organizations boxing groceries for the homeless. They take great pride in helping others they perceive to be needier than they are. Some clients volunteer at stables and petting zoos. A young man with an exceptional memory works one day a week as a docent at a local museum. He is very proud of having memorized the programmed speech he has to deliver.

The typical job, if there is such a thing, would be in a market that is currently shrinking. Many of our clients have enjoyed working in video or music stores. They tend to be collectors of movies and music, so they are familiar with the names of musicians and groups. They like to be around all those objects that they prize, and re-shelving videos seemed the perfect activity for many of our clients. In our area, those stores are closing day by day. There is a growing market in video games and some of our clients love those as well, so we hope to be able to make use of that market for employment. Other clients have jobs washing pots at a nursery, stocking shelves in toy stores and drug stores, and washing cars. A few are successful in restaurant work, mainly as bussers. The quickness required for food preparation, even dishwashing, and for waiting tables is beyond our clients' abilities, for the most part.

Another form of employment that exists for our population is the enclave, or supervised work situation in which a small group of workers accomplish a specified amount of work together, under the guidance of a job coach. In this arrangement, the employer is allowed to make a contract by fee-for-task, circumventing the requirement to pay each individual the minimum wage. The workers divide the task and divide the fee under the supervision of the agency that develops such jobs and negotiates the contracts with employers.

Lest you think it unfair to pay workers a wage lower than minimum wage, let me describe some of the behaviors that are tolerated in enclaves. One man loved the idea of working in a bank, but he most enjoyed talking to himself about being in a bank rather than actually accomplishing any work. Another worker had a compulsion to sniff every document before performing her step of the task. Another fellow wouldn't do the work the way the job coach taught him, thinking he had a superior method. No matter how many times he was shown what to do, he reverted to his own strategy as soon as he thought he had privacy. Eventually, he was observed copying addresses and phone numbers from documents, and it turned out he was planning to use the information in a nefarious scheme. He would have been unable to carry out an effective plan, most likely, but he could have been arrested for stealing the information, and he could have ruined the opportunity for the whole enclave to continue working in a bank.

A unique difficulty for our unusual clients when working in an enclave is that they can be perceived to be capable of better performance than is realistic. Recall Julie, who is so stimulus-bound that she seems to agree with everyone and to be conversant in any subject. She doesn't know when she has lost contact with the actual chain of events, and everything seems equally likely to be true. Julie passes for normal more than any other client in our program because of her fluid, conversational speech. So, imagine her co-workers at a hospital who see her in an enclave. They think a mistake has been made. When they discuss their work, she is so adept at mimicking their way of talking that she appears to understand.

Staff had seen this pattern repeatedly: Julie lost each job in which she was successful because she was promoted beyond her ability. This hospital enclave appeared to be her last chance for success and we were determined to protect her. Nevertheless, she was offered a full-time clerical job in the hospital, a job that would have taken her out of the enclave and qualified her to work unsupervised. We perceived that Julie was uneasy about the opportunity, but her family wanted her to try it.

We have learned over and over again how difficult it is for family members to accept the limits of their loved one's disability. But we were determined not to let this "opportunity" cost Julie her position in the en-clave, so we called a meeting between the parents, CAL staff, and enclave supervisor to secure a guarantee that if Julie failed in the new job, she would be allowed back into the enclave. We were careful to point out that the way she would fail would likely be perceived as a character problem rather than a function of her disability. In the past, Julie perceived when she was out of her depth, and as a consequence she acted out and got fired. For her, that was preferable to having her disability exposed to people who had believed she was normal.

Wisely, the employer allowed Julie to try the new job a few hours a day and continue in the enclave the rest of the time. She failed at the new du-ties in short order, was embarrassed in front of those who had championed her, and was grateful to go back to her comfort zone. Lest it appear that I am simply content with low expectations for our clients, the truth is that the clients pay a huge price when someone else—parent, employer, case manager—needs to see a situation played out in order to be convinced. We can tolerate some trial and error to prove a point, but when it costs the client in embarrassment or in the loss of an opportunity that is a perfect fit, we become very protective. All our clients have had more than their share of failure in life, so we are determined to provide situations that will guarantee success.

The only work opportunity considered "lower," or more supported and protected, than an enclave is a sheltered workshop. From time to time we've had clients who were willing to work in sheltered workshops. For the most part, though, our clients don't want to be seen with those who are, or appear to be, intellectually impaired. For our clients this is a matter of pride, in a world where they have had precious few opportunities to be prideful. This was discussed earlier: we may not admire their attitude but we can understand it.

Even when a client achieves the best fit we can find between individual skills and demands of his job, CAL staff stay closely involved in their work lives, knowing that anything can arise as a problem. Typically, problems occur between people, as they do for all of us. There might be a personality clash with a co-worker or with a supervisor. There may be too many supervisors who issue directives in different ways that are befuddling to our clients. Or a client may be asked to work a different shift and find that the tasks are different on that shift. Sometimes the supervisor with whom the job was developed moves on and the new supervisor doesn't even realize the employee has a disability. Remembering how many times I've said our clients love to pass for normal, you will know that our client, in that situation, will be pleased that the new supervisor doesn't think he's disabled and will ride that misperception right into disaster.

Sometimes, no matter how clearly we portray the client as having a disability, the employer will decide to form her own opinion. One such situation resulted in the client being fired even though accommodations could have solved the problem. A young woman was placed in a stationery store, with the job of stocking the shelves. One day she was told to "face the shelves." Apparently, in retail parlance, this means to bring all the goods forward on the shelf so they can easily be seen by customers. Many of us would not have known that term, but we would have questioned our supervisor. Our client, not wanting to ask a question that made her feel stupid, did what the request sounded like to her. She was found quite a while later, standing and looking at a shelf, "facing the shelf." She was fired and when staff tried to intervene and explain, it appeared that the supervisor was too bewildered (maybe embarrassed?) to continue working with the client.

Most of the time, however, if the job is developed properly, there is a successful long-term outcome for both client and employer. In this day of awareness of diversity, most employers can see the advantage in hiring qualified individuals with disabilities. Our clients will do jobs that many people would refuse to do. What is boring to others may require just the right amount of concentration for our clients, who are juggling multiple challenges with their impaired brains. The proof is in the track record: for our clients who have been thoughtfully placed in their jobs, we see years and years of success. And once the best placement is found, it is usually counterproductive to look for steps to greater success. Success remains where it begins with our population. I have seen only one client who sought advancement actually be capable of moving on. Imagine if you secured the best possible job for your skills and temperament and someone kept encouraging you to look elsewhere! Wait for the individual to express a desire for change. Meanwhile, celebrate his success.

Computers and cell phones

There was a time, about ten years ago, when the management of CAL thought we could ban computers and cell phones because we saw so much potential for danger and abuse through their use. We weren't wrong about the potential for trouble, but we were wrong to think we could fight a trend that was so strong in the general population. Our clients want what their non-disabled peers have. They keep up with cultural trends and fads, and these two useful items have moved way beyond just being trendy. So, we've had to adjust to computer and cell phone use.

Why are they problematic? Because of our clients' poor judgment. Consider all the advice you've heard about adolescents who create personal websites like MySpace and Facebook. And consider the debates you've heard about whether parents have a responsibility to monitor their kids' internet use and the personal information they post, or whether they must respect their kids' privacy. We've all heard anguished discussions of these topics on talk radio and in news stories. Because our clients function below their age level in terms of judgment and self-monitoring, we must consider monitoring the use of computers and cell phones much as we would with children. But the clients are not children, so the justification for monitoring them must be explained over and over, and with sensitivity and respect for their feelings.

Both the internet and cell phones provide motivation and opportunity for our clients to lie and misrepresent the truth. We all know that many people lie about their identity and various aspects of their lives when presenting themselves on the web. The difference for our clients is that even though they lie about themselves, they don't believe that others are lying!

The computer problems generated by our male clients have to do with underage girls and pornography. They create personal spaces and collect "friends" and people to chat with, and they believe every word written by their new friends. We are emphatic and repetitious with our young men about the importance of avoiding contact with girls who are under 18 years of age, as that could cause them to be tracked as sexual predators. Then they go on the internet and have no way of knowing that they may be chatting with teenage girls. Some of our clients have gotten as far as exchanging phone numbers and talking by phone. The girls may live with their parents and talk about high school, yet our young men don't grasp that those are red flags suggesting underage girls.

Our male clients are starved for the acceptance of "normal" young women, and if they can write well enough for chatting, they can have a connection without the pitfalls of actual contact, face-to-face. It is a very seductive way to spend time, which allows them to sidestep real social requirements and achievements. Our female clients are more likely to want real face-to-face friendships, but some of them have also engaged in cyber relationships. Some have found their way to communicating with inmates in prisons over the internet. One woman sent money to a prisoner, before we learned what she was doing.

As with so many other issues, our approach is to discuss consequences in a step-by-step, concrete manner. In the case of the young man talking to teenage girls, we would ask him if he knows what it means to be labeled a sexual predator. If he says he does not, then we assign him a project, on-line, to investigate that term. If he becomes frightened by what he learns, that's good. If he does not, then we may have the police talk with him about circumstances that could cause him to be arrested. If he is already involved with someone he's not sure is safe, we may have him speak to the young woman's parents. If she turns out to be over 18 years old, there may still be a problem, but it is a substantially less serious problem. If the parents of an underage girl learn that she is misrepresenting herself online, that's a good outcome. And they might appreciate our young man having alerted them, however inadvertent it was. Every aspect of the situation is improved, except that our client feels betrayed and interfered with. Usually, he would have preferred to continue the relationship, risks and all. That's why the situation can be dangerous.

Pornography is a particularly troubling issue. First of all, there is disagreement about the moral value judgments associated with pornography. Some people take a pragmatic approach and some a libertarian approach. In other words, everyone knows that women (and men) are being "used" for the sake of anonymous sexual gratification of others. And everyone knows there are people working in that industry solely to make money. Here the agreement stops. Some feel that women, as long as they are over age 18, should be allowed to make the choice to earn money in that manner. Others feel the whole industry is an abomination, is exploitive, and is immoral to all involved. In our program, as a nonprofit organization, we are required to draw lines based on what is legal and illegal, even while we try to take a common-sense approach to moral issues. Yet many parents wish we could tailor our approach to the needs of their loved one, and parents don't agree as to those needs.

Young men who have little success finding real women with whom to have sexual relations appreciate readily available pornography. Pornography featuring adults is not illegal. However, our clients can find pornography beyond their wildest imaginings on the web, and they are unsure when they've stepped over the line separating legal pornography from illegal child pornography. They think that if they found it on the internet, it must be okay. When a young man gets captivated by child pornography and can't be convinced how wrong it is (and illegal), we have no recourse but to forbid him to have internet access. (In our experience, the parental blocks are not effective in allowing some pornography but blocking the illegal kinds.) And there is still the problem of that young man using others' computers and putting them at risk by searching for the illegal material. We generally cannot keep a client in the program when he is obsessed by illegal pornography. Generally such a client needs a more restrictive environment for his own protection.

One other aspect of computer use has already been touched upon in discussions about money. Some clients become very skilled at ordering things online and having no means to pay for the items. Generally we return things when we can; we negotiate payments, and we rely on the reductions in the client's spending money to motivate him to stop the behavior. Usually there is a compulsive element if the client has difficulty stopping the behavior. Then the only recourse is for him to live without internet service. If you think about what you would do when supervising a child, you see how we arrive at our strategies. However, when a parent has to treat an adult like a child, it can lead to bad feelings all around. When staff, not parents, take the same steps, we are better able to preserve the adult's dignity and self-respect.

On the positive side, computers are being used by our clients for learning and for fun. Some use art programs to make cards, calendars, notepads, and other gifts. They are proud when they complete something in the realm of art that doesn't look childish. In addition, they are becoming proficient in using email to keep in touch with relatives and with other clients who have left the Center. I've noticed that the use of email improves writing skills over time. One young man writes to the editor of the local newspaper and has had many letters published. We've promoted writing campaigns in response to political issues of importance to our clients' welfare. Being occupied in a positive manner eliminates much of the time available to use the computer for dangerous, costly, or questionable objectives. Again, a good habit replacing a bad habit is what we strive for.

Cell phones, in their own way, create problems with money and deception. Many clients cannot grasp the difference in cost between the various cell phone service plans. They have been accustomed to using land lines and knowing that their phone bill is an item in their budget that they don't have to think about. Those who have misused land line telephones have been given phone cards, which are easy to understand. You use them until the time (money) is used up. Then you are cut off (and it's time to wheedle phone use from your friends). Parents like the phone cards as a method of control, but some are concerned about the need for a phone call in an emergency. The debate over which kind of phone and which kind of service is best is being won by cell phone over land line use, because cell phones are so popular in the mainstream culture.

Most of our clients now have cell phones. Besides the obvious potential abuse of the budget and the same dangers that attend internet use, cell phones have one more downside. Clients can call staff or their parents from a cell phone and lie about where they are. We have, now, a whole new area of deception to keep track of. We can take cell phones away from clients who misuse them, but then we must revisit the problem of having a phone for emergencies. We can require a land line as well as a cell phone, but that causes extra expense. For most clients, firm reminders of real consequences, like runaway costs and internet schemes, keep them in check; for others the cell phone is the perfect tool for impulsivity. It is right there in pocket or purse and can be used without thought, without judgment. This issue is a work in progress.

Exploitation

I've said a lot about how we handle bad behavior in general. We emphasize real, concrete consequences and then we make those consequences come about. Of course we can require repayment when food and personal belongings are taken. We employ thinking out loud as a technique to provide the kind of deliberation the clients' brains can't do for them. Ultimately we also employ punishments as a last resort. Public apologies, fines, and community service are in our arsenal.

I've said elsewhere that the staff laugh a lot, in our work. We laugh when the clients outsmart us with their unique logic, or by exploiting our failure to be as concrete as they are. At one point we were frustrated about food being borrowed, lent, swiped, begged, mooched and so on. I made a big announcement: there was to be a new rule prohibiting borrowing or lending or giving away food. I provided a forum for explanation, questions, and discussion of the new rule. I felt I had been exhaustive in explaining it. The very next day I got wind of two clients eating each other's food. I asked them if they hadn't heard of the new rule. Yes, they said, but we didn't borrow or lend food…we traded! I had forgotten to say *no trading*. A few days after trading was added to the list, they came up with *offering*. And another few days later we heard of someone being asked to *chip in*. I tell this story to illustrate why we laugh, but it also shows how we learn to give up on certain points of control. The clients who were trading food were not mindful of fair trade value. They might trade a soda for three microwave dinners. That offends our sense of fairness—and it might cause us to receive a call from a parent. The point is that *sometimes we can't stop the clients from behaving in ways that suit them*. We bring them together to live among their true peers and we see them develop real friendships. Then we try to make them conduct their friendships according to our standards. They can't always aspire to the vision we have for them. Then the vision they have for themselves has to be good enough.

Our clients can be exploited by people outside the community. This happens more than you might imagine. Unscrupulous people can spot the disabled and can think of myriad ways to use them and get them in trouble. It can be as simple as being talked into buying liquor for underage drinkers. Or they can be victims of more harmful scams. I mentioned elsewhere the client who had moved out of the program into his own apartment. He met a new "friend" at a bus stop, invited him home, and within a few days had been conned. He told his friend about the problem and was exploited again when the friend offered to "help."

Another form of exploitation is not even illegal: it occurs when offers are made by telephone, online, television, and so on, and our clients can't discern the exploitive aspects of the offer. They constantly sign up for things they think are free and then receive huge bills, which they typically ignore until they go to collection. Or they take a month's free sample of some service, online or by phone, and then find they've entered into a long-term contract they can't afford. Our methods of dealing with these offers have been explained in the discussion of money.

Social interactions between clients can illustrate what we might consider to be meanness or at least lack of kindness and consideration. They break promises and dates; they are tactless and insulting and call it "just being honest." They pass along information that was told in confidence or was not meant to be heard by a third party. They justify telling each other hurtful things on the grounds that "friends tell all." These are some of the effects of executive function impairment that would never be revealed in a structured evaluation. There is no better way to explain the pervasiveness of such impairment in everyday life skills than to see it in our community. And it is completely understandable in the context of frontal lobe impairment. As I have said repeatedly, our clients try to pass for normal. So they use words and phrases they hear in the culture, but they don't know how to temper the catch phrases with judgment. So tactlessness passes for "being honest." And impulsivity replaces commitment to a plan.

Luckily, our clients are also quite concrete in their acceptance of apologies. They even accept from one another the unfortunate fact that an apology does not equal a promise not to commit the same offense again. They do the same wrong things over and over and they forgive one another over and over again.

As long as exploitation remains fairly mutual and consistent between all clients, we live with it while always seeking new ways to replace bad habits with better ones. If a particular client is targeted or scapegoated, we intervene. And when a client is revealed to be truly predatory toward his peers, and others fear him, we have to expel him for the peace and security of the community. This has only happened once in my ten years, and the client was physically aggressive as well as predatory and exploitive.

Stealing

We use the same tactics suggested for children in our attempts to change the behavior of a client who steals. We employ strong expressions of anger and require public apologies in front of the whole community. We require community service while wearing an orange vest like the safety vests worn by construction workers. We remove privileges like computer time and spending money. Of course we require repayment of what was stolen.

These tactics have worked in cases where the stealing was mainly a matter of testing the boundaries and the authority of the program. Clients who have come to us from institutions or therapeutic boarding schools are most likely to engage in this kind of testing. One client stole from his roommate specifically, it seemed to us, to test how his father's authority would stack up against ours. He was able to get his father to call and try to talk us out of the public apology and the community service. We didn't budge and he has not stolen again since completing the various consequences.

The kind of stealing we can work with, albeit reluctantly, is the kind that goes on between roommates. They label it stealing when they are the victim, and sharing or borrowing when they are the perpetrator. I'm talking about eating each other's food and using items like clothing, CDs and DVDs without permission, and perhaps breaking them or passing them along to someone else. Money is usually not left lying around because of the compulsion, already discussed, to spend all money immediately. But occasionally a client will report the loss of money. It is usually transparent who has taken it; typically the roommate of the victim will have gone out and purchased something immediately. Anyone with money or a new purchase on a weekday is suspect. The person who stole has to repay the victim from his next weekend's discretionary money and he has to perform community service.

Hank exemplifies a particularly interesting and difficult aspect of executive disability. He appears to have no moral compass at all. He is not unkind or mean-spirited; he just doesn't behave according to any rules. He seeks what he wants relentlessly and feels no remorse when he steals from friends or breaks items that belong to others. Hank knows he is cute and can be appealing, especially to older women. He behaves like a meek child when he wants women to like him. He can recite moral rules as well as anyone. In fact, in one attempt to curb his stealing, we had him write a paper on punishments for stealing in other cultures. He wrote about a culture in which a person's hand can be cut off as punishment for theft. Hank was struck by this horrific idea and wrote about it with great conviction. But it made no impression whatsoever on his own tendency to steal.

To be fair, Hank doesn't plan to steal. He only steals when the opportunity is before him and he needs or wants an item left unguarded. The more impressive aspect of his moral failure is his complete lack of remorse when caught. In one instance, he admitted under pressure that he had taken an unguarded ten-dollar bill. He was asked to produce it, which he did with little reluctance. He was positively appalled, though, when told to give it back. He felt that the discipline was over when he admitted he had taken the money—wasn't that enough? He was waiting out the reprimand, passively listening and displaying a sheepish expression, with every intention of spending the money! There is no cure for this deficit in this young man. He doesn't have the feelings for others that would lead to intentional good behavior. He lives at the moral level of trying not to get caught.

How do we keep Hank in the program? Again, one of the strengths of the program is its adaptability. The other clients know Hank steals, and they seem to know he can't help himself. So they protect their belongings when he's around and they accept him for his other likable qualities. We have to balance what is best for the program and what is best for Hank. He would be miserable in a more tightly controlled setting, and he is doing relatively little damage in our setting, now that everyone has found ways to manage him. I've often wondered why Hank doesn't steal from stores. I think the answer is that stores employ many cues that remind buyers how to behave in a store. In other words, the setting reminds us that there is a price for every item and we must pass through the cashier aisles before leaving. Hank doesn't steal in stores because he is reminded not to steal and he is aware he would probably be caught. This is speculation, however. I haven't asked Hank why he doesn't steal in stores because I know what he would say: "It's against the law!" He would act shocked that I needed to ask such a question and he would see no irony in the situation.

Deliberate, planned stealing cannot be tolerated in our program. We once had a client who cased the staff offices and the other clients' apartments to see exactly where and when purses and wallets were left unattended. Before he was expelled, he had stolen from virtually all staff and many of his friends. When there has been a long-established pattern of stealing from parents and siblings, and shoplifting from stores, we usually cannot affect the behavior. When parents have repeatedly excused stealing because of the disability, the client has learned to use his disability to "get out of trouble." In one instance when we did expel the client, both his parents proudly admitted they believed in a counter-culture, anti-authority lifestyle. They did everything from lying about the child's age when buying movie tickets to "cheating the system" to get subsidies like food stamps. A child whose disability allows only concrete thinking will be unable to grow up in that atmosphere and choose something different for himself in adulthood.

Physical aggression

We have had a few clients who hit someone else in the program, once. Our reaction is swift and strong. "We don't have hitting in this program," we say. Hitting once seems to be about the same as stealing once. It is a behavior brought from elsewhere to test the limits of the program. Many young men feel a need to push against the rules, possibly to convince themselves there really are rules. We talk about social and legal consequences rather than about rules per se. We stress that it is against the law for adults to hit one another "out in the real world." If they imply they are hitting due to their disability and cannot control themselves, then they need tighter containment than we provide, and will have to live in a more controlled environment. When told that, they generally "discover" that they do have enough self-control to stop hitting.

Another kind of hitting occurs when a stable, well-known client is pushed beyond his limits. That can occur when we make an error in placing a new, perhaps rambunctious young man as roommate with a more tentative or anxious older man. If there is a lot of teasing, borrowing, incessant chatter, messiness and so forth, the older client might lose his temper and bop the younger one. We assess the situation and either make a roommate change immediately, or provide counseling toward respect for boundaries in the apartment. We've never had a client develop into an aggressive person unless he was already inclined that way.

We have clients who have outbursts as part of their disability. They may yell and curse and appear very scary, but they don't hit. They are taught strategies for managing their outbursts, much as you would teach a child how to ride out his tantrums. They often have a PRN medication that they take in those situations. It is a wonderful thing to see individuals, whose outbursts would not be tolerated in a work or public setting, following strategies for managing themselves, and being tolerated and accepted by their peers who understand that they can't help it.

When we make a mistake and accept a client who is truly physically aggressive, we have to expel that client. We are saddened by these rare expulsions because joining the program represents a monumental life change for the whole family. Hopes are raised, belongings are packed, parents dare to look forward to a normal retirement lifestyle. If there is a failure to adjust to our program, often there are no other good alternatives. The disappointment is huge. Fortunately, in over ten years we have expelled only two clients for aggressive behavior toward others, one for self-injurious behaviors, and one for a pattern of spectacular glass-breaking.

Chapter 18

Teamwork with Parents

This chapter may be of limited interest to those readers whose children are still very young, or to those who don't expect ever to be part of a therapeutic community like the CAL program. However, it does provide information about the complex relationships that inevitably develop when an adult with disabilities goes out into the greater community to live. Perhaps you will be designing a program of your own. Any situation short of complete independence will most likely include caregivers, a case manager, or a designated payee or conservator in your adult child's life. The following information should therefore be of interest.

Ideally, staff and clients' parents or other family members work together. *The best teamwork occurs when there is mutual trust and a similar evaluation of the client's disability.* Trust is essential whenever we put a loved one in the care of others; and a similar evaluation of the disability is essential because it determines the expectations that all parties will have for the client.

Teamwork between staff and parents is a complicated relationship, one that is affected by many variables, like the age of the client, prior experience in living away from parents, geographical distance, issues of privacy, alliance, and triangulation, the skills of the staff, the expectations of everyone involved, as mentioned above, and the temperament of the client and family. And, sadly, sometimes funding issues override all others.

The client's age and experience

Individuals who have just reached their eighteenth birthday may be too immature to fulfill the requirements of a program offering supported independence. At that age, they tend to treat the program as if it were boarding school. Imagine having your own apartment, and spending money, and no one to tell you what to do when you were 14 or 15 years old. You might be wildly out of control, whether you had a disability or not. We have found that waiting until clients reach age 20 or 21 generally produces a better result. But while we are concerned about their age, there is also the question of what else they may have been doing in those first two to three years after high school.

Clients who have been at home for up to three years after high school are generally chafing for a new experience. They know their non-disabled peers are doing more than they are doing. Developmentally, they should be yearning for greater autonomy, social experiences, romantic relationships, and sex. If parents are unusually resourceful they may have taught their child to cook and do household chores; they may have secured a job for their young adult child. They may have taught him to drive and supervised the process of getting the driver's license. They may even have found some kinds of social activities through a church group, Special Olympics, or adult education. All of these accomplishments enhance his chances of being successful when he reaches a program like ours.

On the other hand, if the adult child has entered into one of the less functional scenarios described earlier, then the adjustment to life at CAL will be more problematic. In scenarios like the rebellious youth and the compliant child, the level of enthusiasm for our program will depend upon the client's ability to imagine what he might gain in autonomy, experiences, and relationships with peers. For some adults with disabilities, seeing is believing. In other words, they may protest and resist the new plan until they have seen the program, the apartment, and their new friends.

Let's consider young adults who have lived away from their parents. When clients have lived away from home already, perhaps at a boarding school or in a therapeutic facility of some kind, they have had some experience of managing homesickness. They also may have had the odd experience of learning that not everyone sees them as their parents do. Some families develop such idiosyncratic ways of accommodating their kids that it surprises them when other adults won't do those things their parents have always done. Some clients have greater awareness of all the world has to offer, and they are more ready to live in a new place and learn the lay of the land.

The reason the client has lived away from home makes a difference too. Some have been to special-ed, private secondary schools. That generally means they've seen large numbers of other kids similar to themselves. They've learned jargon related to disability and special education, maybe even psychological or psychiatric terminology applied to themselves and others like them. They've been acquainted with a number of adults who feel comfortable around kids and young people with disabilities. All of these experiences affect their adjustment to life in our program.

Some young people have been incarcerated in juvenile facilities because of behaviors stemming from their disability. In the case of young males, the behaviors will typically have been related to sex, drugs, aggression, or minor law-breaking. These clients are usually pretty inept at whatever sexual or aggressive activity they engaged in, and commonly a misinterpretation of their disability has led to the extreme consequence of incarceration. Our clients' typical sexual offense would be something like sneaking into a women's restroom in a public place to attempt to see women undressed. Or peeping into windows in the neighborhood in a similar attempt to satisfy sexual curiosity. Incarceration with true sex offenders or predators is a bad experience for our population as they are great mimics and will take on the behaviors and attitudes they see around them.

Violence in our population is about as inept as the sexual "crimes" reported above. Generally a young male in our population might take on the image of a tougher type of kid because he thinks it makes him appear cool. But he will be poor at producing the behaviors associated with the image. He might become frightened or intimidated, and he might be carrying some kind of weapon, like a knife; he might show the weapon at the wrong time and the wrong place. Our clients can appear violent if they have emotional dysregulation and become overly angry at the wrong time and place. They may seem to be threatening when they are simply losing control of their frustration or anxiety. The appearance of being threatening is, of course, exacerbated if the client is physically intimidating in some way, such as being exceptionally tall, big, or muscular.

The types of care available for young people with behavioral manifestations of disability vary widely around the country, the world, and between urban and rural areas. Being treated together with members of psychiatric populations is, for our clients, an opportunity to learn new behaviors that may have no real meaning to them. They will learn from mentally ill individuals in the same way they learn from "normals," by imitation, without understanding. Learned behaviors are the result, such as acting out for attention, labeling one's inner experiences negatively ("I have low self-esteem"), trying self-injurious behaviors like cutting, or describing themselves as mentally ill. Some clients have come to us exhibiting signs of institutionalization, meaning they have adapted to dependency upon staff for every decision, and need staff to provide structure, guidance, and permission at every moment.

Finally, another way clients may have been away from the parental home is the most chaotic option. They can have landed "on the street" due to failing an ultimatum from parents to get a job or get out. Or they may have stormed out after an argument and, if they were over 18, the parents could not legally compel them to return home. Being out on their own with no support is a terrible situation in which our clients are apt to be exploited and abused. A good disposition and some social skills may lead to their being sheltered by well-meaning people, at least for a while. But these clients usually gravitate toward people who are not much higher-functioning than they are in terms of judgment. They fall into situations which can result in all kinds of exploitation and abuse, such as drug use, sexual favors, unwanted pregnancy, disease, crime, and even death. The best outcome is that the young adult goes home voluntarily and the event becomes the catalyst to seek a placement. Our experience at CAL has been that a young person who has faced *some* hardship in the world is receptive to the opportunities presented by the program and therefore is likely to work hard and do well.

To summarize, then, clients can have spent time away from home because they were sent to special boarding schools, treatment programs, or because they were being punished or incarcerated. They may also have spent time in psychiatric facilities if, again, they had difficulty with emotional outbursts or extreme anxiety or depression. Or they can have run away from home and spent time on the streets. The specific effect of all this on the teamwork between staff and parents has most to do with whether the parents can stop feeling guilty. Guilty parents engage in protecting their kids from reality and from the reasonable judgments of others. They try to conceal events they consider to be their mistakes, not realizing the sooner we know about the past, the better we can begin to combat it. They make excuses for behavior, based upon beliefs that the adult child is depressed or has low self-esteem, even in the absence of evidence for those feelings.

Guilt over the past is not helpful in getting on with the teamwork required to secure success for a new member of the CAL community.

Parents who are more accepting and matter-of-fact about past experiences have a better chance of moving forward and facing their child's future realistically. We try to cultivate the expectation that we will brainstorm together, but not judge one another's efforts, in the search for the best treatment approach for each adult client.

Shared assessment of the disability, alliances, and triangulation

Rarely do parents and staff have exactly the same assessment of a client's disability. Parents may have an inflated sense of their child's abilities based upon not realizing how much they cue the young person. Or they may have put off teaching essential skills because they didn't believe the child to be capable, when he or she actually was. Staff have the advantage of employing critical observation with no personal feelings about the conclusions. The absence of feelings like disappointment, guilt, shame, or pride is a huge asset when starting to work with a new client.

When parents think their child is less able than staff think in some important area, the outcome is generally a good one. If staff can get the client to cook better than the parents thought possible, or if she lands a job that parents never imagined, or if she loses weight or has her first boyfriend, in short, any success that was unforeseen by parents is a happy outcome. On the other hand, when parents think the adult child is more capable than staff think, the outcome is more problematic. Failures in that case are thought by parents to be the staff's fault. Excuses are made for the adult child and she usually understands the potential for exploiting her parents' feelings against staff. This kind of standoff can go on for years. Parents can't bring about the results they want, and they may believe there is no other option for their child than our program. So they leave their child in the program and they continue to be critical and to undermine attempts to achieve the results we think are appropriate and possible. Interestingly, the client in this situation often learns to adapt to the expectations of each side of the triangle: in the presence of his parents he is critical of the staff and the program, endorsing their stance; yet he continues to enjoy his apartment, his friends, his independence, and the services provided by staff. He tends to avoid being in a room with both parents and staff, as his adaptation of playing one side against the other might be exposed.

Of course, the best working relationship occurs when there is close agreement as to the strengths and limitations of the client. Some clients who have been with us for many years benefit from a warm, trusting relationship between parents and staff that allows any member of the triangle to offer a suggestion in a climate of safety, knowing the other two participants will give it a fair hearing. We have had a client ask for a bicycle and both staff and parents judged it a disastrous plan; we have had parents suggest a particular job and staff and client found it an ingenious suggestion. Teamwork allows for more adventurous ideas than would emerge in an adversarial relationship.

Triangulation is an important concept that can exert a negative influence in any relationship between a client, parents, and helpers. Triangulation is the use of two-against-one alliances that can occur whenever three parties enter into a relationship. The triangle in the case of adults with disabilities will always be made up of client, family, and staff. Any two can and do form an alliance, and sometimes the alliance works to leave the third party out. In my early years, before I understood the close connection between most people with Asperger's and their parents, I participated in an instance of triangulation. A client insisted he was not close to his mother; in fact he said he hated her. He told stories in which his mother did seem to have mistreated him. I didn't do anything to actively work against this parent, but I never consulted her on behalf of her son because I believed his statements that she was unreasonable and abusive. Several months into this misunderstanding, I found out that this client and his mother saw one another every weekend, without fail. Because he was dependent on his mother and because he has Asperger's, he felt no contradiction in "bad-mouthing" his mother and also insisting on seeing her every weekend. Had I known what I do now, I would have taken every opportunity to work with the young man as to the inconsistency of his behavior and his exaggerated statements about his mother.

When parents act in alliance with their adult child against staff, they generally do it because they are afraid of something. They may fear their child will be rejected by a provider of services for not learning fast enough. So a mother may show up and clean her son's apartment on weekends, thus sabotaging his progress. Or parents may disagree with an aspect of staff goals for the client and surreptitiously allow him to do things a different way, also telling him not to tell staff. Parents think they can enlist their child in a secret against staff and he will keep the secret, especially if he is receiving something he wants from his parents. *The client's disability is such that he cannot keep a secret from the people he sees every day.* Instead, the client usually tells staff all about the agreement with his parents, often adding some details that are not true. Or if he does try to keep the secret, he will feel as if he is lying to staff and it will weigh heavily on him.

This example represents inadequate alliance between parents and staff, but the more important alliance that is damaged is that between the client and the staff, because parents have said to their child, in effect, *we must be more loyal to one another than either of us is to the staff.* Staff do not want to usurp the position of love between child and parents. These two relationships are, and will always be, different. But clients will be confused about how to feel toward staff if they see that their parents don't trust the staff. *Clients can't feel very safe if they believe their parents have put them in a program where they, the parents, don't trust the very people they chose to care for their child.*

Certainly there are times when all three parties to the triangle, client, parents, and staff, meet together and say everything that needs to be said in front of one another. But there will always be some decisions that must be made in the client's best interest, and out of his awareness. Our belief is that those decisions should be made by parents and staff, pooling their knowledge of the client's disability as well as his strengths, his likes and dislikes, and especially based upon figuring out what will work.

Privacy issues

The clients' privacy is another factor related to open communication with parents. I've said a lot about privacy and confidentiality in the description of our counseling methods. The stated purpose of the program is to help adults lead the most independent lives they can achieve. Clearly, then, they may feel it is not fair or justified for staff to tell their parents about every misstep. Given the executive deficits, the clients' judgment will always be an area of difficulty, and purposefully, therefore, we do not hesitate to discuss their poor judgment with them. Sometimes we point out that their desire not to tell their parents something *is* an instance of poor judgment. There are times, though, when we honor a request not to tell the parents something, often because it may be motivating for the client not to repeat the behavior. At other times, we may discuss issues with the parents as clinical team members, expecting them to maintain confidentiality with the staff and not the client. This is only done in the client's best interest.

There is another side to the issue of privacy. Adults on the autism spectrum are not known for their discretion. They tell staff *and each other* anything and everything that occurs to them from their 20-plus years of living with their families. The last thing on parents' minds when they send their adult child to our program is privacy for their family secrets. We have heard about intimate arguments, near-divorces, child abuse, domestic violence, miscarriages, and acts of petty theft, as well as how the parents vote and how they eat and how they spend their money. It is as if the whole family were engaged in family therapy and had agreed to tell all, but they aren't all present to hear the revelations.

I generally handle this by telling family members, before anything happens, that they have given up their privacy by placing their adult child with us. I also tell them I will assume their child probably got some portion of the story wrong anyway. Some realize they should probably ask *exactly* what I've been told so they can correct the parts the client may have gotten wrong. Most parents are remarkably able to laugh about it and move on. Most of these revelations have been resolved with trust intact. Parents who are happy with the progress their child is making are generally willing to sacrifice their privacy to that end.

Geographical distance

Open communication is definitely complicated by distance. Granted there are many easy and inexpensive ways to keep in touch; nevertheless, talking by phone across time zones can be troublesome. Email is easy and effective, but sometimes nuance and tone are misinterpreted in emails. When the information to be communicated is troubling or even shocking, it is always preferable to talk with parents in person. Also, from the parents' point of view, it is reassuring to those who are close by to know that they can drop in without notice and therefore get a view of the program, and of their child, that is spontaneous and not staged for them.

Distance means homesickness for some clients and excessive worry by some parents who have been accustomed to taking care of their child on a daily basis. Visits must be planned to fit into the program schedule and eventually to the employment schedule of the client. Some parents have a hard time grasping that their grown child's job is real, expecting them to be given time off whenever the parents want to see them. Visits and traveling can be very disruptive when attempts have been made to impose structure on chaotic lives. Parents must realize that their child's travel plans may send a ripple through the whole community. Parents who visit the program may ask to stay in their child's apartment. This is usually disruptive to the roommate. Parents may try to be extra nice to their child's roommate for a variety of reasons, both good and bad. Being nice to other members of the program usually translates to taking them out for meals, movies, or shopping. Imagine the feelings of those clients who never receive such a benevolent visitor. Knowing it is difficult, we ask parents to keep in mind the welfare of the whole community while they are intensely focused on the well-being of their own child.

Another feature of distance is that parents don't see changes in their child in the gradual manner that they occur. Instead, they see what may appear to be huge changes, sometimes in directions the parents had not predicted. Generally these changes are related to greater maturity and are in every way positive. But a parent who last saw a 27-year-old young man dressed like a teenager may be shocked to see him dressed appropriately for his age group. Changes in hair style can make a dramatic difference in the look of a young man or woman. And some clients even change their names, from the more childish Bobby to the more mature Bob or Robert, for example. Parents would take each of these changes in their stride if they didn't have to encounter them all at once. Some of the most welcome changes are those that truly reflect new accomplishments, like securing a job, or managing aspects of life that were unmanageable before. But the change that presents a mixed blessing for long-distance parents is what they feel when their adult child first says, "I've had a good time visiting, but I'm ready to go home." How should parents feel when the new place has become "home?" Hard as it may be, they should feel good!

Skills of the staff

At CAL, our founder and Executive Director is the backbone of our staff. Over the 20 years of the program's existence, she has moved consistently toward a more professional operation, in every way. This is due partly to stringent licensing requirements, but mainly to the academic climate pervading the various associations that support clients on the learning disability spectrum and the autism spectrum. Genevieve reads widely in the disability literature and is a politically informed advocate who has lobbied in Washington to secure rights for our clients. But her approach will always be informed primarily by her experience of her son and all the other clients she has known.

Genevieve has taught staff to trust their powers of observation. If she thinks someone on staff is making assumptions rather than observations she will ask them to find an opportunity to learn by observing. It is unforgettable to see something as mundane as a client washing a frying pan without interfering (that was the hardest part). All the executive deficits you would ever want to learn about were there on display, and the client was oblivious to them. I learned how that particular woman would perform many tasks by observing one.

Another of Genevieve's teachings is that any task, no matter how simple or trivial-seeming, can be broken down by task analysis. The way to teach a task is by knowing the steps and the logical way they follow one another to completion. Then we must be flexible enough to see that logic can be turned on its head and the outcome will still be all right. If your child already knows how to do something, and the outcome is acceptable, it is usually not good to try to change the way he does it.

Talking with people who are best at concrete thinking and who have poor short-term memories is another talent our staff must master. We don't say to a client, "Tell me what happened last night." We say, "Tell me who decided to buy beer." That gets us right past the step where they deny everything. Then when they mention a name we might say, let's go tell him you said it was his idea. That might produce something like, "Well, he'll probably lie and say it was my idea." Now we know whose idea it was and we might proceed by attributing responsibility to both clients.

Clients who have spent their whole lives maneuvering around a parent will, of course, try the same tactics with us. One recent example was provided by a client who had been in several programs and had been expelled from all of them. He is a young man whose learned interpersonal behaviors are actually more of a liability than his brain-related disability. Among other things, he likes to get others in trouble. Recently he awoke at 4:30 in the morning to discover his roommate's girlfriend sleeping on the couch. He called the emergency phone number to report this and was reprimanded for using that number for a non-emergency. His entire message was recorded on voice mail. The next day he told his counselor that someone might say he had called the emergency number, but he had not. The counselor took him to the office of the person he had called, where he repeated that he had not made the call. They played the recorded message, at which point he got angry and said the staff talked to each other too much. His next tactic was to say he was confused. The counselor asked him if this kind of manipulation used to work with his father. He readily said that it did. Then she asked him if he could tell that it wasn't working here in the program. That concept was a bit difficult for him to grasp, but the counselor found ways to restate the premise until she was sure he understood: the lies that worked with dad are not working with staff. That was enough of a message for one day.

It will take a long time for this young man to learn to be honest, if he ever does, because he has had great success with lying for over 20 years. He is not the same as Hank, described earlier as a man without a moral compass. This young man has learned that his father can be convinced of the most improbable lies, and he wants the rest of the world to function the same way his world with his dad functions. The talent of the counselor is to be logical with him, to confront his story one piece at a time, and to tell him which part needs to be changed. At no time does he appear to feel that she is not on his side.

Another technique in working with executive function impaired individuals is to get *them* to explain things rather than explaining or lecturing to them. Suppose a client has caused a ruckus by borrowing her roommate's clothes. She maintains that they both borrow clothing whenever they want to so it was okay to take her favorite blouse when she wasn't even home. As a parent or staff, we might be tempted to launch into a lecture covering the whole topic, beginning to end. Instead, we ask the client simple, concrete questions that lead down a logical path. The point is to lead to an understanding of the roommate's feelings, to the idea of taking responsibility for one's own behavior, and to a plan for a better outcome next time. *The more we can get the client to say all those things in her own words, the more likely she is to have "heard" the message.* In this instance the questioning began with asking why the roommate was angry if this is something they both do all the time. What might be different this time that made her angry, and so on.

Most techniques utilized in staff training stem from the same principles. The principles are that client behaviors are caused by impaired brain functioning, for the most part, with some environmental modeling thrown in; that strengths can be built upon more easily than limitations can be overcome; that observation is the best way to know what really happened; and that responsibility is usually shared by all clients involved in anything that goes wrong. Overall, the qualities that make the best staff are compassion, tolerance, curiosity, flexibility, respect, and commitment. A sense of humor is indispensable as well.

Temperament of client and family

Temperament is an interesting concept. We don't really know why children may or may not be similar to one or both of their parents in temperament. We've heard of situations where a person feels he just doesn't fit into the family he belongs to. A young person might feel more bold or more humorous or more idealistic than his family's style; or she will not fulfill the generations-long commitment to a particular life's work, such as a long line of pastors or doctors. We suppose there is a genetic or hereditary component to these issues; and there is certainly an element of learning as well. How does this concern our population? Many of our clients are exaggeratedly similar to a parent in temperament.

We see this similarity particularly when a client is anxious by nature. A parent will likely be anxious as well. Anxiety in the family affects our ability to provide services. The client may be excessively fearful about trying new things, but usually he will be positively persuaded by peer pressure. There is strong motivation to try things their peers are doing, with the reward of doing new things with friends. The parents have been anxious far longer than the client, and, when worried about something their child might attempt, they don't have the positive element of peers cheering them on. In these cases, staff can expect to receive many calls expressing concern about everything the client might be newly exposed to. Parents express fear of the wrong job being attempted, of public transportation, of spoiled food being eaten by their unsupervised adult child, of exploitation by other clients, including sexual coercion, of strangers gaining access to the apartment complex, of dirt and germs in the environment, and of the staff not being patient enough with their sensitive child.

To enhance an anxious parent's ability to work with the team, I suggest finding a support group of other parents who are not particularly anxious. She should deliberately surround herself with parents who take a more casual approach to life's uncertainties. If she will present her worries in a safe environment and then listen, not only to the words but to the tone of voice of a less fearful person, she can learn to do a reality check with these trusted individuals. How many of their kids have gotten sick from spoiled food, or have gotten lost on public transportation? They may in fact have done these things, but what was the outcome? Did they learn something new, did they rely on a kind stranger, and did they get home safely after all? Life is full of uncertainties and we all have to reach our own balance between boldness and self-protection. A person with disabilities will definitely need guidance, but can, nevertheless, achieve a balance point that feels comfortable and does not represent capitulation to lifelong anxiety. A client in a safe environment may have a better chance to overcome innate anxiety than does his parent who has lived with it much longer, after all.

It is a joy to encounter a whole family of sunny dispositions. The client with such a temperament is extremely fortunate because these people are naturally likable. Being easily liked paves the way to securing assistance and tolerance when needed. I know a young man with Asperger's who, uncharacteristically, has a sunny disposition. He does have the rigidity and the odd interests typical of Asperger's. He would like to talk endlessly about Civil War battles, but he does so with such charm that he is a delight to everyone who meets him. The first time I had him in my office for a counseling session, he received a call on his cell phone. He very politely asked if he might take the call as it was from his former employer and he would be brief. I watched with fascination as he paced across my office while talking on the phone. He used a rather loud voice and seemed sort of "official" in his manner. When he hung up the phone he said, casually, "When I'm on the phone I like to pretend I'm a neurologist." I've never heard a sentence that was more unexpected than that one!

One more temperamental type deserves a bit of discussion. The word "entitled" is heard a lot lately. The word suggests an expectation of getting everything one wants and, moreover, deserving everything one can imagine. In addition, the word suggests that other people should acknowledge and cater to the deserving person. I don't know what gives rise to people feeling this way, but I do see that it runs in families. When a client has feelings of entitlement, one or both of his parents are sure to exhibit the same trait. A mother called us to say that since her daughter had been in the program for over a year she "deserved" to live alone in a one-bedroom apartment. Never mind that we only have two of those and both were occupied by clients who had very specific needs to live alone. And never mind that the client actually could not afford a one-bedroom unit. A feature of entitlement is the lack of logic behind the demands.

Entitlement becomes an issue in an adult child's out of home care when parents expect the program design to be altered to fit their child's needs. We've been asked to modify the whole food program for one client, to accompany clients with travel plans on Christmas Day, to alter the hours of a client's job or to arrange for time off work at the parents' convenience, to change roommates or not to change, and on and on. If you have this temperament, you probably cannot see it realistically as someone outside you would describe it. But if you suspect that you might, and are willing to examine it, again I would advise getting a reality check from a trusted friend or another parent. If someone else says they would never make the kinds of requests you have in mind, have the courage to ask them to explain why they say that. The answer will likely include the notion that you are asking for too much, or expecting to be catered to. In our program, we accommodate when we can, and we do not comply with completely unreasonable requests; and there have been times when a client had to leave because a parent became a morale problem for staff. That is a sad outcome and should not have to happen.

Summary

This chapter has covered disparate elements that contribute to teamwork between clients, family members, and staff who serve adults with autism spectrum disabilities. Some elements stem from the experiences of the client and the expectations of the family. Some evolve over time and emerge from factors like temperament, trust, and growing maturity of the client. Personal attributes and lucky accidents can result in lifelong partnerships between staff and families. Sometimes the most unexpected but important element is that the client makes it known she has made a home away from home. This is to be celebrated.

A New Idea: A Variation on the Model of Group Home Living

I've given a great deal of attention to describing the model program provided by the Center for Adaptive Learning in California. But I am aware that most states do not have sufficient financial support committed to these clients. Most parents cannot depend upon a similar program being developed near them. Although all states in the US are required to have some support in place for the mentally retarded and those with other disabilities like cerebral palsy and epilepsy, other diagnostic groups are not so fortunate. Those who are currently diagnosed PDD-NOS, and others on the autism spectrum, are not specifically supported (financially) by any organization.

Autism is the disorder that has pulled the focus of the whole country, and much of the developed world. Financial support and creative options for adult care will be needed in the near future in unprecedented numbers. Whether the whole spectrum will be treated equally in deserving services will have a lot to do with the way diagnoses are considered. I have personally heard several of the most important leaders in the field tell conference rooms full of parents, teachers, and service providers to seek and to give the diagnosis that will best lead to services. This is undoubtedly an act of advocacy, and therefore an ethical position to take with regard to caring for clients. But in terms of diagnostic accuracy it is confusing, to say the least. If clinicians are following that advice, and I believe they are, it must account for part of the current epidemic of autism diagnoses.

My proposal for a new diagnosis that clarifies and highlights the differences between Autistic Disorder, Asperger's Disorder, and those who default to PDD-NOS, would be meaningless if it did not also highlight the need for services tailored to such a diagnostic population. There is much work and advocacy to be done to bring about this change in service delivery. For now, I have one more suggestion related to services.

Parents of adult children who can access only the funding provided by social security benefits, or Supplemental Security Income (SSI), could maximize the value of those funds by forming small groups, and networks, of clients who would live together in adulthood. The first decision to be made is whether the clients should live with or without in-house staff, which is the defining element of a group home. If they were to live without staff on hand, it would still be imperative that there be some paid service providers involved in key positions of support. In addition to their shared housing, services could be provided to three to five or so young people at a time. Forming a network of several such homes or apartments near one another would be key to meeting the social needs of the clients, the most important being the selection of clients who have similar diagnoses and who function similarly.

It would be important for parents contemplating this kind of solution to begin as early as possible by creating networks with other parents. Your children would then be friends before they reach adulthood, which is a circumstance none of my current clients have enjoyed. And you would have a sense of which parents you could work with successfully. You must anticipate that there will be difficult decisions to make and incomprehensible situations to mediate. Most parents of kids with spectrum disabilities have spent their kids' whole lives being protective and feeling that they are the only advocate for their child. Trusting your fellow parents will allow you to be more open to advice and less defensive and fearful for your child when she needs something extra in terms of services. It will be important for all parents to develop a somewhat dispassionate view of their own child and the others in the network. In other words, there will come a time when you feel your child needs special consideration in some way, and therefore you will need to see when to grant the same to another member of the group.

At all costs, there should be one or more paid service providers who are not related to any of the clients. This will guarantee a more objective point of view toward your child and the others, an invaluable point of view. Remember, you are preparing for the day when you will not be there for your child.

I'm picturing this arrangement for clients who would be capable of living in the homes or apartments without live-in supervision. But they would need services similar to those we provide at the CAL program. The most important element of successful adult life is the separation from parents, in one's living arrangement and in terms of decision-making. To sustain that all-important independence, it would be essential for parents not to provide services to the home in which their own child lives. But parents could provide services to other homes in the network, where their child's friends live. The services would have to be tailored to the needs of the clients, and, whenever possible, hired staff should provide the most hands-on or intrusive services. In other words, if someone has to remind your son to make his bed, it had better be someone he considers "staff" rather than mom or Jason's mom. That way he is not thrust back into the role of child with each reminder. Instead, he can see himself as an adult with disabilities *and* a staff to assist him.

Similarly, when it comes to managing money, the best way to set up the service is to have someone other than a parent provide a no-nonsense explanation of the facts and the consequences related to managing a limited amount of money. Most likely each client would have a payee, meaning they would not be able to spend their money at their own discretion. Their household bills like rent and utilities could be paid from an account which all pay into equally. Their discretionary money could be given to them once a week or several times a week, with the natural consequence that when it's gone, it's gone. If you've ever been begged for money by your adult child, who has made the same impulsive mistakes over and over, imagine the relief in knowing that someone who doesn't have strong feelings about the situation is going to tell your son that there isn't any more money right now, period. Your son might then call you as his last resort. This is the time when it will be crucial to have a prepared speech. You could say something like this: you knew that living on your own would sometimes be difficult, and you agreed that we would all go by the rules. The staff has given you an answer and I can't break the rules. End of conversation. If you stick to this approach from the very first time, your adult child *will* adjust to it.

You can use the CAL model, described in Part Four, to enumerate the many kinds of services you will need to think about. Clients who can thrive in this model of supported living will need to have some areas of pretty high functioning. By high functioning I don't mean smarter; I mean better able to manage tasks related to daily living and less dominated by executive function deficits. For example, you would hope that issues related to food and health could be well managed by clients living in independent homes, those without in-house staff. The clients must either be able to shop for groceries themselves or accept healthy groceries ordered online and delivered to the home. They must be able to cook reasonable meals day after day, and remember when to eat and when not to eat. They must manage eating as a group, or be able to keep their foods separated and respect each other's habits and possessions, even down to individual food items. If all of this seems too difficult, then someone in a staff position (not mom!) must arrive each evening and oversee cooking and eating. That would be a good time to supervise preparation of the following day's lunches as well. Breakfast is generally the simplest meal and most clients can prepare a reasonable breakfast day after day. (Besides, if you've followed my advice in earlier chapters, you're already raising an adult with reasonable cooking and eating habits.)

The biggest difference between this model and the CAL program model is the amount of supervised time during the day. Time management is a difficult issue for adults with disabilities. For clients to flourish in this model they must have structure built into their day. If they are not capable of working, preferably part-time, then they must have a structured and supervised day program available to them. Without either of those options in place, I cannot see this living arrangement being successful. Like those clients I described who stay in the parental home but have no structure and no direction to their lives, they will end up mismanaging their time. Television, video games, and the computer, with its pull toward pornography, are the downfall of these clients. Lack of physical activity likewise leads to boredom and premature health problems. Time management, then, is inextricably linked with work and with social life.

The network of several homes with similar clients, clients who are true peers, is the most important feature of this arrangement. Many communities have leisure activities designed for adults with disabilities. If your community does not, you must advocate for them. In the meantime, this will be one more service you will have to provide through your parent network. Dances, bowling, hiking, swimming, sports events, and visits to museums on the free days are options. And of course there are always movies, but increasingly movies are being watched at home and therefore not regarded as much of an outing. You will have to think about and experiment with the level of supervision required to make these outings a success. It will be more than you think.

If your network consists mainly of male clients, you must make efforts to find families with young women who are the peers of these men. If you don't make efforts to find suitable romantic (and sexual) partners for your adult children, they will make those efforts themselves. I cannot emphasize this enough. Many of our young men seem childlike and completely unsuited for adult relationships. The more socially inept they are, the more likely they are to be enthralled by pornography on the internet; and they are eager to experience what they've seen. Even without pornography, their sexual drives are usually one of the normal things about them. Their social skills make them unable to find romantic partners from the normal population, therefore it is important that you steer them toward relationships with their true peers.

If, however, your adult children are much higher functioning, for example holding full-time jobs in the competitive market, their social skills might be at a different level than the clients I'm discussing. You might think some nice young woman your son describes as a friend at work will enter into a romantic relationship with him. I advise extreme caution in such a situation. Generally, a well-meaning young person might offer friendship, but will eventually move on with her life, leaving her friend with disabilities behind. It is best that you think about these things ahead of time, so your children don't have to learn every lesson "the hard way."

And finally, because safe sex cannot always be guaranteed, birth control must be in place. This is more difficult for parents of men because of the lack of a birth control method that can be in place *before* any decision-making is needed. Vasectomy is the best choice, but many parents and young men with disabilities hold out hope that things will change enough for them to consider parenthood. If you are quite convinced that is not likely, you should consider discussing vasectomy with your son.

Given all the social and interpersonal issues to be managed, it would be good if the paid staff in your housing network were people with counseling backgrounds. Group meetings in the various homes, and even larger meetings comprising the network of homes, would provide the clients opportunities to connect and discuss social issues at their own level. Counseling could be undertaken with the CAL model as a guide. At regular intervals, once a week, or once a month, a 45-minute group meeting facilitated by staff could be held and followed by TV or music and popcorn.

Employment will probably be the issue of most concern to parents. Clients' employment would ease the financial burden on the whole network. In addition, work would fill their time productively, as well as enhancing their satisfaction. Most importantly, for those closer to the autistic and Asperger's end of the spectrum, they sometimes experience enough social contact through the workplace that they are content or even prefer to be alone in the evenings. They may be tired from the work day and also from the added burden of trying to behave normally, and thus they are less likely to spend their down time getting into trouble. Their idiosyncratic hobbies are a great comfort to them after a day in "the real world." Finally, work gives shape and meaning to an adult's life, and allows him to see his life as separate from, but similar to, that of his parents. Seeing his life as separate from his parents goes a long way toward his being able to tolerate their eventual deaths.

Clients' employment will need support from time to time. The paid staff, or parents acting as staff for clients *other than their own child,* could make periodic visits to the job site to trouble shoot and to maintain a connection with the employer or supervisor. Employers tolerate more eccentricity when they know there is a responsive adult they can call for help when they don't understand the way the employee with disabilities is behaving. As you can see, all aspects of the clients' lives require ongoing support. Leaving your child alone in the world is the one thing I know you worry about most.

Summary of the new model

- Clients ideally come from a network of longstanding friendships.

- Parents realize trust and cooperation will be essential.

- Several homes with clients who are peers make up a social network.

- Independent evaluation should be considered for new members of the network.

- Parents must not provide direct services to their own child.

- Contracts should be in place providing for smooth transitions when necessary.

- There should be at least one staff person unrelated to any of the clients.

- Long-term financial care such as Special Needs Trusts should be in place.

- Services must include:

  ○ oversight of food management

- money management
- supervision of living skills
- monitoring of medical needs and medications
- social opportunities and leisure activities
- employment given ongoing support
- emotional support provided by counselors or paraprofessionals who understand the diagnosis.

Appendix II

Resources

Resources in the United States: online

The Autism Society of America: www.autism-society.org
National Autism Association: www.nationalautismassociation.org
Yale Child Study Center: www.info.med.yale.edu/chldstdy/autism
The Social Security Administration: www.ssa.gov (financial assistance)
National Council of Independent Living (NCIL): www.ncil.org
Online Asperger's Syndrome Information and Support—OASIS: www.udel.edu/bkirby/
    asperger
MIND Institute: www.ucdmc.ucdavis.edu/mindinstitute
Autisminfo.com: www.autisminfo.com
MAAP Services for Autism, Aspergers, and PDD: www.maapservices.org
Autism Speaks: www.autismspeaks.org

International resources

The National Autistic Society of the UK: www.nas.org.uk
393 City Road
London, EC1V 1NG
Phone: +44 (0) 20 7833 2299
This website will provide a list of almost 100 references to services in over
60 countries.

The International Association Autism Europe: www.autismeurope.org
Rue Montoyer 39 11 1000 Brussels
Belgium
Phone: +32 (0) 2 675 7505

Autism Spectrum Australia: www.aspect.org.au/default.asp
41 Cook Street
Forestville NSW 2087
Australia
Phone: +61 (0) 2 8977 8300

Autism Society Canada: www.autismsocietycanada.ca
PO Box 65
Orangeville
ON, L9W 2ZS
Canada

Irish Society for Autism: www.iol.ie/~isa1
Unity Building
16/17 Lower O'Connell St.
Dublin 1
Republic of Ireland
Phone: +35 3 (01) 874 4684

Autism New Zealand Inc.: www.autismnz.org.nz
PO Box 7305, Sydenham
Christchurch 8002
New Zealand
Phone: +64 (0) 3 332 1024

The National Autistic Society in Scotland
Central Chambers, First Floor
109 Hope Street
Glasgow, G2 6LL
Scotland
Phone: +44 (0) 141 221 8090

The National Autistic Society in Wales
Glamorgan House, Monastery Road
Neath Abbey, Wales, SA10 7DH
Phone: +44 (0) 1792 825 915

Action for Autism: www.autism-india.org
T370 Chiragh Gaon, Third Floor
New Delhi 110 017
India
Phone: +91 11 29256469

References

American Psychiatric Association (1994) *Diagnostic and Statistical Manual of Mental Disorders*, 4th edn. Washington, DC: Author.

Barkley, R. A. (1995) *Taking Charge of ADHD*. New York: Guilford Press.

Barkley, R. A. (1997) *ADHD and the Nature of Self Control*. New York: Guilford Press.

Grandin, T. (1995) *Thinking in Pictures and Other Reports from My Life with Autism*. New York: Doubleday.

Lezak, M. D. (2004) *Neuropsychological Assessment*, 4th edn. New York: Oxford University Press.

Luria, A. R. (1973) *The Working Brain*. New York: Basic Books.

Sacks, O. (1995) *An Anthropologist on Mars*. New York: Alfred A. Knopf.

Sapolsky, R. (2000). "*The Beast Within*." Talk at CorText Educational Seminars, November 11, Sacramento, CA.

Stuss, D. T. and Benson, D. G. (1986) *The Frontal Lobes*. New York: Raven Press.

Index